JEAN ANOUILH
THE COLLECTED PLAYS
VOLUME I

Jean Anouilh

THE COLLECTED PLAYS

VOLUME I

The Ermine

Thieves' Carnival

Restless Heart

Traveller without Luggage

Dinner with the Family

METHUEN · LONDON

Contents

The Ermine

Characters

MR BENTZ

FRANTZ

MONIME

PHILIPPE

FLORENTINE

MRS BENTZ

MARIE-ANNE

MAID TO MRS BENTZ

LA DUCHESSE DE GRANAT

HER MAID

URBAIN

JOSEPH

FIRST POLICE OFFICER

SECOND POLICE OFFICER

THIRD POLICE OFFICER

Original Title: L'Hermine
Translator: Miriam John
First produced in 1931

Act One

MR BENTZ *and* FRANTZ *stand facing each other.*

BENTZ (*extending a hand*): Well, Monsieur Frantz, it was nice seeing you. And I thought your friends were quite charming.

FRANTZ: Mr Bentz, you can't let me go like this!

BENTZ: That little cousin of yours is delightful. Gentle, too, I should imagine. I always longed to have a gentle wife; Mrs Bentz is a demon.

FRANTZ: If I still haven't got the money by the day after tomorrow, the business will fold up. This is my last chance. I can't let it slip through my fingers.

BENTZ: You're young.

FRANTZ: Not any longer.

BENTZ: Bit of a romanticist, I guess. (*Pause. Sounds as of a vain effort to start up a car.*) What are they up to, those friends of yours? Still trying to start the car? What's the idea of having such an old crock?

FRANTZ: We're poor!

BENTZ: I haven't got a car at all. (FRANTZ *shrugs.*) Oh, it isn't that I want to be a miser. I know very well I could have several cars if I wanted them; but to reach that happy state I've had to build up scores of businesses and watch them all collapse; I've had to make scores of fresh starts, my friend.

FRANTZ: I haven't got time to make scores of fresh starts. I've got to save this business, and to do that I must have money right away.

BENTZ: I know how you feel. But you must have patience, too. Why always resort to me, instead of to patience?

FRANTZ: You've been saying that over and over again for the last two years. But don't you realize I'm at the end of my tether now – I just can't go on any longer!

BENTZ: All young men say that.

FRANTZ: Very well.

Silence.

BENTZ: You're going to sell?

FRANTZ: Yes. Tomorrow.

BENTZ: I'm not the monster you think me, you know. I like helping people. I might buy, if that would be any use to you. Oh, I don't say I could give you much for it. You won't get a great price for the business anyway, you know. Probably not even as much as you put into it. In fact, I'm very much afraid that all you'll get out of it in the end will be debts.

FRANTZ (*looks at him and murmurs*): Swine!

BENTZ: Tut-tut! Cigarette?

FRANTZ: Mr Bentz, you're a rich man. All I want is enough money – just enough to live on and be happy.

BENTZ: You're a sentimentalist, you know.

FRANTZ: All I know is that I'm a young man wanting to buy a little happiness. It would be so easy for you to put that happiness within my reach. All it needs is a —

BENTZ: I have visits like yours every week.

FRANTZ: But you said I was your friend. . . .

BENTZ: You are my friend, Monsieur Frantz. Both my wife and I think a great deal of you. Why the devil do we always have to be talking about money? You're the one that makes it difficult for us to be friends. (*He helps himself to a drink.*) Why can't we just quietly enjoy the pleasure of a good drink and intelligent conversation? I like talking to you.

FRANTZ: How I detest you.

BENTZ: You shouldn't. Someone like me could be very useful to you – help you to give of your best.

FRANTZ: I don't want to give of my best. I want to be happy.
For that, I need money.

BENTZ: Would it be a girl friend, I wonder? You can confide
in me. I might be able to help you. I have a very wide
experience in such matters.

FRANTZ: I'm asking you for money, not advice.

BENTZ: How extraordinarily tactless you are. First of all you
appeal to our friendship – you want me to part with a sizeable
sum of money for purely sentimental reasons – and then a
while later you talk to me as though I were some petty pawn-
broker about to snatch your watch from you.

Pause.

FRANTZ: I lost my temper. . . .

BENTZ: Right. I'll prove to you that I have better manners
than you. Maybe the well-bred Frenchman can take a lesson
from the self-made Yankee. I'll save you the humiliation of
apologizing by warning you right away that there's no point
in it. I can't do anything about your business. But I'm still
your friend.

He holds out his hand. Enter MONIME.

Ah! The little cousin.

MONIME: Frantz, something awful has happened. Philippe
says he'll never be able to get the car to go. Could you go
and help him?

Exit FRANTZ, *muttering 'Oh, all right', etc.*

BENTZ: You don't smoke, mademoiselle?

MONIME: I try. But I don't really like it much.

Silence.

BENTZ: This must have been very jolly for you and your
friends, this little moonlight treasure hunt. Frantz has some
charming ideas. . . . You're quite a happy little band, by
the look of it.

MONIME: Yes. Philippe and Florentine are great fun. Florentine is a friend of mine. She came with us from Granat.

BENTZ: I thought you were all at Vichy?

MONIME: No, Granat. At my aunt's château.

BENTZ: I had some business dealings with a Duc de Granat some time ago – a long time ago, in fact.

MONIME: That must have been my uncle. He got killed in a riding accident.

BENTZ: And the Duchess – is she related to Monsieur Frantz?

MONIME: No, she's my aunt, not his. As a matter of fact we're not really cousins. Frantz is the son of a friend of my aunt's and was brought up with me.

BENTZ: I see. And of course she always treated him like one of the family.

MONIME: Well, not really. . . . He always wanted to go his own way . . . and when she tried to arrange a marriage for him, he wouldn't have anything to do with it.

BENTZ: I see. . . . Your aunt was anxious to get him settled, then?

MONIME: Yes, but it was a very bad match. She wanted him to marry the local miller's daughter. A great, tall, skinny girl who puts on the most awful airs just because she's got a bit of money. Oh, it was stupid! Besides, Frantz doesn't want to marry.

BENTZ: He doesn't? All the same, his affairs are in a bit of a mess at the moment – I suppose you know – and it would be a way out. I rather gather that Madame de Granat has never thought of supporting him herself? (MONIME *looks hard at him.*) I must apologize for asking such a question, mademoiselle, but the fact is I seem to be getting myself mixed up in business discussions with Monsieur Frantz; he came to see me this evening to ask me to help him – financially. He was extremely pressing.

Pause. Enter FRANTZ. *He stands looking at them.*

FRANTZ: Were you requiring any more information, Mr Bentz?

BENTZ: I was simply expressing my surprise to this charming young lady at the fact that the Duchess is making no attempt to help you out of this spot you're in.

FRANTZ: You don't need to express surprise to anyone about what Madame de Granat does or does not do.

BENTZ: How very quick-tempered you are – and tactless as usual!

The whole party comes in. FLORENTINE, *fair and laughing.* PHILIPPE, *obviously glad to be alive.* MARIE-ANNE, *an elderly companion, apparently frightened out of her wits. And* MRS BENTZ.

PHILIPPE: I think the old bus really *has* had it now. We might as well chuck it.

FLORENTINE: This is *the* very end.

MRS BENTZ: I must say I'm rather glad about it. It means that you'll all have to stay the night.

MARIE-ANNE: Oh, but that's quite impossible. Think of it, madame. Her Grace is expecting us. Eleven o'clock already! We should be back by now, and there are still sixty miles to go.

PHILIPPE: On foot, too!

FLORENTINE *bursts out laughing.*

FLORENTINE: Idiot!

MARIE-ANNE: What are we going to do, Monsieur Frantz? Whatever will Madame de Granat think?

FRANTZ: Isn't there a garage anywhere?

MRS BENTZ: There is one on the way to Moulins, about six miles from here, but you'll never get a mechanic in the middle of the night. No, my snare is well and truly laid. I'm going to keep you all here.

MARIE-ANNE: Oh, this is really most unfortunate! The Duchess is waiting up for us. . . .

FLORENTINE: I think it's wonderful, don't you?

PHILIPPE: Terrific.

FLORENTINE: We shall all sleep in the same room. . . .

JACP–B

MRS BENTZ: Never fear, my dear. I have three rooms upstairs and you can have one each. As for your men friends, they can take potluck. One of them can shake down here on the divan. I'll have it made up. And the other can sleep in the summer house – there's a divan there, too. My husband will be delighted to lend them some pyjamas. Don't pull such a face, Frantz, Mr Bentz has some very fine pyjamas.

MARIE-ANNE: I'm sorry, Mrs Bentz, it really isn't possible. We really must get back. The Duchess would never forgive me. . . .

MRS BENTZ: But how can you possibly expect to get back?

FRANTZ: Isn't there at least a bicycle? I'm going to try to get to that garage.

MRS BENTZ: No, there is *not* a bicycle. And the mechanic wouldn't come anyway. I know him. He's a lout. You may as well resign yourself, my dear Frantz. Now don't make those cat's eyes of yours. Give in with a good grace, there's a dear boy.

FLORENTINE: That's very good – he *does* make cat's eyes!

MONIME: Cat's eyes?

MRS BENTZ: My dear young lady, you don't mean to tell me that you're his cousin and you didn't know that he makes cat's eyes when he's angry? (MONIME *gives him a long look.*) But why are we all standing up? At least let's make ourselves comfortable.

MARIE-ANNE: Oh, dear me, this is most unsettling. Her Grace will simply not speak to me tomorrow. . . . She made me responsible for these young people, Mrs Bentz. . . .

MRS BENTZ: I promise you to return them unscathed.

BENTZ: Too bad I haven't a car. But there is at least a telephone. I have to have that, to keep in touch with the stock market. Couldn't they phone to Granat?

MRS BENTZ: Toby, you're the only one with any sense. You see, now everything can be arranged. The Duchess will forgive you, after all.

MARIE-ANNE: I wonder whether it is really advisable to tell her this way. . . .

MRS BENTZ: We have no choice. I shall go and prepare the rooms. (*Exit.*)

BENTZ: What number is it?

MONIME: Granat 5.

BENTZ (*on telephone*): Give me Granat 5, please.

FLORENTINE: Oh, Mr Bentz, would you please ask for 7 as well, so that I can warn my mother?

BENTZ: Hullo! Hullo! Give me Granat 7 as well. Thanks. (*He leaves the telephone and comes back to the others.*) Now, in a few minutes from now we shall all have our minds at rest and be able to enjoy the charm of this little unexpected party in peace, eh, Monsieur Frantz?

FRANTZ: Yes.

Silence for a while. BENTZ *hands round cigarettes.*

MARIE-ANNE: Monsieur Frantz, do you think the Duchess will ever forgive me?

FRANTZ: What else could we do? You don't think I want to stay here, do you?

BENTZ: As I was saying, your cousin is charming, but you will have to teach her to enjoy smoking. There is no moment at which a woman is more seductive than when she is smoking a cigarette. Properly, of course.

FLORENTINE: Do you find me attractive when I smoke, Mr Bentz?

BENTZ: Enormously.

FLORENTINE: You see, Philippe? Please note that I can be enormously attractive.

PHILIPPE: Duly noted.

BENTZ: I should like to see my friend Frantz and his cousin in the same good spirits. Would they be hiding some secret grief, I wonder? Aha! If my wife were here, she'd say you were making your cat's eyes, young man. . . .

MONIME *looks furiously at* BENTZ, *who bursts out laughing.*

PHILIPPE: Mr Bentz, you mustn't forget that when Monime's about, Frantz is labelled 'Please do not touch'.

MARIE-ANNE: These children must be wondering what sort of welcome we shall have from the Duchess tomorrow, Mr Bentz. That is if it is a welcome. I must say I wonder too. . . .

BENTZ: This woman seems to be an ogress. (*Telephone rings.*) Ah, you see? . . . Hullo! Hullo! Granat 5? Hold on a moment, please. Now, which of you is going to take it?

MONIME (*getting up*): Is that you, Urbain? . . . It's Mademoiselle Monime. Is Madame de Granat in her room? Oh, she can't sleep . . . she was worrying . . . oh . . . would you please ask her if she could come to the telephone, Urbain?

MARIE-ANNE: You see, Mr Bentz, she's still up! Oh, good gracious me, what a state of affairs!

BENTZ: Please don't get upset. Everything will be all right.

MONIME: Is that you, Aunt? . . . Yes, it's Monime.

FLORENTINE: Now for it!

MONIME: No, Aunt, I'm dreadfully sorry . . . we're with Mr and Mrs Bentz. Frantz had some business to discuss here this evening. . . . We thought we should be back by eleven, but Philippe's car broke down. . . . Philippe Luc . . . We can't possibly get back. . . . No, I'm afraid not. There's no one to repair it. Mrs Bentz has very kindly said we can stay here for the night. . . . We can get it repaired tomorrow. . . . But, Aunt . . . no, but really, Aunt . . . Well, if you wish, then, Aunt, send Albert. But we're more than sixty miles away and he wouldn't get here before two in the morning . . . we shan't be home before four and we shall be terribly tired. . . . Yes, really, Aunt . . . Very well, let him leave early in the morning . . . we shall go to bed soon, and we'll expect your call. . . . Yes, I think that really would be better. Yes, Aunt, Marie-Anne is here. I'll put you on to her.

MARIE-ANNE: It's all my fault . . . I know it only too well, it's all my fault. . . . Good evening, your Grace. But, your Grace . . . but, your Grace . . . but, your Grace . . . Yes, I'll ask him to come to the telephone, your Grace. . . .

She holds out the receiver to FRANTZ. FLORENTINE *blows out her cheeks with laughter.*

BENTZ: She certainly seems to be a fierce lady.

FRANTZ *listens respectfully, then hangs up.*

MARIE-ANNE: Oh, Monsieur Frantz, you hung up!

FRANTZ (*shrugging*): So did she.

BENTZ (*moving close*): Tact, my boy, tact. Why kill the goose that lays the golden eggs?

MRS BENTZ (*reappearing*): The rooms are ready. Has everything been settled?

MONIME: Not very satisfactorily, I'm afraid, Mrs Bentz. We're being called for at five o'clock. I do hope that's all right for you. It seems awful to abuse your hospitality like this.

MRS BENTZ: Five o'clock? Madame de Granat seems very anxious not to leave you at my mercy any longer than she can help.

MARIE-ANNE: You must admit, Mrs Bentz, that it is a little unusual for a young lady of noble birth to spend the night at a strange house.

MRS BENTZ: But you are here, too, mademoiselle. Young girls go anywhere with a chaperon, even in France.

MARIE-ANNE: I quite realize that, Mrs Bentz. But for a great lady such as her Grace, there is always tradition to think of.

BENTZ: Now that's the sort of thing we Yankees find quite fascinating, isn't it, darling?

The telephone rings.

BENTZ: Here's the other number, laughing lady!

FLORENTINE: Hullo! Is that Emile! Would you ask my mother to come to the phone, please? Hullo . . . is that you, Mummy? . . . Oh, Mummy, such an upheaval . . . we've had a breakdown about sixty miles away. There's Monime, Marie-Anne, Frantz, and another young man – rather charming. We're spending the night with some awfully nice people Frantz came to see. Yes . . . yes, I shall be home at about six in the morning. Yes, six. 'Bye then, Mummy. (*To the others.*) Well, that's that.

BENTZ: Nice work.

FLORENTINE: Oh, I'm used to this sort of thing.

BENTZ: And how about Mademoiselle Monime – is she used to it?

MONIME: I don't go out very much.

MARIE-ANNE: It is evident that you do not know her Grace, Mr Bentz! Oh, I am not looking forward to our return!

BENTZ (*to his wife*): You know, I figure, my dear, that we've become unwilling accomplices in some sort of family drama. Mademoiselle Florentine, you don't seem to me to be the timid type. . . . Does the lady really deserve this baleful reputation?

MARIE-ANNE: Oh, Mr Bentz!

FLORENTINE: You couldn't imagine a sweeter old lady!

MARIE-ANNE: But, Mademoiselle Florentine, that's absurd. . . .

Everyone laughs, except FRANTZ *and* MARIE-ANNE.

BENTZ: I can't help feeling relations must be extremely strained between the Duchess and our moody young friend here, who loses his temper so easily.

PHILIPPE: You should see them together – it's too absurd for words. The Duchess fixes Frantz with a stony stare from behind her fan, and Frantz just sits there and scowls back at her. They hardly ever speak to each other, or, if one of them does say something, the other never answers.

MONIME: My aunt treats Frantz very badly. When he is at Granat, hardly a day passes without her finding some way or another of annoying him.

BENTZ: Looks like Granat is steeped in melodrama. How very fortunate that you are there to console him, mademoiselle.

MONIME: Oh, yes. . . .

They all smile.

FRANTZ (*rising abruptly*): Mrs Bentz, please forgive me –

but it's past midnight, and we have to leave very early. May
I ask you to show Monime her room – she'll be very tired in
the morning. . . .

MONIME: Frantz! You must be mad! I'm perfectly capable of
sitting up like everyone else. . . . Oh, now I feel embarrassed. You make me look an idiot.

BENTZ: Be assured we understand everything, mademoiselle.
You were treating us to some charming details, and I guess
our friend Frantz was afraid they might become a little embarrassing for him.

MONIME: What on earth is the matter, Frantz? I don't want
to go to bed. . . .

MARIE-ANNE: It is true that at Granat her Grace insists that
everyone should retire at eleven o'clock.

MONIME: But we're not at Granat.

FRANTZ (*gently*): *Please,* little one, for my sake . . . go to
bed. You'll be tired in the morning.

MONIME (*who has been looking at him*): Yes . . . I'll say good
night then, Mrs Bentz . . . if you'll excuse me. . . .

BENTZ: How docile the little cousin is. . . . Courage, mademoiselle. He looks very frightening, but I know him . . .
his bark is worse than his bite. . . .

MRS BENTZ: Do be quiet, Toby; you're being very silly.
Frantz is quite right. We shouldn't be keeping them here
talking when they have to get up so early. . . .

FLORENTINE: Oh, we're used to it.

MRS BENTZ: No . . . you'll be dead tired tomorrow and the
journey will be dreadful for you. No, I should never forgive
myself for enjoying your charming company at that price.
(*She rings.*) Good night, monsieur, we shall meet again
tomorrow morning. At five, I shall be out in the garden in
overalls, cutting roses. You'll be sleeping, I suppose, won't
you, Toby?

BENTZ: Definitely. (*He shakes hands with* MARIE-ANNE *and*
PHILIPPE. *To* FLORENTINE.) Good-bye for the present,
mademoiselle. You know, I really do find you very attractive
when you smoke; and when you smile, too.

FLORENTINE: Thank you. I'll try to do both at once.

BENTZ (*to* MONIME): Good night, mademoiselle. You'll never be happy if you let him frighten you.

MRS BENTZ (*to the* MAID): Louise, show Monsieur the room you have prepared in the summer house and make up the divan here for Monsieur Frantz. Now (*to* FLORENTINE *and* MONIME) if you will follow me, I will show you your rooms.

Farewells all round. FRANTZ *is left alone with* BENTZ.

BENTZ: You're in love with Mademoiselle Monime, aren't you – and you need money so that you can marry her?

FRANTZ (*making towards him*): Mind your own damned business! You say I'm tactless with the people who could help me – well, so I am!

BENTZ: You seem to be furious. Maybe I hit the nail on the head? (*Pause, while they stare at each other.*) I think it's charming.

FRANTZ: If you've kept me here to talk about that after refusing me the money, you really are a skunk.

BENTZ: A-ah! May I point out that the only reason you are here is that your car broke down. Just that. Perhaps I might also point out that I don't have to be a skunk, as you put it, just because, having refused you money, I want to talk to you about yourself. In the eyes of the world we're friends, and that sort of conversation is quite usual among friends.

FRANTZ: It's what is known as a confidence. That's something that's given, not asked for.

BENTZ: As opposed to money, which is asked for, but not always given.

FRANTZ: Quite so – as opposed to money. In other words, it's a subject you're not qualified to discuss.

BENTZ: Come now, we're getting things mixed up and expressing ourselves clumsily as usual. Just now you were talking business. You asked me for money. I replied in kind. Now I've lost interest in your enterprise – I want nothing further to do with it. Right. But there's nothing to prevent our discussing personal matters, is there?

FRANTZ: What are you driving at?

BENTZ: I am your friend, young man, and yet you won't confide in me.

FRANTZ: Your use of the word 'friend' doesn't deceive either of us.

Enter MRS BENTZ.

BENTZ: Isn't that so, darling? I was telling him he is our friend.

MRS BENTZ (*taking* FRANTZ *by the hand*): Did he dare to doubt it?

BENTZ: Yes. And he keeps on making those cat's eyes.

MRS BENTZ: We must make him sit down and talk to us.

BENTZ: We must. (*He serves drinks and passes them cigarettes.*) You see, my dear, I've guessed everything. This attachment of our young friend to that hopeless business of his, that he keeps on wanting money for, amounts to something much more than the vanity and greed that usually prompt people in such matters. . . . This will appeal to you, my dear – you're a sentimentalist. . . . As I say, it was more than that. It was in order to achieve the conquest of Mademoiselle Monime that the young man has been making such desperate efforts these past two years.

MRS BENTZ: Oh! Frantz, dear, is that true?

Pause. FRANTZ *lowers his eyes and remains silent.*

BENTZ: Come now, my boy, answer the lady.

FRANTZ (*who has got up abruptly and walked away from them*): You said I was to sleep in this room, didn't you, Mrs Bentz? Do you think your maid could please prepare my bed? I'm tired.

MRS BENTZ: Toby, you are an idiot. . . . Frantz . . . Frantz, dear, you know what a terrible tease my husband is. He just couldn't resist the desire to pull your leg. Frantz, I do apologize for him. I'm sure he's sorry.

BENTZ: I beg you not to be angry with me.

MRS BENTZ: It's going to cost him a lot of dollars to buy his pardon. Come back, Frantz dear, I promise you he'll help you. (*They all sit down again.* MRS BENTZ *continues after a silence*.) I'm your friend, Frantz. You can talk to me, absolutely frankly. Give me your hand. Now, tell me honestly, do you really love Monime, and is it for her you're working so hard?

FRANTZ: Yes, I love her.

MRS BENTZ: How thrilling! They make such a delicious couple, don't you think, Toby?

BENTZ: Yes. Does she love you?

Pause.

MRS BENTZ: Oh! Could anyone not love the dear boy?

FRANTZ: Yes. She loves me.

BENTZ: Fine. But – do forgive the question – does she love you the way little girls love the first young man that talks to them one fine evening at some party or other – you understand me?

MRS BENTZ: Toby! I won't let you be stupid tonight! One doesn't love Frantz that way. . . .

BENTZ: I ask you that as a father might ask it. I don't believe it can ever be a good thing to encourage a union based on a little girl's whim.

FRANTZ: Monime loves me. I know.

BENTZ: That's better. Said like that, it's believable. I know you're too intelligent to be mistaken about it. Now, can you tell me exactly what relation you are to the Duchess?

FRANTZ: I'm not any relation to her. My father was her doctor for twenty years. She helped me finish my studies when he died.

BENTZ: U-huh. I didn't know how you stood. So Madame de Granat isn't expecting her niece to marry money?

FRANTZ: No. She's rich.

BENTZ: I see. So obviously she's on the look-out for titles?

FRANTZ: Yes.

BENTZ: Which you, as obviously, don't possess.

FRANTZ: No. (*He puts his head in his hands.*)

MRS BENTZ: Frantz darling, don't be sad. Everything will be all right. We'll help you.

BENTZ: One more thing. Has Mademoiselle Monime much influence on her aunt?

FRANTZ: No. What are you driving at?

BENTZ: I've got a shrewd idea that, even if you have the money, you'll never get the Duchess's consent to the marriage. Is your cousin under age?

FRANTZ: Yes.

BENTZ: Are you sure the money is hers and not her aunt's?

FRANTZ: Oh, Monime hasn't any money. Her father went bankrupt and killed himself. The fact is, all the money belongs to her aunt.

BENTZ: I see. Well, of course that makes the whole thing impossible!

FRANTZ: But when I have money I shall take Monime away, and then when she comes of age, we can get married!

BENTZ: But her aunt won't give her a sou.

FRANTZ: No, but if my business goes well, I shall have enough.

BENTZ: Yes.

FRANTZ: Don't you see that patience is just not enough? I must have money right away. The business isn't too bad, you know, Mr Bentz. It's already doing better this year. If I can clear off this payment the day after tomorrow, I shall be able to make some money.

BENTZ: No, Monsieur Frantz. That business of yours is no good.

FRANTZ: But you were saying just now—

BENTZ: Oh, you might have been able to flog the dead horse for a bit, and keep up the appearances of a large income. But what's the good, since you admit yourself that nothing will persuade the Duchess to accept you?

FRANTZ: But it doesn't matter to me whether she accepts me or not!

BENTZ: I beg your pardon. It does to me. I can't put into this thing the considerable sums of money that are needed, with no other guarantee than your possible future success. I should have a lot more confidence in the nephew by marriage

of the Duchesse de Granat. Even though he may not possess
your personal qualities.

FRANTZ: Then . . . you still refuse to help me out?

BENTZ: I'm sorry. I thought you were going to reveal a more
or less official romance – something it would have been
possible to risk money on. But as things are, your situation
is extremely tricky. In fact, if you ask my advice as a friend,
I'd say give the girl up.

FRANTZ: Oh! I hate you. . . .

He hurls himself at BENTZ, *but* MRS BENTZ *holds him back.*

MRS BENTZ: Frantz, darling . . .

FRANTZ: Let go of me!

MRS BENTZ: Frantz, I don't want— Go away, Toby, leave
him alone . . . he's beside himself. . . .

BENTZ: I'm sorry.

FRANTZ: You . . . scum! To think I've told you everything
– things I've never said to anyone else. It hurt, too, but I
thought you were going to pay for it in good hard cash.
. . . And now you refuse me money . . . you . . . you
. . . thieves! Let me go! Do you think you'd have got all
this out of me if you hadn't promised me money? I've told
you everything. . . . You've *got* to pay now . . . thieves!

MRS BENTZ: Get out, Toby. . . . Please Frantz. . . .

BENTZ: You forget yourself. You are under my roof. I shall
refrain from taking the obvious course.

He bows and leaves.

FRANTZ: Thief . . . thief . . .

MRS BENTZ: Frantz, my little one . . .

FRANTZ: Leave me alone . . . you disgust me, too.

There is a knock. It is the MAID *with the sheets and blankets.*
MRS BENTZ *helps her to make up the divan. She glances at*
FRANTZ *from time to time, secretly. When the* MAID *leaves, she*
goes up to him.

MRS BENTZ: You mustn't harbour these hard feelings against

me, darling. You can count on me as a friend. My husband is a businessman, and you know what they are – they only understand money. I'm a sentimentalist. I get very upset about his way of doing things.

FRANTZ: Go away.

MRS BENTZ: I don't want to leave you in this state. Oh! you're feverish! Lie down on the bed – you'll feel better. (*He throws himself down on the bed.*) There . . . I'll stay at your bedside, like a nurse. . . . You mustn't give up hope. His bark is worse than his bite. He's really very weak. I can do just what I like with him. When I go to him for money to help some young man I'm truly fond of, he always gives it me. He says he's buying his freedom. I make it very expensive sometimes. How much do you need to clear off your debt, Frantz?

FRANTZ: A thousand dollars.

MRS BENTZ: *Really?* Do you mean to say it's for that that you and my husband have been hurling insults at each other for the past hour? Toby really is unforgivable. But you know what businessmen are like. Money is money, no matter how much or how little. In private life it's quite different. He sometimes gives me checks for larger amounts than that without even asking me what I'm going to do with it. . . . I can't understand why you bother with these stupid business matters that bring you in so little money. That sort of thing's all right for Toby, but you're worth something much better. The idea of you scribbling away at figures and screaming your head off at the stock exchange – it's repellent! You should always be as you are now – lying there, with your arms behind your head, looking like a sulky child . . . you're adorable like that, darling. (*She sits down close to him and touches a stray lock of hair on his forehead.*) I'll help you myself, if you like, and you can give up that silly old business.

FRANTZ (*sitting up and looking at her. She also gets up*): Get out.

MRS BENTZ: What's the matter, Frantz? What have I said to hurt you?

FRANTZ: I said, get out.

MRS BENTZ (*going toward the door*): Sweet little idiot. Come back and see me when the megrims have gone. I'll always be happy to take an interest in you.

She goes out. FRANTZ *stays motionless for a while. Enter* PHILIPPE.

PHILIPPE. Aren't you asleep yet?

FRANTZ: No, what about you?

PHILIPPE: Your little Florentine's got under my skin.

FRANTZ: Go and find her then, she's bound to be waiting for you.

PHILIPPE: You think so?

FRANTZ: Yes. Don't be shy – she sleeps with everybody.

PHILIPPE. I'll stay and talk a bit.

FRANTZ: That's very decent of you. But you go on and find her.

PHILIPPE: You look fed up. What did Bentz say?

FRANTZ: He refused.

PHILIPPE: Refused? (*Silence.*) You're going to have to sell?

FRANTZ: Yes.

PHILIPPE: Oh, I'm sorry, old man . . .

FRANTZ: Two years. This farce has been dragging on for two years. And all for this.

PHILIPPE: What are you going to do? (FRANTZ *shrugs his shoulders.*) I told you when you first plunged into this thing that you weren't cut out to be a businessman.

FRANTZ: I knew it, too. But I can't just be content to earn a few hundred francs a month on a newspaper the way you do. I must have money.

PHILIPPE: Who mustn't?

FRANTZ: I know, but for you it's just something to make jokes about. I haven't the strength to laugh about it any more. What a sinister sort of farce life is when you're young and poor!

PHILIPPE: To be young and rich is a farce, too.

FRANTZ: I know, I know. No contact with life. Poor people have to invent that sort of myth to console themselves. But they don't mention what it's like to be the sort of young man that women don't smile at – that doesn't know how to behave with waiters and whose every gesture is studied and calculated. . . . Oh, yes, we've had contact with life all right! It's taught us not to be careless or wasteful. To be rational, sober, prudent. . . . Coming back from my father's funeral, I knew the whole business had been more than my family could afford. . . . Since then . . .

PHILIPPE: I know something about that, too.

FRANTZ: Less than I do, it seems, since you're not prepared to do anything about it.

PHILIPPE: 'Do anything about it.' . . . There's nothing one can do. I want to be happy, too. Meanwhile I shall make the best of what I've got.

FRANTZ: Not me. . . .

Silence for a while.

PHILIPPE: When we were studying, two years ago, you were the cheery one.

FRANTZ: Life is easy when you only talk about it in cafés. . . . But you have to face the real thing sooner or later.

PHILIPPE: You're not really unhappy, though, are you?

FRANTZ: I'm poor.

PHILIPPE: All the same, you've got a bit of money. And you have girl friends and men friends. . . .

FRANTZ: Do you really believe that's enough? (*Pause.*) When every day, at every single turn, you knock your head against the same old brick wall: poverty! When you know there's no way out. That you've got to choose between being either the sort of upright, straightforward youth who brings up his brothers and sisters and maintains his old mother and gets pushed around by all and sundry, or else becoming a sort of travesty – like a draper's assistant on holiday. Imagination, idleness, generosity are vices for us, Philippe. We're specimens of 'the poor'. The sort they write books on morality for.

PHILIPPE: Frantz, what's got into you? I've never seen you like this.

FRANTZ: I've been holding myself in for two years. Two

whole years I've waited patiently. . . . I've clothed myself in all their virtues – put them all on as a worker puts on his overalls. I've been economical, prudent, practical. I've been lying for two years. I've cheated myself for two years and this is where it gets me.

PHILIPPE: Why didn't you stay with us?

FRANTZ: The very reason I want money is to get away from you.

PHILIPPE: Come back. We manage to be happy enough.

FRANTZ: Back to Lili, for instance, to the occasional round of drinks, sparkling conversation over coffee, earnest political discussions, the flicks. . . . No thanks.

PHILIPPE: Not only that. There is such a thing as friendship.

FRANTZ: With you, perhaps . . . to some extent . . . in so far as you are sane and fabulously good-humoured. But as for the others – now be honest.

PHILIPPE: You've been growing away from us for quite a while now. But you'd soon take up the threads again.

FRANTZ: I'd rather leave the threads where they are. What am I missing? That great bore Martial, for instance, always wanting to drag you off to a brothel. Clement babbling politics all the time. And Jacques, with his lectures on literature. You certainly have to gird up your loins to resist that bunch. I couldn't do it any more.

PHILIPPE: What are you going to do?

FRANTZ: Keep going. Live alone, I suppose.

PHILIPPE: What will you do about money?

FRANTZ: What is there to do?

PHILIPPE: Frantz! It's not as bad as that.

FRANTZ: It is.

PHILIPPE: *You* haven't any money? Look at us. None of us has any money.

FRANTZ: You don't even begin to understand. You're still living the life of the Boulevard Saint Michel and the Quartier Latin! Or else you've become resigned. I've been struggling for two years, understand? Two years, at a dead loss. I know what's what. And I'm not resigned.

PHILIPPE: Well, then, there's nothing lost, my dear old chap.

He stops short at a look from FRANTZ.

FRANTZ: Because I'm not resigned?

PHILIPPE: The way you say that! (*A gesture from* FRANTZ.) Frantz!

FRANTZ: I can't stand it any more.

PHILIPPE: Well, then, you must take some sort of action.

FRANTZ: Ah! These good friends who give encouraging advice. . . . What sort of action?

PHILIPPE: My dear chap, you're not twenty-five; at our age there's a solution to everything. Work . . .

FRANTZ: I've tried to believe in that one for two years.

PHILIPPE: I don't mean that sort of work. There's all your ideas. Your novel – what about that?

FRANTZ: Oh, I've said good-bye to those illusions long ago. I haven't any talent. You're barking up the wrong tree, Philippe. You seem to think I'm suffering from some sort of belated *mal du siècle* – that I'm just looking for something to keep me employed. But I'm not. I'm the sort that wants to live and be happy. I need money to build up the kind of happiness I'm aiming at, and I know now that there is no way of getting it.

PHILIPPE: And yet you were jolly near success. . . . If Bentz hadn't refused his help at the last minute.

FRANTZ: Any failure could tell you how many times he very nearly succeeded. But for me it'll be only once.

PHILIPPE: You can't just cave in like that, old man.

FRANTZ: I just haven't any guts left, Philippe – can't you understand the feeling? This was a last chance, and it slipped through my fingers. It's all up now. It's harder this time because it's the last. That's all there is to it.

PHILIPPE: How could you *not* succeed, with all the wealthy people you know?

FRANTZ: Another little illusion you'd better discard. Rich people never lend their friends money. They only offer them cups of tea and dainty sandwiches.

JACP–C

PHILIPPE: Get married then.

FRANTZ: Why do you say that?

PHILIPPE: It'd be a solution.

FRANTZ: To whom, for instance?

PHILIPPE: A wealthy heiress!

FRANTZ: Look, I've no name, no looks to speak of, I'm not famous. . . . Besides, I should despise myself for the rest of my life if I were to go about it that way. Making love to a woman who doesn't attract you is as sordid as working.

PHILIPPE: All the same, Charles got himself out of the same sort of mess by marrying that Argentinian.

FRANTZ: Mrs Bentz has just given me to understand that if I were to sleep with her she would make her husband advance the money I need.

PHILIPPE: And you refused? I'd have thought you'd take any chance that came.

FRANTZ: This isn't so much a chance as a superstition. In any case, I'm having nothing to do with it for the moment.

PHILIPPE: Is it your little cousin that's having this effect on you?

FRANTZ: Possibly.

Silence.

PHILIPPE: Frantz, do you realize that for two years we haven't talked about ourselves to each other at all?

FRANTZ: I know.

PHILIPPE: It's you who've forced our friendship into this conspiracy of silence that'll probably be the death of it.

FRANTZ: Yes, it's me. (*Long silence, which* FRANTZ *eventually breaks, in formal conversational tones.*) Have you got a good story to cover at the moment?

PHILIPPE: Yes. Two kids who've murdered an old woman, the grandmother of one of them, to get the money for a trip to Paris.

FRANTZ: What are they getting?

PHILIPPE: Reform school. The older one may get a spot of jail.

FRANTZ: How old is he?

PHILIPPE: Sixteen.

FRANTZ: Poor, I suppose? Will he stay there?

Silence.

PHILIPPE: Pretty sure to.

FRANTZ: If I landed in jail one day, would you do anything about it?

PHILIPPE: If I happened to have any money at the time, yes.

FRANTZ: Do people get very miserable in prison, I wonder?

PHILIPPE: Our sort does, I imagine. Inside, as in the army, there are no pips for intelligence.

FRANTZ (*absently*): Their grandmother. She'd probably been good to them when they were little. What did they say when the judge expressed the usual indignation?

PHILIPPE: That an old woman isn't any use anyway.

FRANTZ: You know, one can admire that, Philippe! To kill your grandmother because you want to go to Paris. Don't you feel how terribly simple it is? – so much simpler than we imagine.

PHILIPPE: Are you crazy?

FRANTZ: Not crazy enough, I'm afraid. However, that is one solution that's still open to me. If only my childhood were not so smothered in priests, and pious books, and mother love. . . .

PHILIPPE: Are you trying to be funny, Frantz?

FRANTZ: Yes, I'm trying to be funny. I'm trying to live. Suppose I were to kill someone, too, in order to get my happiness? Do you think I could commit a crime, Philippe? Seriously. Don't answer right away, and don't joke about it. You know me very well. Think, and then look me straight in the eye and tell me. Do you think I could commit a crime?

PHILIPPE: No, Frantz.

FRANTZ: You mean from the moral point of view. Do you think that would stop me?

PHILIPPE: No. Don't be angry, Frantz, but I simply think you wouldn't have the guts.

FRANTZ (*after a pause*): Oh, I'm not angry.

PHILIPPE: You'd have enough guts to talk about it probably and even to prepare it. But not to go through with it.

FRANTZ: You're probably right.

PHILIPPE: In my job, I often get the chance to follow these things very closely. Killing's a tough business. Sometimes it's a long business, too. You have to have the sort of nerve that'll last to the bitter end.

FRANTZ: And you think I'm too much of a coward?

Silence.

PHILIPPE: Why worry? . . . Look – why are you asking me all this?

FRANTZ: No reason. I was joking.

PHILIPPE: You weren't, you know.

FRANTZ: No, that's true. I *was* toying with the idea, just to see how my nerves and muscles would respond. Now I know. I'm too much of a coward. You're right. There's nothing more to be said. (*He puts his head in his hands.*)

PHILIPPE: Frantz, what is it? What's the matter?

FRANTZ: I'm too much of a coward. . . . I've managed to see where my happiness lies and blaze a trail to it across all the phony ideas I was brought up on, and I shan't have the guts to hold on to it. Philippe, we're friends. We talk for hours every day and yet I've never told you anything. Philippe, I'm in love with Monime. It's for her that I'm trying to get money. If I give up the idea of money, I must give up the idea of her as well.

PHILIPPE: Is Monime rich?

FRANTZ: Her father died poor; all the money belongs to her aunt, and you can imagine Madame de Granat wouldn't think twice about me. I needed money to get Monime away from there so that we could live together. Bentz refused. I haven't a sou. I've got to sell my business. Monime can't belong to me because Bentz refuses me money. Can't you see how odious and inadmissible it is! Can't you understand why I want to shout myself hoarse? (*Silence.*) You can look at me. You didn't say what I expected just now. You felt I was too wretched for you to say what was in your mind. You can say it; I've been prepared for it for a long time. Go on, say it. I know it already; it's because of that that I've grown away from you over these two years. You say you've noticed it. For two years, we have been having the sort of conversation that strangers have. Once, remember, we talked for a whole hour about how they make tar. You and I. Just the two of us, alone together. During the whole of that conversation I was feeling wretched and hopeful. I wanted to tell you about it – about my wretchedness, and about my hopes.

PHILIPPE: Why didn't you?

FRANTZ: Because I was afraid of your thoughts, the way I'm afraid of them now. I knew them already then. I knew what turn they were going to take. What words you would clothe them in. I could see a certain twist of your mouth that I knew so well. One of those looks of yours – the one I dislike most. I imagined all the futile explanations I should— (*He has been almost shouting, but stops suddenly. Silence.*) This scene surprises you, I suppose? We must have been in short pants when I last threw one. Living that café life, you've grown up, Philippe, without noticing it. You've become a man. You're already incapable of understanding me. Through the expression of amazement on your face, I can read in it the signs of your manhood. Signs of indulgence and irony that have frightened me for two years. Come on, say it, say it!

PHILIPPE: But Frantz, what on earth's wrong with you?

FRANTZ: You know what's wrong with me. Say something! Be amazed! Pity me for being in love with Monime!

PHILIPPE: I'm not amazed, and I don't pity you.

FRANTZ: Don't pretend! This very minute you're remembering how shy I was with women when we used to go to Montparnasse, and how they would always go off and leave me, saying I was crazy. They'll have a good laugh when you tell them, won't they? A better laugh than you, probably, because you're a bit frightened of me at the moment. . . . 'Falling in love with a little girl!' you'll all say . . . 'that

would happen to *him.*' . . . Go on, laugh, why don't you?
Are you afraid to? You wouldn't have fallen in love, I
suppose? You'd have seen the red light and cleared out in
time? No nonsense. Little girls when one's thirty-five and
ripe to settle down. (*Pause.*) All right, I'll try to pull myself
together. Otherwise you'll never say anything. And tonight
I've got to talk. Just talk and talk and talk my head off, like
a whore. And I'd rather it was to you than anyone else, after
all.

PHILIPPE: I don't know what's wrong with you, Frantz.

FRANTZ: Yes, you do. I'm at rock bottom, tonight, and I'm
lonely.

PHILIPPE: In spite of the way we've drifted apart these last
two years, I'm still your friend.

FRANTZ: Yes, but all you can offer me is intelligent advice,
and that's what I need least. It's a luxury. Any stranger could
give it to me. What I was hoping you could do for me – just
for tonight – was what the truest and simplest friends do –
take some of my unhappiness on yourself. It's too much for
me to bear alone. (*He has seized* PHILIPPE's *hands.*) Philippe,
they'll take her away from me. Go on, laugh – you'll be
perfectly right. I've lived for two years on the love of this
girl, trusting in my success, like a fool. When Bentz refused
me the money just now I felt utterly lost and desperate. I
realized for the first time how flimsy my hopes really were.
If I've no money to take her away, she'll be snapped up by
someone else, now that I can't make a decent bid for her.

PHILIPPE: But you say she loves you.

FRANTZ: Oh, she's fond of me all right. But the first time the
Duchess produces some titled feller-me-lad for her to marry,
what's to prevent her going off and leaving me in my poverty,
even though she is still fond of me?

PHILIPPE: Wouldn't she follow you without money?

FRANTZ: Oh, I suppose she'd follow me on an impulse. But
what should I do with a millionairess, if I hadn't any money?
No one in his senses could expect her to be able to put up
with the petty irritations of that sort of life, or hope that I

could go on loving her, poverty-stricken and humiliated. I know poverty, and I'm not going to introduce her to it. I'd rather marry her off myself to some rich man.

PHILIPPE: You're letting your own pride lead you off at a tangent. If you really love her, you can still marry her.

FRANTZ: It's useless. I might have known it. Everyone will tell me that. I do 'really' love her, Philippe. Why do you always talk, all of you, as though money were something nasty from under a stone, when actually it's the only thing that can protect you from nastiness? I love her too much to do without money.

PHILIPPE: That's blasphemous, Frantz. Real love can do without money.

FRANTZ: Oh, for God's sake – don't start moralizing. I tell you I'm suffering. You say you're my friend. Can't you try to understand what I'm going through, instead of just churning out ready-made answers? Poverty made my childhood a long train of pettiness and disgust, and now I don't trust myself. My love is too beautiful, I expect too much of it to risk infecting it as well. I want to surround it with a protective wall of money.

PHILIPPE: It's sheer madness, Frantz.

FRANTZ: Yes, isn't it? I want my love to be spotless. I want us to love each other without calculation or fear or shame. Sheer madness. (*Silence.*) I sometimes think there are probably people about who have too much money. Who are afraid it will spoil their love, just as I am afraid mine will be spoiled by poverty. It's ludicrous.

PHILIPPE: Frantz. I know you'll say I'm talking like an uncle, but . . . be patient. It will probably all come right, one day.

FRANTZ: There's something else. It's not easy living at close quarters with a young girl. I can't wait any longer. I need her as much as I need air and water.

PHILIPPE: Take her as your mistress at Granat, then. . . .

FRANTZ: I suppose that's what will happen. I can feel the moment approaching, irresistibly, inevitably, when she will have to belong to me. The only true link between us, our

tenderness, is at the mercy of that moment now. I know the
value of tenderness, Philippe. I know there is no compromise
possible with love, and that any little drab in the streets has
only to lift up her arms and show off her breasts for tenderness to be utterly futile.

PHILIPPE (*in a hard voice*): Frantz, there's another solution.
Be a man. Have the pluck to get out.

FRANTZ: No, Philippe. . . . My love isn't perfect, but I have
the feeling that somewhere out of sight, though very near
me, there is another love spreading enormous wings, and
that this other love will perhaps be mine one day if I prove
myself worthy of it. You think it would be courageous to
resign myself, don't you? – not to snatch at it and drag it
out of the shadows? But it would be cowardly. We all have
one chance of love. What we should do is to seize the chance
as it passes, and then build up our love humbly, relentlessly,
even though it cost a year of our life – or perhaps a
crime.

PHILIPPE: But are you sure there is no other solution than
the success of your business?

FRANTZ: Her aunt's death would be one.

They stand looking at each other for a long time.

PHILIPPE: Frantz!

FRANTZ: What's the matter? You told me yourself I should
never have the courage to commit a crime.

PHILIPPE: Were you really thinking—?

FRANTZ: Just now, yes. I was quite wrong to believe for a
moment that it was possible. You saw for yourself.

PHILIPPE: Frantz! You're making me feel guilty! I feel like
someone who's pointed out the wrong road to you and gone
calmly on his own way.

FRANTZ (*rising, with a smile*): Don't be too remorseful. For
sensitive people the parting of the ways always comes sooner
or later. And we shall have gone a long way together.

PHILIPPE: Why did you want us to separate? I'm sure things

would have been different if we had stayed friends. Frantz –
drop all these mad ideas . . . let's carry on together, help
each other.

FRANTZ: One could always try, I suppose.

FLORENTINE (*appearing with a coat over her pyjamas*): There
you are, you two! I was looking for a man. Country houses
give me the creeps. Of course, there's a spider in my room –
there always are spiders in country bedrooms. It's as big as
a house. I'm terrified of spiders. Won't anyone come and
kill it for me?

FRANTZ: Go on, Philippe. Florentine knows how bad I am
at killing spiders.

FLORENTINE: Oh! If I had to count on you! But I'm sure
your friend is much nicer than you are.

PHILIPPE: Yes, I'll come. In a minute. Frantz and I were just
talking – something rather important.

FLORENTINE: As important as that?

PHILIPPE: Yes.

FRANTZ (*gently*): No. Not so important. Off you go, Philippe.

PHILIPPE: I can't leave you like this, old man.

FRANTZ: Of course you can. I swear it's all right. Please.

PHILIPPE: I'll come back in a minute, I promise.

FLORENTINE: My God, there's chivalry for you! I'd better
go and find Mr Bentz. He's older, he won't be such a heel.
(*She goes out.*)

FRANTZ: Go on, old man. Please. You've been very decent.
Truly. Now you go with Florentine – *I'm* asking you to.
Go on.

PHILIPPE: You're not angry? I'll be back.

FRANTZ: Yes.

PHILIPPE: I feel terrible about it. But I really do want to know
what she's getting at. This little manoeuvre's been going on
ever since you introduced us.

FRANTZ: Hurry up and catch her.

PHILIPPE: Do cheer up. You're exaggerating, really, you
know. . . . We'll talk more about it. You'll see. We'll
think of something.

FRANTZ: Yes.

PHILIPPE (*going out and coming back again*): You're not angry with me?

FRANTZ: Of course not.

PHILIPPE *goes out.* FRANTZ *sits down and holds his head in his hands.* MONIME *enters suddenly.*

MONIME: Aren't you in bed, Frantz? You'll be tired tomorrow.

FRANTZ (*sitting up*): What about you? Why aren't you asleep?

MONIME: I wanted to talk to you. I was waiting till the other two had gone.

FRANTZ: Are you pleased with the trip, little one?

MONIME: Yes.

FRANTZ: It's fun, isn't it, to drop in on people one doesn't know of an evening and then have to stay the night? Is your room all right?

MONIME: Yes.

FRANTZ: You don't look happy. If I were a girl boxed up in a castle all the year round with an aged aunt, I should feel highly delighted at having so many things happening in one evening.

MONIME: I am happy.

FRANTZ: Then why the sigh?

MONIME: You came to ask them for money, didn't you?

FRANTZ: Don't you worry about that, Monime. Let me fight it out by myself. You mustn't know anything. I swear I'll manage to get hold of enough for us to be happy.

MONIME: As you say that, I can hear that your voice doesn't believe it any more. Why won't you tell me? They refused to give it you, and you're too proud to say so. (*Pause.*) I let you alone at first because I thought that after all it might be better that way, but do you really believe that our happiness depends on that money? Do you, dear silly one?

FRANTZ: Yes, I do.

MONIME: Well, you're wrong. We can be very rich if we want to, and still turn up our noses at money.

FRANTZ: You're such a little girl, Monime.

MONIME: I know, I know – you can be terribly older and wiser just because I'm younger than you, but I know a lot.

FRANTZ (*smiling*): What do you know?

MONIME: Sit down. S-sh! Don't say anything. And you're not to smile at me or shout at me, and above all – above all, you're not to interrupt me with one of those bitter remarks of yours that you're so proud of and that make you miserable for the rest of the day when you've said them. (*She is standing behind him, her head against his.*) Frantz, I don't want you to be sad any more. Don't say anything. You'll only start lying and telling me you're not sad and that you're earning a lot of money and that you'll come one day in a huge bottle-green car, the sort I like, to carry me off miles and miles away from my horrible old aunt. . . . I know your little story. . . . Don't tell me . . . It wouldn't be true. You are sad. One thing I must say for you, you play your part well. Breaking the branches off trees as you pass them, just to infuriate me; sneering at the books I read; pulling down my hair seven times a day – the same old ritual as when we were children. And yet, underneath all this byplay that hasn't changed a bit, I can see perfectly well that you're unhappy, Frantz. (*She places her hand over his mouth.*) You were going to lie. Ever since we started out this evening you've had a face as long as a fiddle. Do you think I didn't see all those horrid figures you were scribbling in your notebook? You are unhappy, Frantz. Do you think I don't know why? You jumped, didn't you, and you tried to move your lips. But I've got my hand tight there, and you can't say a word. You know very well I'm as strong as you, my boy! My boy. Frantz, you're not my boy any longer. You don't look at me the same way. Or kiss me the same way. You're frightened to take me on your knee or hold me in your arms. Go on, go on, try to talk. You'll only tell me that I don't understand. . . . Just because you were brighter than I was at school you've got into the habit of thinking you're the cleverer one still. Idiot! Dear idiot! I know what's wrong. (*Pause.*

She has her cheek against his head and is murmuring, far too tenderly.) I'll be your mistress, Frantz, whenever you like. S-sh! Don't talk. Don't move your lips – you tickle my hand. Just stay like a little boy and let me rock you to sleep with what I've said, until you're not unhappy any more. I'll be your mistress whenever you like. You want to talk, do you? I know what you're going to say. But it doesn't matter. Nothing matters. I want your arm to find its way back to my waist and your head to find its way back to my shoulder – freely and openly. I'm taking my hand away. You can talk now. Only don't look at me for a moment. (FRANTZ *remains motionless for a moment, then turns abruptly and holds her to him. She feels ashamed.*) Oh, Frantz!

FRANTZ: I'm looking at you. The same eyes, the same mouth as when I was a child. You are Monime, with the wildest of looks and the reddest of lips. Trembling lips, too. My everyday Monime, is it really you?

MONIME: Yes, Frantz, it's me.

FRANTZ: Stand up straight now. I'm looking at you. You're very beautiful today. Is it for the great occasion that you've got on your new dress and put up your hair? But you've forgotten to make yourself some grown-up fingernails. . . . These are your tree-climbing nails! And your great decision hasn't taught you to make up your face . . . you've put your lipstick on any old how, as usual. . . .

MONIME: Oh, Frantz, you're laughing at me. . . .

He has drawn her towards him. She hides her head.

FRANTZ: My little one, I'm glad it was my wild one that came to tell me this, with her hands all scratched and her lipstick all awry. (*Pause.*) Dear, silly girl. Coming without thinking to stop me from being sad. Without stopping to ask yourself any questions. Do you think I don't know everything? You don't love me as a man, Monime. You came to find your lost comrade, and you offered your body in exchange, the most precious ransom you could give. Our friendship never hurt you. You've never dreamed of a tyranny stronger and gentler than that of childhood friendship. Don't hide your head. What are you ashamed of? I love you for it all, my girl with the quiet voice . . . Monime, who knows everything and nothing.

MONIME: I know that I want to be your mistress. I want you to make love to me and hurt me. I want to hear you laughing and singing again.

Silence. He takes her in his arms.

FRANTZ: Idiot, I love you. You've come to give me a wonderful present; but what could I give you in exchange?

MONIME: I'm not a little girl. I don't want you to laugh at me. I want you to take me.

FRANTZ: But you don't love me, Monime.

MONIME: I love you the only way I know how to. I shall soon change, Frantz. I swear I shall learn terribly quickly. Take me, Frantz.

FRANTZ: You must go to bed.

MONIME: You're not well. I can see it in your eyes. Your hands are trembling.

FRANTZ: Go along, little one. It would be too stupid if anyone found us together here.

MONIME: I don't care.

FRANTZ: Please go.

MONIME: Touch me, at least. Kiss me. I don't want to be just your friend any more, your poor little playfellow that hasn't any claim on you. You said once that I should be your wife. . . .

FRANTZ: When we are rich, and when you love me with a woman's love.

MONIME: But I *shall* love you that way, I know I shall. (*She goes up to him and says to him softly, awkwardly.*) Kiss me, please. Kiss me as you would kiss someone you had just met and loved. (*He makes as if to push her away.*) Just once, only once, so that tonight begins another sort of life. You want to, Frantz, you want to. You're trembling and you haven't the courage to tear me away. Why don't you kiss me? Ah! (*He gives her a long kiss.*)

FRANTZ: Go along now, Monime.

She goes.

Curtain

Act Two

SCENE: *The* DUCHESS'S *antechamber, in semi-darkness. It is a huge bare room, with tapestries and armour about. A french window leads to the grounds, where large trees are to be seen.*

TIME: *It is evening, near nightfall.*

MONIME *and* FRANTZ *come in from the garden and put on the lights.*

MONIME: She didn't ask any questions during dinner, because of Urbain. But she certainly will. Frantz, don't pull that awful face. I was a stupid little goose before, but I'm a very good liar now. You taught me that.

FRANTZ: Yes.

MONIME: Why are you unhappy every time we come back from there?

FRANTZ: Because you're a very good liar, and because I taught you.

MONIME: You're mad! I'm very happy.

FRANTZ: That's not true.

MONIME: It is.

FRANTZ: No doubt you can lie well enough to your aunt, but not to me. Since we've been lovers, you're not happy, Monime.

Long silence. MONIME *gets up, and speaks with forced cheerfulness.*

MONIME: There must be some water in her room. I'm going to take the famous pills before she arrives; with her water – what a joke!

FRANTZ: Don't take them. It's not worth it now.

MONIME: But, Frantz, the doctor told you – it's our only chance.

FRANTZ: There's another, that he didn't think of. Don't take them. It's not worth it.

Silence.

MONIME: What's the matter, Frantz?

FRANTZ: I've had enough of living in this constant state of apprehension. Telling lies. Making furtive trips with Florentine.

MONIME: We won't go any more.

FRANTZ: You know very well we shan't have the courage. We're prisoners now, Monime. We must love each other now, at all costs. Every day. Laboriously. Scrupulously. Taking pills to murder our children and smiling to deceive the old woman.

FLORENTINE *appears at the french window, coming from the garden.*

FLORENTINE: Hullo there! Aren't you coming to Vichy with me? I've got a midnight pass. Good evening, pale and interesting!

FRANTZ: Good evening.

FLORENTINE: It's marvellous in the evening, you know – there's a whole crowd of us going, the oddest collection you ever saw. But of course you don't like it. God, how difficult conversation is with you! So you really aren't coming?

MONIME: You know we can't. Aunt Caroline has forbidden us.

FLORENTINE: What? Isn't the old dear dead yet? She really has no sense of propriety. Tell her to hurry up and not hang about so.

MONIME: Florentine. . . .

FLORENTINE: I'm off, dear girl. Frantz is glaring at me quite terrifyingly. Hang it all, Frantz, I was only joking. 'Bye, darling. Good-bye, pale and interesting.

She goes off into the grounds, laughing. MONIME *watches her go. Then she fetches a glass of water from the adjoining room and takes the pills.*

MONIME: There you are! A little water; two pills at midday, two pills at night, and the babies die off like flies. I have no shame – no shame at all. (*She makes a little curtsy.*) Expert infanticide, at your service.

FRANTZ: Why do you make fun of it?

MONIME: We've got to be happy any way that we can now. Even if it's just by making fun of things.

FRANTZ: You're better than I am. And not such a coward.

MONIME: I won't have you saying such things. Just because a poor idiot of a girl loves you and plays the clown to try and make you laugh. It doesn't happen often.

FRANTZ: I'm miserable, Monime.

MONIME: You see the reward I get.

FRANTZ: We were wrong to love each other this way. It's all right for Florentine.

MONIME: Frantz, there mustn't be any regrets. . . .

FRANTZ: But it's over now. We're going to get out of this dead end, I promise.

MONIME: You're going to have some money? Your business is starting up again?

FRANTZ: No. Something else.

MONIME: Something else? But we've thought so hard – there can't be a solution, however tiny; it could never have slipped through the mesh.

FRANTZ: Yes, there is. There was another solution I told you about.

MONIME: Which one?

FRANTZ: Get up, there's your aunt coming.

The DUCHESS, *a larger-than-life, almost fabulous personage, comes in, followed by* URBAIN, *the major-domo, carrying a fur rug.*

DUCHESS: So there you are, both of you! I must say you are most difficult to find these days. You seem to have a way of disappearing as if by magic. (*She installs herself in her enormous wing chair, a slow, meticulous ceremony.*) You may go now, Urbain. And bring me my sleeping draught when I ring.

URBAIN *goes out. Pause.*

Now, I quite understand that you should have a taste for long walks and solitary excursions. The poor Duke was just the same. Except for meals, he was never to be found. Always prowling about the woods with nothing but his cane for company. . . . But is it perhaps possible that you are a little too fond of them? Pray don't interrupt me, Monime. I am not your nurse, of course, to follow you about and spank you when you are naughty. Nor am I at all put out by your close association with this dear boy, please be assured of that. But seeing you flying off to Vichy and here, there and everywhere by motor-car, as you do, just the two of you, I've been thinking – the people in this part of the country are so stupid – they might begin to imagine there was some sort of relationship between you other than mere friendship. . . . It's ridiculous, I grant you, my dear Frantz, and being as intelligent as you are, you will be the first to laugh at it. . . . Quite so. That is a compliment I really have to pay you! You have always known your place and kept to it. I am sure it is only thoughtlessness on your part, and were it not for the grotesque – you will agree that grotesque is the word – were it not as I say for the grotesque gossip it might occasion, I should certainly not allude to it. However, there *is* this outlandish gossip in the air. And you know how quickly it can take hold of these small provincial places. The curé, who by the way is a perfect fool, is already heaving ecstatic sighs in anticipation of the marriage service.

MONIME: Aunt Caroline—

DUCHESS: I know. He's been dreaming of that service ever since your first communion, and he would die of chagrin if we were to go to the bishop – which we probably shall, by the way. But from the way he gushed over me last Sunday it would seem that he thinks the ceremony is likely to take place at any moment. And I am sure you will understand, my dear Frantz, that that is quite impossible. I have the friendliest of feelings towards you, but all the same, and in spite of the great respect I had for your poor father, I cannot allow Granat to imagine that I would have my niece marry the son of my late physician. It would be comical, as the poor Duke used to say. It was the only adjective he knew.

MONIME: Aunt Caroline—

DUCHESS: Now don't interfere, Monime. Frantz is an intelligent boy. He wouldn't dream of taking offence at anything so obviously reasonable. Isn't that so, Frantz?

FRANTZ: Most certainly, madame.

DUCHESS: You are a fine boy, Frantz; I have always appreciated that. I realize that at the moment you are not managing your affairs particularly cleverly – however, let us not go into that now, we can discuss that later – but you are a charming young man in every respect, I must say that. A little weak, of course, both morally and physically. . . . When I think of your father, who could pretty well fell a tree with a few blows of his stick, I must say I am baffled. How is it possible that he begot you? . . . It is true your mother was nothing to speak of. . . . He married her against my advice . . . she hadn't a penny to bless herself with and then she had that chronic cough, it seems. I say 'it seems', for I could never be bothered with her – never set eyes on her, in fact. If he had taken the wife I had in mind for him, his son would have been quite another proposition, if I may say so, and he would not have died penniless. But we are straying from the point. You are a good boy just the same. I am very fond of you, and have every respect for your excellent qualities. But once having said this, I cannot possibly have people thinking that you are about to become my nephew. Were we in Paris, among sophisticated people, everything would be quite different. It would not enter anyone's head that I could possibly marry you to my niece. But here we are dealing with people stupid enough to think anything possible – and if I were to announce tomorrow that I had chosen you for Monime, it would not in the least surprise them. They are quite absurd. I know them only too well. That is why, my dear children, I am going to ask you to space these outings more discreetly, and make yourselves a little less conspicuous.

MONIME: But, Aunt—

DUCHESS: Now do let us leave this ridiculous subject, Monime my dear. I feel sure you have both understood perfectly well what I have been trying to say. Let us talk about you now, Frantz. You have had to sell your business. At a loss, I understand.

FRANTZ: I have nothing left but debts.

DUCHESS: You would have your way, and now of course you have come a cropper. Were you my own son, I could forgive you for having neither business sense nor a taste for study. But you have neither the fortune that makes idleness possible nor the breeding that makes it imperative. What do you propose to do?

FRANTZ: I don't know. I don't know what to do.

DUCHESS: A bad reply if ever there was one. You must work, my dear boy. For people of your sort, it is the only thing to be done. I mean, you can't turn thief or murderer. (FRANTZ *gives her a long look.*) It would get you nowhere – and in any case you would be caught in the end. If only you would bring yourself to marry some fat moneybags. But you will bring in sentiment. Think it over, my dear Frantz. I am always happy to have you at Granat – but I should not like you to take for granted a leisure and luxury which are not yours by right.

MARIE-ANNE *appears, with red-rimmed eyes and handkerchief in hand. She is torn between distress and timidity.*

MARIE-ANNE: You must excuse me, your Grace, for disturbing you.

DUCHESS: What is it, woman?

MARIE-ANNE: Oh, your Grace, it's dreadful.

DUCHESS: Really. Is this going to be another of your tedious stories?

MARIE-ANNE: Oh, no, your Grace . . .

DUCHESS: I suppose this time you want me to supply knickerbockers for some village brat you've taken pity on?

MARIE-ANNE: Oh, no, your Grace . . .

DUCHESS: Take that pitiful look off your face, woman. You know it drives me to distraction. Well, come along, what is it?

MARIE-ANNE: My cousin, your Grace . . .

DUCHESS: Ah, this is a new one. Now what has he been up to? No doubt trying to extort money from you in his usual manner?

MARIE-ANNE: Oh, no, your Grace . . . I've heard from the hospital at Toulon, where he has been taken; he's very ill; he's going to die.

DUCHESS: And you really believe that? How much does he ask for? He must be wanting quite a tidy sum.

MARIE-ANNE: But he didn't write to me, your Grace – it was the hospital. . . .

DUCHESS: An accomplice, of course. Anyone can fool you. Show me the letter. . . . Obviously, they've used the hospital writing paper. . . . My good girl, what do you expect? – we're all going to die.

MARIE-ANNE: Might I perhaps ask you to allow me a few days' leave, your Grace?

DUCHESS: Take it. Take it, my good woman; one can never rely on you anyway.

MARIE-ANNE: I shouldn't like to displease your Grace.

DUCHESS: Oh, my displeasure is of no importance! We all know that here. I shall just have to look after myself; take my medicine by myself, play piquet by myself, and—

MONIME: But I'll take Marie-Anne's place for you, Aunt Caroline. . . .

DUCHESS: It is true you will have plenty of time, my dear child, now that you are giving up your walks. You may go, then, Marie-Anne. These two children are wearing the most appalling expression, but as they declare themselves willing you had better take advantage of it. It won't last. When are you leaving?

MARIE-ANNE: There is a train at ten o'clock.

DUCHESS: Take it then, and try to be back on Monday. . . .

MARIE-ANNE: Oh, your Grace, I thought I might stay until—

DUCHESS: Of course, of course. But be as quick as you can. . . .

MARIE-ANNE: Good night, your Grace. . . . I must hurry and pack my bag. I'm so afraid I might arrive too late, poor boy. . . . (*She goes out.*)

DUCHESS: So the creature's going to die. Good riddance to bad rubbish. The old fool's been giving him all her money and he of course has been drinking it away, with the able assistance of any trollop he could find. I never have been able to understand why she stuck to that seafaring Casanova.

MONIME: Was he her cousin?

DUCHESS: So she said, to cover up her little game. I have never for one instant believed it. Or if he was her cousin, it was certainly not as such that she flew off to see him every time he came into port and gave him all her savings.

MONIME: I don't understand, Aunt Caroline.

DUCHESS: I know what I'm saying. She was engaged to him once . . . let's hope to God that's all it was . . . and yet at over fifty, she still weeps when he doesn't write. What do you think of that?

MONIME: Poor Marie-Anne! Perhaps they were in love once, and couldn't get married!

DUCHESS: Pshaw! – is that all? I was to have married the Duc d'Orléans. Ring for Urbain, will you, please, dear boy? It never came to anything because his mother unearthed a Spanish princess for him. But did I spend the rest of my life weeping and wailing?

MONIME: It isn't the same, Aunt Caroline. . . .

DUCHESS: Be quiet, you are a little nincompoop. You really are being most provoking, and I want to get a good night's rest. (URBAIN *comes in, carrying a glass on a salver.*) Ah, here is my medicine. Ugh! It's disgusting. You will not forget to inform the kitchen maid, Urbain, that she should choose between that boy and her situation. Send my women in. . . . (URBAIN *goes out and comes back later with the maids.*) It would be a fine thing if I were left to the mercy of all my servants' whims. Not to speak of having to put up with their marrying those of my mortal enemy. One of the kitchen maids, if you will believe it, wanted to marry Dr Fernot's valet-de-chambre! Dr Fernot – a man who makes me long to pour a little something into his wine. The ninny maintains she's in love with him! Quite magnificent. What is the matter with them all? Let them give their minds to doing their work properly and being honest, and leave the rest to the street girls. Good night, Monime my dear. . . . (*Noise of a merry-go-round in the distance.*) Now, of course, there's that hubbub. . . . This fair is a positive martyrdom. Scores of times I've asked for it to be postponed until August, when I take my cure at Plombières. But the Mayor says it is impossible, that it's been at this time since the twelfth century. But he is so negligent. . . . Ah well, my sleeping draught has quietened me down. . . . Good night, my dear Frantz. You are quite pale, what is the matter? Perhaps you need a tonic? Good night. . . .

She goes into her room, followed by two MAIDS. URBAIN, *having closed the door, comes back to* MONIME.

URBAIN: I beg pardon, mademoiselle. But as you are being kind enough to replace Mademoiselle Marie-Anne this evening, I ought to tell you that her Grace has given us all permission to go off to the fair for a while. . . . There will only be old Joseph here. But you know he's deaf, mademoiselle, and always dropping off to sleep. So I should be very grateful if you would be so good as to send for me if her Grace should need anything. I shall not go far.

MONIME: Very well, Urbain. (*He bows and goes out. Silence for a while. The two* MAIDS *leave the* DUCHESS'S *room and curtsy as they go off.*) It will be nice alone together.

DUCHESS (*calling*): Monime. . . .

MONIME (*in the doorway, through which can be seen a bed with a canopy*): Yes, Aunt Caroline?

DUCHESS (*who can be heard but not seen*): If I move during my sleep, please make a note. My doctor claims it is very indicative. As a matter of fact I believe the man's a lunatic. But we have to submit to these people. . . . Make a note, there's a good girl.

MONIME: Of course, Aunt Caroline.

DUCHESS: Your eyes look haggard, Monime. These walks are tiring you. Where were you this afternoon? At Vichy? Don't overdo this dancing.

MONIME: But on the contrary, Aunt Caroline. We went for a very quiet walk in the country with Philippe and Florentine.

DUCHESS: Very well, then. Good night.

MONIME: Good night, Aunt Caroline. . . . (*She has closed the door, and comes back to* FRANTZ *on tiptoe. She drops a curtsy, laughing.*) Good night, Aunt Caroline. . . .

FRANTZ: Let's see your real smile again now. Look at me with your real eyes. Be yourself.

MONIME: Don't you think I'm a very good liar?

FRANTZ (*looks at her*): My Monime with the white dress. . . . Yes, you *are* the same girl. The girl that's such a good liar. The girl that can undress in a flash, take her lover, and dress again in a flash – the girl that's always drinking water.

MONIME: I love you, Frantz. . . .

FRANTZ: Forgive me. That false smile that I reproach you for – I put it there myself.

MONIME: What does it matter?

FRANTZ: I've made you into so many of the things I detest. All because I was too cowardly to give you up and too cowardly to get the money at all costs. It's because I was every sort of coward that we're afraid now. (*Pause.*) Can't you feel them all around us – filthy hands, greasy hands, old wrinkled abortionists' hands . . . ?

MONIME: How can they harm us, Frantz, since we love each other?

FRANTZ: My climber of trees, my girl running in the grass, my little one. I don't want some vile old woman to hurt you and make you feel frightened and ashamed. I don't want it. I don't want it. (*He puts his head in his hands.*)

MONIME (*goes to him*): Let's go away, Frantz. We'll go and

live in a big town and get some work. I don't mind a bit about being poor.

FRANTZ (*without moving*): We shouldn't be able to love each other if we were poor.

MONIME: Why do you say that? I should love you even if you were ugly and poor and sick.

FRANTZ: Oh, my God, what a monster I am. Other people believe in an eternity of love, in a humble cottage, with clear cold water. Why am I blessed with this love, but not the credulity to feed it on?

MONIME: You don't love me, Frantz.

FRANTZ (*taking her by the arm and shouting*): I forbid you – do you understand – I forbid you to say that!

MONIME: You're hurting me!

FRANTZ: I know there'll come a time when other people will say those things. I can hear them sneering already . . . and I don't care. But you mustn't doubt me, not you, not even for a second. (*On his knees.*) I love you, Monime.

MONIME (*stroking his head gently*): Why are you afraid then?

FRANTZ: Because I love you. Because I know what petty things can kill the greatest love.

MONIME: Ours can't die.

FRANTZ: Yes, it can. Even ours. Try to understand, my little one. People don't love each other like lovers in stories, naked and for ever. People who love each other are constantly battling against hordes of hidden forces that attack them from within or from the world outside. Against other men and other women.

MONIME: We are strong enough to fight them.

FRANTZ: Not with poverty to fight as well. Poverty will line up with our enemies, with all the fatal germs that love has to resist from the very first moment. Oh, you're talking like a spoiled darling. . . . You don't know the way that poverty goes to work; how ingenious it is – how persistent. For twenty years now I have had it at my heels like a snarling dog – I know that nothing can resist it, even youth, although youth is as vital and as strong as love. I'm afraid of it. I'm afraid of the beautiful women we shall pretend not to notice when you are poor and ill dressed. . . . I'm afraid of seeing you diminish every day – taking orders from a boss or doing sordid chores about the house. I know that that shouldn't matter and that I shall feel all the more tenderness for you because of it. But I'm afraid of that very tenderness, too, because little by little it will take the place of love.

MONIME: Perhaps if we're happy you'll stop being afraid. . . .

FRANTZ: You're not listening. You're following your own sweet dream. No one will listen to me. No one will believe me. . . . But what if I know that we have no right to take this thousand-to-one risk of spoiling our love? Supposing I know that one morning we shall wake up in our room and look at each other with hatred; and that you will ask yourself if it wouldn't have been better to go on leading the peaceful, happy life of the rich?

MONIME: Oh, Frantz!

FRANTZ: You will ask yourself that, whether you want to or not. . . . You'll look at me quite differently when my back is turned. And I shall watch the almost imperceptible marks of poverty at the corners of your mouth and on your hands, and it will be enough for our eyes to meet for our love to be killed.

MONIME: Oh, how can you know all that in advance?

FRANTZ (*crouched on the ground, clasping her legs, stays wrapped in thought for a while*): Monime, I should like to believe in fairy tales too. . . .

MONIME: Frantz! You're crying.

FRANTZ: You won't be able to understand it all perhaps, but promise me that if one day you see me hauled up for judgement and you find that I fill you with disgust – promise me you'll remember these tears.

MONIME: What's wrong with you?

FRANTZ: They'll tell you I was a weakling; that I hadn't the courage to work and endure poverty; they may even tell you I didn't love you, as though they had the right to judge me. . . . But you won't listen to them. You will think of these tears and of how much I longed for perfection.

MONIME: I don't understand you.

FRANTZ: I don't need you to. I need you to believe in my love, even without understanding it.

MONIME: I do believe in it, Frantz, and we'll do whatever you like. You must never cry any more. (*A long silence. They remain motionless close to each other, looking very small in the great hall, surrounded by armour.* MONIME *looks thoughtful.*) Oh, why haven't I any money of my own? Everything would be so simple. . . .

FRANTZ (*raises his head and looks at her*). When your aunt dies you will be rich.

MONIME: Why do you say that? We shouldn't wish she were dead.

FRANTZ: We can wish we were happy. And it's the same thing. Monime; if you want us to love each other, you will wish for her death. Every morning, like a prayer.

MONIME: Oh, Frantz, no!

FRANTZ (*taking her face in his hands*): Look at me. There is only this one chance left for us. Will you dare not to wish her dead so that we can be happy?

MONIME (*turns her head away*): I love you.

FRANTZ: Look at me. Please.

MONIME: I'm ashamed.

FRANTZ: What are you thinking?

MONIME (*hiding her head on* FRANTZ'S *breast*): The same as you, but it makes me unhappy.

FRANTZ: There's no need, silly one. It's never been known for wishes to interfere with destiny, even for a second. . . . Besides, I may be wrong. We may be able to love each other for a long while the way we are. . . . (*He takes a few steps away from her.*)

MONIME: Frantz, you say 'we', but you still mean yourself! Is it true that you could stop loving me because of it being this way? (*He shrugs his shoulders.*) Oh! Then let her die . . . let her die quickly! I don't want you to stop loving me.

FRANTZ *goes slowly to the door of the* DUCHESS'S *room, opens it a fraction, and looks in. After a moment of silence—*

FRANTZ (*softly*): There she is lying in state. . . . You're asleep. . . . Your old heart is beating feebly, but doggedly, of course. You can't even be dreaming . . . except perhaps of social caste. You take every possible precaution, don't you? You're on your guard; you're holding on like glue. . . . You'll squeeze out another twenty years yet, day by day, as cleverly as you squeeze bargains out of shopkeepers with your highfalutin talk. You're alive, you old thief. . . .

MONIME: You'll wake her up. Come back.

FRANTZ: She'll stick it out. She'll stick it right out to the end if someone doesn't see to it. She's spent all her life preparing this glorious old age; not devoting herself to anything – love, charity, not even wickedness. Every act of pleasure or devotion or enthusiasm cuts us short. She knew that all right; she was on the look-out all the time so as to last a little longer. (*He laughs.*) The old miser. . . .

MONIME: Frantz, please! Come back.

FRANTZ: She's never had a cough, has she? Lungs in perfect order. Never taken cold in a garden at night, or in a church. . . . Her liver functions splendidly. She could have been a glutton, but she denied herself that as well. What about her heart? She's never complained of any trouble there, has she, Monime? Answer me, Monime – she's never suffered with her heart, has she?

MONIME: I don't know. This is horrible. Stop it.

FRANTZ: What intense joy or suffering do you think could arouse that old carcass? She can have hardly any blood in her at all.

MONIME: Frantz!

FRANTZ (*suddenly coming back to her*): Have the courage to admit to yourself what her life is worth compared with our love. She's never been kind to you. Never a smile or an affectionate word. Never a hand stretched out to protect you from some childish heartache. . . .

MONIME: No, never.

FRANTZ: It was not thanks to her that you learned to live and love; you were brought up by servants, below stairs.

MONIME: Yes.

FRANTZ: You can't remember a single thing she did to make you happy. All you associate with her is harshness and meanness.

MONIME: Yes, Frantz.

FRANTZ: Well, then you must have the courage to wish she would die. Die, and let go of all that money that she's been hanging on to ever since she was young, for no reason at all, all that money that represents our happiness. Look at me, Monime. . . .

MONIME: I'm ashamed, Frantz.

FRANTZ: Surely you don't love her?

MONIME: No.

FRANTZ: Then why don't you answer me?

MONIME: I'm frightened.

FRANTZ: You must take a tight grip of your fear. It's like a dog that tries to jump at your throat. You must strangle it and kill it. Take hold of it – turn it to face you, press yourself against it, mouth to mouth, until your hair stands on end and your teeth chatter. It isn't fear any longer then. You'll see. It's something else. Silence and darkness become one's accomplices. Then it's possible to go to bed, and sleep, even though there's a corpse near by.

MONIME (*stares at him and cries*): Frantz! We must go upstairs and put on all the lights! Something is happening that I don't understand. Why did you say that just now? Give me your hands, I'm frightened. They're all cold. . . . Let's get away from here. Please!

He remains motionless. Silence for a while. The noise of the fair can be heard.

FRANTZ: Why are you afraid? You used not to be so timid. We used to play hide and seek at night in the antechambers. Shall we play it now? Remember, how we used to hide behind the armour?

MONIME (*pressing herself against him*): Don't leave me.

FRANTZ: I shan't leave you. I don't ever want to leave you. Only for one minute. One long, terrible minute. Then I shall never leave you again as long as I live.

MONIME: What are you saying?

FRANTZ: Nothing. Just talking. I'm listening to my voice. It's the same as ever. It's astonishing.

MONIME (*crying out suddenly like a mad thing*): What does all this mean? What are you talking about?

MARIE-ANNE *appears, dressed for the journey and carrying an old-fashioned suit-case.*

MARIE-ANNE: Good-bye, mademoiselle, monsieur. . . . Is her Grace asleep? I do hope she will not be upset about my leaving. But I had to go at once. Poor boy, it will be the last time perhaps, the last time. . . .

MONIME: Will you be at Toulon tomorrow?

MARIE-ANNE: Yes, some time tomorrow. . . . I'm afraid it may be too late. My poor dear, my poor dear. . . .

FRANTZ (*suddenly*): Did you love him, Marie-Anne?

MARIE-ANNE (*stops short, nonplussed*): Why do you ask me that, Monsieur Frantz?

FRANTZ: Madame de Granat told me he had been your fiancé.

MARIE-ANNE: Yes.

FRANTZ: Why did you never marry? Were you lovers? Tell me. What are you afraid of? Is it your one-time fiancé you're going to see, or the man who made you into a woman? Taught you to love, made you suffer? Why won't you answer me?

MONIME: Frantz, leave her alone.

FRANTZ: Answer me, Marie-Anne.

MARIE-ANNE: That is my grief, not yours. . . . You have no right to ask me.

FRANTZ: He's going to die, and when you're dead as well, no one will know that you were happy once. Tell me. Wasn't he your lover? (*Pause.*) Marie-Anne, you can tell me.

MARIE-ANNE: He wouldn't have wanted me to be his mistress. . . .

FRANTZ: Why not?

MARIE-ANNE: Because he was proud . . . and I couldn't be his wife.

FRANTZ: Why?

MARIE-ANNE: We had no money to set ourselves up, or even to go away together. He earned barely enough to live on, and that kept him at sea all the year round. I was already serving the Duchess, who would not have kept me on had I married. We simply had to resign ourselves. There was no other way of getting money. We could hardly have murdered someone for it, could we?

FRANTZ (*taking her forcibly by the arm*): Are you sure?

MARIE-ANNE: What are you saying? What is the matter? Let me go.

MONIME: Frantz, let her go. What's the matter with you?

FRANTZ: Are you sure he loved you?

MARIE-ANNE: Oh! yes, he loved me. . . . You have no right to doubt it; he would have taken his own life for my sake.

FRANTZ (*softly*): That wouldn't be any good. If he had loved you he would have taken someone else's life for you.

MARIE-ANNE: You are mad! Do you know what it means to kill someone, that you talk so glibly about it? He knew. He had been in the war. . . .

FRANTZ (*suddenly*): I know, too. To kill is to take a knife or a club and deal blow after blow until there's not another sound, not another twitch.

MONIME: Frantz! Stop it! You're out of your mind! (*She clings to him, but he tears her away.*)

FRANTZ (*shouting at the top of his voice*): You think I'm raving, don't you? Do you think I'd dare call him a coward if I hadn't thought and thought and thought about it? Yes. I know what it means to kill someone. I know every way there is of doing it. I can tell you the best and the worst.

MONIME: Frantz, what are you saying?

FRANTZ: I know what you're going to say! But don't try and

fool yourselves with ready-made moralizing. It's because we're cowards, that's all. What else stops us killing? You simply don't have to look at your hands when it's done; you just wash them very thoroughly, and then you've earned the right to be happy.

He is positively yelling. MONIME *suddenly cries out loud and runs to shut the door of the* DUCHESS'S *room. She flattens herself against it as though to prevent* FRANTZ *from passing.*

MARIE-ANNE (*stammering, panic-stricken*): I don't know what's the matter with him. . . . I don't know what's the matter with him. . . .

FRANTZ (*continues hollowly*): Do you think I don't know what killing means? Do you think I don't feel the cringing of every muscle at the very thought of it? Do you think I don't know how the blood would stick to your fingers, and how the screaming would echo in your ears for days? I know it all. I know all about it, but it isn't going to make any difference.

MARIE-ANNE: It grieves me to have upset him like this. I don't understand it.

MONIME: You must forgive him, Marie-Anne; he is ill.

MARIE-ANNE: Yes.

MONIME: It's not true what he's been saying. You mustn't take any notice. It doesn't mean anything, does it, Marie-Anne?

MARIE-ANNE: No, mademoiselle.

MONIME *crosses to* MARIE-ANNE.

MONIME: I'll come to the gate with you. You must hurry, or you'll miss your train.

MARIE-ANNE: Yes, mademoiselle. Au revoir, monsieur.

MONIME: Leave him. Leave him. He's ill.

They go out. He remains where he is, completely spent. MONIME *comes running back.* FRANTZ *has not moved. There is silence for a while.*

Frantz!

FRANTZ: It's true, Monime. I didn't tell you because I knew the secret would be too much of a burden. I've quite made up my mind; in a few minutes from now, I'm going to kill her.

She has not allowed him to pronounce the word 'kill': she has sprung at him and taken him in her arms – her hand over his mouth.

MONIME: Be quiet. You mustn't say that word. They would take you away afterwards and kill you. We'll go away; we won't see each other any more. We'll do anything, but not that. . . . They would kill you. (*Pause.*) Come upstairs to my room. We'll put on the light and then we'll think. But not until we're up there. Come.

FRANTZ: I want to stay here.

MONIME (*falls on her knees*): Frantz, please, I beg you to.

FRANTZ: Get up. Don't cry. It's no use. Don't raise your voice. I'm staying here. (*He lifts her up and lays her on a couch. She is in a half-fainting condition.*) S-sh! I'm here. Close beside you. Don't try to talk. No, I shan't go away. I'm here, holding your hand. (*Long silence. He strokes her forehead now and again; she makes a few nervous movements. He tries to soothe her.*) You must keep very calm and listen to me. . . . You mustn't make me lose heart. I've thought of everything. S-sh! Don't move. . . . I've had something ready for a long time – something wrapped in cloth so that there won't be any blood or any noise.

MONIME: Frantz, you're talking like a murderer.

FRANTZ: I'm talking like a murderer because I'm going to be a murderer.

MONIME (*struggling with him*): I don't want you to! I don't want you to! I don't want you to!

FRANTZ (*holding her*): Be quiet. Don't move. I must, Monime. . . . Tears and shouting will only take away my courage and my nerve. My hands mustn't tremble while I'm doing it; I'm calm now, very calm. Don't say any more. It must be tonight. . . .

MONIME: Let's get away from here. Frantz. It's not true. . . .

FRANTZ: Yes. It will be true. We shall love each other and have nothing to be afraid of. This little one of ours, this hidden life that is struggling and growing inside you – we'll let it live if you'll let me do as I want. An old woman will die, but our child will live; that will be our justification, Monime.

MONIME: No. I don't want it! I'm frightened.

FRANTZ (*watches her struggling*): I know you. You're my own kind. Those wild eyes; those trembling lips – they're my own cowardice.

MONIME: You're afraid, too!

FRANTZ: Yes. I'm afraid. I'm a coward. But I've been trembling for months now. I'm used to my fear.

MONIME: Go away! I don't want any more to do with you!

FRANTZ: I want you all to myself, every day. I can't do without you any more. Life would be pointless and empty without you. You're going to go up to your room and go to bed as usual. I'm going to mine to disarrange my bed. Then I shall come down here, and come straight back to you afterward.

MONIME: No! I won't do it.

FRANTZ: I order you to.

MONIME: I won't go.

FRANTZ (*getting up*): Very well. Stay.

MONIME (*also getting up*): Frantz! You shan't go in there. You're mad.

FRANTZ: Let me pass.

MONIME: You shan't go in there. I'll call for help!

FRANTZ: There's no one there. And if she wakes up, I shall knock her senseless.

MONIME: You can't do it, Frantz!

FRANTZ: Come away from there.

MONIME: No, I shan't come away.

FRANTZ: You're shouting. Stop it!

MONIME: Yes. I'm shouting. I'm shouting!

FRANTZ: Have I got to hurt you?

He has taken her violently by the wrist and gives it a violent twist. She falls at his feet.

MONIME (*crying out wildly*): I don't love you, Frantz!

FRANTZ: It's too late to say that now. Let me go. (*He opens the door.*)

MONIME (*she is clinging to his leg. She talks rapidly, and in a low voice*): You shall listen to me, or you'll have to drag me right up to her bed and kill me first. I realize now. We don't love each other. You said so yourself. We don't love each other enough. . . . Our love is a lost cause. I'm not beautiful; you're already looking at other women and wanting them. . . . You only half-desire me, and I can't love you. We come back tired and miserable from that beastly room. If we really loved each other, do you think we should be unhappy and ashamed every time we made love? Do you think we should have been together so long without becoming lovers and that we should have been afraid of being poor? We didn't really love each other, Frantz. . . . We only felt tenderness for each other, and one doesn't kill for that.

FRANTZ (*pulls her violently toward him*): You're lying. . . . You're lying. . . . You know there's something else that's eluding us, passing us by . . . something we've wanted madly ever since we've been lovers. You know that there is a part of us that belongs together now and that it's only for the two of us that love means anything. We are bad lovers, bad friends, but all the same you know you'll never have any other lover or any other friend as long as you live. So why are you lying? (*He kisses her passionately. She submits.*) You see, tenderness can be forgotten for a while. We'll escape that too. . . .

She has fainted in his arms; he carries her off. The stage remains empty for a moment. Then one of the lower servants, old and half-witted, dodders up to the door and knocks.

SERVANT: Monsieur . . .

FRANTZ (*coming back alone*): What do you want?

SERVANT: It's me, Monsieur – Joseph. I've been left in charge. It's a telegram for you; a lad from the post office has just brought it by bicycle. To be delivered even in the night, he said.

FRANTZ: Thank you.

The servant leaves. FRANTZ *opens the telegram, reads it, and crumples it up without any expression having passed over his face.*

DUCHESS (*calling from her room*): Monime . . . Monime, are you there?

FRANTZ *has started violently at these words. He goes to the door and answers the* DUCHESS, *who can be heard, but not seen.*

FRANTZ: Monime has gone up to her room. She wasn't feeling well, but she'll be coming down again.

DUCHESS: Is that you, Frantz? I woke up with a start. I thought I was alone. I was frightened.

FRANTZ (*suddenly*): Are you frightened of being alone?

DUCHESS: It seems to be stormy outside.

FRANTZ: Are you afraid of death?

DUCHESS: Why do you ask me that? We mustn't talk about death. (*Pause.*) Get along now, Frantz. I want to go to sleep.

FRANTZ (*stares at her without moving, then murmurs*): I don't hate you.

DUCHESS: I don't know what you mean.

FRANTZ: Thank God. I don't hate her any more now. . . .

DUCHESS: Now go along, my dear Frantz, I don't know what you're talking about. . . . What are you doing standing there staring at me like that?

FRANTZ (*with a sort of appalling tenderness*): Poor old woman! We're trembling with fright, both of us. But it'll soon be over, you'll see. . . . (*He approaches like a sleep-walker; suddenly he falls on his knees.*) Oh, please! I beg of you! You're old now, you can't be deprived of love or of strength. There's only hatred left for you to give up. I love Monime; she loves me. Give us a little of your money and let us be happy! It's of no use to you.

DUCHESS: Aha! At last I understand. That's what you were

leading up to. . . . Ha! ha! ha! You are joking, my young friend!

FRANTZ: Don't laugh. I assure you you shouldn't laugh. Look how my hands are trembling. Look at my eyes. I'm afraid. I'm afraid now. I implore you to let us be happy, quite simply, with your blessing. We are two poor sweethearts like any others and we'd prefer it that way, after all. Listen – let me marry Monime. It would be better that way, I assure you. It would be better.

DUCHESS: This scene is ridiculous. You're asking the impossible. I'd rather see her dead than married to a little good-for-nothing like you, do you hear? (FRANTZ *has got up. There is silence for a while.*) There now, you've quite made me lose my temper, I shall have to take another sleeping draught if I'm to get any rest now. . . . Call Urbain.

FRANTZ: He's at the fair.

DUCHESS: So he is. Go and fetch Monime and tell her to come and give it me.

FRANTZ: I'll give it to you myself.

DUCHESS: Why you?

FRANTZ: Why not me?

DUCHESS: But you're not going to come into my bedroom. I'm in bed! I forbid you to!

He goes in and closes the door. Nothing more is heard. The stage remains empty for a moment. MONIME *appears in a distraught state.*

MONIME: Frantz, where are you? (*She goes to the door, but dares not open it. She goes out calling.*) Frantz! Frantz! Frantz!

She can be heard slamming doors and calling further off. FRANTZ *has come out of the* DUCHESS'S *room, very pale. He remains in the middle of the room, motionless, staring straight ahead of him. He draws the crumpled telegram from his pocket and looks at it.* MONIME *comes back.*

Ah! There you are! What is it, Frantz? (*She takes the telegram from him, reads it, and throws her arms round his neck with a cry of joy.*) Oh, Frantz! I knew it wasn't possible, and that something would turn up first. We're saved, Frantz. We're saved! Oh, I'm laughing and crying at the same time! So Bentz is offering you five hundred francs a month to help run your old business; isn't that wonderful? You see, he's not so bad after all. Now we shall be able to go away and be happy, thanks to him. . . .

FRANTZ: Not on five hundred francs a month.

MONIME: But you're mad. We shan't have to be poor any more.

FRANTZ: You've had that much every month to buy your dresses. Just try and see whether you can live on it. . . .

MONIME (*drawing back*): I detest you. I never want to see you again!

FRANTZ: It's too late, now.

MONIME: What are you saying?

FRANTZ: I'm saying it's too late.

MONIME (*falls back, crying*): You killed her just the same. . . . You killed her just the same.

FRANTZ: Don't shout. . . . Come along, we must get back to our rooms. I say we must get back to our rooms. . . .

He tries to drag her away, but she lies on the ground, sobbing.

MONIME: You killed her just the same. . . . You killed her just the same. . . . You killed her just the same. . . .

Curtain

Act Three

SCENE: *One of the central rooms of the château. It is circular and scantily furnished. Three exactly similar doors lead off it. The small hours. The lights are still on.*

FRANTZ *is sitting on a chair, deathly pale and exhausted, with his clothes in a state of disarray. Opposite him, at a table, a* POLICE OFFICER *is going through a batch of papers. Another is seated beside the table, legs crossed, manner detached. A third is pacing up and down the room.*

SECOND POLICE OFFICER (*in a low voice to the* FIRST POLICE OFFICER): He's a tough nut. He did it, I'll bet you anything. But God knows whether we'll ever pin it on him.

FRANTZ: What's the time?

THIRD POLICE OFFICER: Six o'clock.

FRANTZ: How is Mademoiselle de Granat?

THIRD POLICE OFFICER: There's a doctor with her.

FIRST POLICE OFFICER: Well, now. We'll proceed with the evidence. I've been acquainting myself with the answers you gave my colleague in my absence.

FRANTZ: You're rested and fresh. I want a drink. Let me call a servant. I'm dead beat.

FIRST POLICE OFFICER: Later. Let's first of all get a few things straight. You say it was at half past ten that you went to bed.

FRANTZ: I've already told you it was half past ten.

FIRST POLICE OFFICER: You went to sleep immediately?

FRANTZ: You've already asked me all these questions at the beginning of the inquiry.

FIRST POLICE OFFICER: And I'm asking you again. Let's assume I'm afraid I shall forget what you said.

THIRD POLICE OFFICER (*stops walking and stands behind* FRANTZ): You said the first time that you couldn't get to sleep right away.

FRANTZ: I beg your pardon, I said, and I say again, that I went to sleep very quickly. Whereas usually, as a matter of fact, I don't go to sleep immediately.

SECOND POLICE OFFICER: Did you read?

FRANTZ: I told you – I usually do read in bed. But yesterday I was tired, and didn't.

FIRST POLICE OFFICER: A light was seen in your window at half past eleven. According to the first investigations, this is just about when the crime was committed.

FRANTZ: I didn't put the light on; I've already told you that. The witness who says he saw a light in my window must have been confusing it with the next one, which is the window of the entrance hall. There's a lamp burning there all night.

FIRST POLICE OFFICER: The witness insists that he is not mistaken.

FRANTZ: That surprises me. All the more because, as you can check for yourself, my window is not visible from the town side. So we can only conclude, can't we, that the witness in question was in the castle grounds at the time of the murder?

THIRD POLICE OFFICER (*between his teeth*): The bitter-end type. (*Coming up to* FRANTZ.) The old man saw you in the antechamber at a quarter past eleven. . . .

FRANTZ: That's unusually precise for Joseph. He's a doddering old half-wit whose sole claim to distinction is that he can't tell the time and never knows what day of the week it is. Ask the other servants. They'll confirm it.

FIRST POLICE OFFICER: You never carry a hunting knife?

FRANTZ: No. I abhor hunting.

FIRST POLICE OFFICER: It has been established as a result of this inquiry that the Duchess was killed with a knife.

FRANTZ: With a knife?

SECOND POLICE OFFICER: That surprises you, doesn't it?

FRANTZ (*recovering himself*): No. It only confirms my first impression that it must have been one of the gipsies camping out in the market-place.

THIRD POLICE OFFICER: But of course you know that it was a hammer that finished the old woman off?

FRANTZ (*not batting an eyelid*): A hammer? But you've just said it was a knife.

The POLICE OFFICER *resumes his pacing.*

FIRST POLICE OFFICER: You are very stubborn. But it is quite useless for us to go on playing cat and mouse. You say you went up to your room at half past ten.

FRANTZ: I didn't look at the time. I must make that clear. But I imagine it was about half past ten.

FIRST POLICE OFFICER: In your previous statement, you said exactly half past ten.

FRANTZ: That surprises me. But I may have said it inadvertently.

FIRST POLICE OFFICER: Why are you going back on it now?

FRANTZ: I'm not going back on anything. I'm simply telling you that I couldn't possibly have known the exact time. I never wear a watch and there are no clocks, either in the Duchess's antechamber or in any of the other rooms between there and my bedroom.

SECOND POLICE OFFICER: So you admit being in the antechamber after half past ten.

FRANTZ: You're twisting my words again. I admit nothing. I have never denied being in the Duchess's antechamber before going up to my room. And I suppose it was 'about' half past ten when I went up.

FIRST POLICE OFFICER: I'll just take this one point; you were in the antechamber, alone, at about half past ten?

FRANTZ: Yes.

FIRST POLICE OFFICER: Can you tell us what you were doing?

FRANTZ: I had spent the evening with Mademoiselle de Granat. She had gone up to her room a few minutes before, not feeling well.

SECOND POLICE OFFICER: At twenty past ten. This time we actually have precise information, thanks to the statement of a maid who came back for a few minutes to do her hair and met Mademoiselle de Granat on the stairs.

FRANTZ: That's possible.

FIRST POLICE OFFICER: How long do you think you stayed in the antechamber after Mademoiselle de Granat had gone?

FRANTZ: I repeat, I can't say exactly. Perhaps ten minutes, perhaps less.

SECOND POLICE OFFICER: What did you do in those ten minutes?

FRANTZ: I was getting ready to go to bed.

SECOND POLICE OFFICER: Do you mean to say you really need ten minutes to make up your mind to go to bed?

THIRD POLICE OFFICER: Come now, admit it. The old lady saw you. What have you done with the hammer?

FRANTZ (*coolly*): You're asking me several questions at once. To which do you wish me to reply? (THIRD POLICE OFFICER *withdraws*.) I can well understand that you are surprised at my taking ten minutes to make up my mind to go to bed. But your surprise is due to the fact that – by force of professional habit, no doubt – you *will* look at the situation from an angle that has no relation to real life. Obviously it didn't take me ten minutes actually to make up my mind to go to bed! But you know yourself that between intending to do something quite without urgency or importance and actually doing it, there is often quite a time lag. It's the same with everyone. I must have been sitting in the arm-chair dreaming, or even just simply finishing my cigarette. I don't remember anything else.

FIRST POLICE OFFICER: You don't remember anything else?

Silence.

THIRD POLICE OFFICER (*between his teeth*): Bastard.

FIRST POLICE OFFICER (*calls him over*): Gérard?

The other comes up and the FIRST POLICE OFFICER *says something in his ear. He goes out saying:*

THIRD POLICE OFFICER: Right, sir.

FIRST POLICE OFFICER: Let's go over your statements again. Mademoiselle de Granat went up to her room feeling unwell at twenty past ten. You stayed in the Duchess's antechamber alone for about ten minutes, and you can think of nothing – not one single thing – that you did during those ten minutes. Agreed?

FRANTZ: Agreed.

FIRST POLICE OFFICER: You then went up to your room, and at about the time of the crime, that is at about eleven o'clock, you were asleep?

FRANTZ: Yes.

FIRST POLICE OFFICER: Good. Now can you tell me how it is that a telegram arrived for you at the Granat Post Office at ten-thirty? I repeat, ten-thirty. And – fortunately for the purposes of our investigation – the Post Office, which, by the way, keeps exact national time, can supply precise details. The messenger took ten minutes to reach the château. It was therefore at ten-forty that he handed the telegram to the servant in charge. Is the telegram in your possession?

FRANTZ: Yes. I forgot it. Here it is.

FIRST POLICE OFFICER: Funny thing to forget.

SECOND POLICE OFFICER: May I see it, please?

FIRST POLICE OFFICER: How can the telegram be in your possession, if at ten-forty you had already gone up to your room, where, according to your statement, no one came to find you?

FRANTZ: But I've already told you I couldn't say precisely at what time I went up to my room. I left the antechamber as soon as Joseph had handed me the telegram. So it was at ten-forty that I went upstairs.

SECOND POLICE OFFICER: So your 'time lag', as you call it, was twenty minutes? Rather a long time to be just hanging about. Plenty of things could be done in twenty minutes.

FRANTZ: It's quite possible that I stayed there smoking and thinking for twenty minutes, and that it seemed like only ten. I'm quite sure such things must have happened to you.

Silence.

FIRST POLICE OFFICER: Let us leave that point for the moment. I see the name Bentz on the telegram. You had to sell your business as a result of the refusal of this man Bentz to advance you some money?

FRANTZ: That's correct.

FIRST POLICE OFFICER: And you sold it at a loss, if one is to believe the witnesses. You were in a desperate situation.

FRANTZ: Not in the least. The telegram offered me five hundred francs a month. Moreover, I would point out, gentlemen – in order to assist the calculations this will no doubt give rise to – that the telegram, which puts an end to a financial situation that, if not exactly desperate, was obviously straitened, was handed to me at ten-forty; we have, thank God, your own word for it that that has been exactly specified. So I had been reassured for quite a while at the time of the murder, and there was every reason for me to sleep soundly, as I assure you I did.

SECOND POLICE OFFICER: Your reasoning is very persuasive. But this crime could have been committed much earlier than you seem to think. We have not yet heard the conclusions of the medical expert; we can only be sure that by eleven o'clock everything was over.

FIRST POLICE OFFICER: We are also justified in asking whether five hundred francs a month is adequate for the needs of a young man like yourself.

FRANTZ: But a young man like myself, who is poor and has always been poor, and who would probably not become any richer on the death of Madame de Granat, could be very happy with five hundred francs a month. Judge for yourself. Without wishing to be indiscreet, may I ask how much you earn in your profession?

SECOND POLICE OFFICER: That's not the question.

FIRST POLICE OFFICER: How much longer are we going to carry on this battle of wits?

FRANTZ: I don't know what you mean.

A POLICEMAN (*enters abruptly*): Excuse me, sir. Drop this one for a moment. We'll take him up again if need be. I've just come from the boss. He's had a complete confession from the old man. It's him that did it. He says he threw the hammer in the lake. They're checking up on it now. The boss wants both of you to come. (*He goes out.*)

FIRST POLICE OFFICER: That'll be all for today, then, sir. Sorry to have kept you so long.

FRANTZ: That's all right.

SECOND POLICE OFFICER: I'll keep your telegram as evidence. The alleged murderer handed it to you here at ten-forty, you told us. It's a point that might prove interesting.

FIRST POLICE OFFICER: I would ask you, sir, not to leave this room, please, and to remain at our disposal until the first inquiry is over; it won't be long now.

FRANTZ: Of course. And *I* would ask *you* please to have the first servant you see bring me something to drink.

FIRST POLICE OFFICER: Certainly. You must be very tired.

FRANTZ: Yes. Very tired. (*When he is alone, he passes a hand over his eyes.*)

A POLICEMAN (*coming in*): Shall I send in the journalists? They're asking to see you.

FRANTZ: No. I don't want them here.

The POLICEMAN *goes out and comes in again.*

POLICEMAN: There's one that insists on seeing you. He says he knows you.

PHILIPPE (*who is in front of a crowd of journalists*): Frantz – it's me.

FRANTZ: Oh, you. Come in then. . . .

Exclamations of disappointment. The door closes.

PHILIPPE: You're going to give me a jolly good scoop. It's

good of you to remember a friend. What's up, Frantz? . . . Do you want me to call someone?

FRANTZ (*has fallen, half fainting, into an arm-chair*): No. It'll pass. They've reduced me to pulp. They've been questioning me since midnight.

PHILIPPE: The old man confessed this morning.

FRANTZ: Yes.

PHILIPPE: Strange, isn't it – about the old man? I'm glad he spat it out, though.

FRANTZ: Yes. Me too. They won't need to question Monime.

Silence.

PHILIPPE: His confession had everyone floored. He had an absolutely watertight defence. They were going to let him go. Suddenly – a burst of dramatics and there he is accusing himself with a wealth of the most extraordinary detail. I think he's dotty.

FRANTZ: You think so?

PHILIPPE: What's the matter? You've gone so pale?

FRANTZ: You sound like the walking-on part in a melodrama. That's exactly what he always says, remember? But the other character doesn't reply. He leans back in his chair, very pale, as you astutely observed. And the walking-on part becomes very suspicious. . . . (*He walks toward* PHILIPPE.) But *you* happen to know that it was me.

PHILIPPE (*recoils*): Frantz!

FRANTZ: What have you come here for with your newspaper and your questions? Just to see me suffer, to stage a free show for yourself? Look at me. Pretty good, aren't I? They didn't get me, you see. . . .

PHILIPPE: Frantz, it's impossible.

FRANTZ: On the contrary, it's perfectly possible. Come on, sit down. Pull yourself together. Have a drink. Give me a cigarette, I haven't got any. I shan't even be getting the one they give the condemned man.

PHILIPPE: You're loathsome.

FRANTZ: Yes, aren't I? I can still manage to be loathsome. Of course, the thing that's lacking is remorse. I'm not conscious of any of these hidden eyes. Did you see how I answered their questions? For six whole hours. . . . (*Pause.*) You said I shouldn't have the courage.

PHILIPPE (*taking him by the arm*): Frantz, what's this game you're playing with me? It's all over now. The old man has confessed. You're free. You'll be able to go to bed now, and tomorrow, when you get up, all this will have been just a nightmare.

FRANTZ (*in a low voice*): I did it, Philippe.

PHILIPPE: You're ill. This business has cracked you up. Either that or you saw the doubt in my eyes when I came in and you want to frighten me. Frantz, this is a horrible trick to play. You're lying. It wasn't you. . . . The old man has confessed. . . . It can't have been you.

FRANTZ: The truth must scare you pretty badly if you can't face it. Do you find it easier to believe that it was that old scarecrow that can hardly stand up and who had nothing to gain by the old girl's death? It's fantastic. You have to want your happiness badly to become a murderer . . . and what's more you have to have a fist on you, let me tell you. . . .

PHILIPPE: My God, it's frightful. . . .

FRANTZ: Oh, yes, frightful. More frightful than you can imagine. (*He looks at* PHILIPPE *for a while, then in a hard voice*) Put down that stick. And your hat. And that infernal notebook. Something tells me you won't want to take any notes now and that what I'm going to say wouldn't be of interest to your newspaper. I killed her, Philippe. There's nothing to it, you know. You have no idea. I had a hammer wrapped in cloth. I lifted it. . . . She watched me all the time. It's a long time, you know, a second. The first blow didn't kill her. I clubbed her and clubbed her because she was still moving. I was kneeling over the old witch. Lying on her in her bed. We fought like animals; like two monstrous lovers straining after some unthinkable union. When she was finally quite motionless, I got up. I had to walk, open the door, shut it again, go up to my room, pretend to sleep, pretend to wake, give the alarm myself, and then spend the entire night answering their questions – all without making a single slip.

PHILIPPE: Stop it.

FRANTZ: Am I frightening you? I was frightened, too. (*Silence.*) And now it's all over. But I wanted you to know what it was like to kill someone – to have killed someone. Have you got some idea of it now, with your poor little smug imagination? The screams, the blood, the convulsive movements, the spine-chilling looks they give you – can you feel it all? (*He takes him by the lapel and stares hard into his face.*) Now listen. I let you in, rather than the others, because I needed to say this to someone! I'm glad I killed her. I don't regret anything. If they get me, I shan't defend myself. I have nothing to say that a judge would understand. And yet I must shout it out while her body's still warm in there. . . . I hate crime . . . I hate death. I believe it's a vile collusion with nature even to be glad when someone dies, however much one hates them. . . . In other circumstances I might have thrown myself in the river to save the life of this old hag, much as I hated her. But I killed her – not for her money, but because her money, in the mysterious balance of things, had become the exact price of our perfection. Philippe, don't think people kill for money because they haven't the courage to work. Look at my hands – how they're trembling still. Better ten years' hard labour than one second of crime. Only I wanted my love to live, to be beautiful, to be perfect; and to enable it to live, I would have done even more terrible things.

Long silence. PHILIPPE *goes slowly toward* FRANTZ.

PHILIPPE: Frantz . . .

FRANTZ (*turns, as though surprised to see him there*): What do you want? Go away.

PHILIPPE: I'm your friend.

FRANTZ (*looking steadily at him*): Yes, I suppose that's true, you are my friend. Or should I say you've taken the place of a friend. You've occupied that difficult position without lifting a finger, where someone else more conscientious or more simple might have offered me a helping hand. You shouldn't have reminded me of that!

PHILIPPE: I don't understand. I don't know what all this is about.

FRANTZ: Oh, don't worry! I'm not blaming you. I've killed her and I'm glad.

PHILIPPE (*still stammering*): But it wasn't you, it was the old man.

FRANTZ: However, since you've come here uttering pious clichés and brandishing friendship at arm's length to get the truth out of me, you can have it. Who knows? Maybe you'll be the one to regret it. Maybe *you'll* suffer from the famous remorse that all the moralists say follows inevitably on any crime – because *I* don't. Are you a true friend, Philippe? Real friends share joy and sorrow, you know. Fine – you take the remorse and leave me the rest. (*He laughs.*)

PHILIPPE: You're terrifying. Why are you laughing?

FRANTZ: Because it's funny. Drama is a mixture of the tragic and the comic. We learned that together, remember? (*Pause.*) It's a mistake to remember you as you were then – a kid in short pants, sitting next to me in the gods. I shan't be able to indulge in the magnificent tirade I promised myself.

PHILIPPE: What's going on, Frantz?

FRANTZ: The old Philippe was making me sentimental. It's true, we were friends then. Real friends. (*He becomes thoughtful.*)

PHILIPPE: What were you going to tell me?

FRANTZ (*shrugs*): What's the good? Go on now, Philippe. I'm going to try and get some rest in case they start questioning me again.

PHILIPPE: What were you going to say? I'm asking you to talk now.

FRANTZ (*looking at him*): It was partly because you were my friend that I killed her.

PHILIPPE: But you're mad! You don't realize what you're saying!

JACP–F

FRANTZ: Ah. Whites of the eyes showing, beads of sweat at the nostrils, hair standing on end. . . . I promised myself I would provide this spectacle as a proof of our friendship. Yes, it was because I had a friend like you that I was able to kill her.

PHILIPPE: You're mad! It's not true! You're lying! It isn't true! It couldn't have been because of me! (*He is breathless and shouting.*) I always gave you good advice! . . .

FRANTZ: True. You always gave me good advice, but it's immoral that those who give good advice should be eternally sheltered from blame. I just wanted to tell you that this morning, so that for once at least it's been said to what is known as a good man. Go on, now, get out.

PHILIPPE: What's going to happen to you? I'm frightened for you!

FRANTZ: I said get out.

PHILIPPE *goes toward the door, looking embarrassed. From the doorway, he murmurs.*

PHILIPPE: All right, then, Frantz. See you later.

FRANTZ: You'll go back to your women, your friends, your cafés. You must pluck up courage one day, Philippe. You'll see how easy it is. You'll see how easily the answers come when the police start questioning. How one feels like the lord of creation afterward. . . . (*He goes and opens the curtains; the morning sun floods the room.*) Ah! it's morning. That horrible night – it's over. I've done it. It's finished. It's finished.

He has forgotten PHILIPPE, *who again stammers.*

PHILIPPE: *Au revoir*, Frantz.

FRANTZ: Good-bye, my boy. Make it a good story.

PHILIPPE *leaves. Enter* URBAIN. *He, too, is looking dishevelled and haggard. He is carrying a drink.*

URBAIN: I'm very glad it is all over for Monsieur. It must have been most fatiguing to be questioned all night like that;

I tried several times to make them let me bring Monsieur something to eat, but they wouldn't let me in. They didn't keep me long, because I was seen at the fair at the time of the— But who would ever have thought it could be Joseph, monsieur? He had been serving her Grace longer than I.

FRANTZ: Yes. What is Mademoiselle Monime doing? Is she up?

URBAIN: Poor young lady. They haven't questioned her at all. Fortunately so; in the state she was in last night it would have killed her. . . . The doctor came and gave her an injection. She is up now.

FRANTZ: Tell her that I have to stay here in case they want to question me further, but that I should like to see her immediately. Ask her to come down.

URBAIN: Very well, monsieur.

FRANTZ *goes to the glass, studies his reflection and smooths out the lines on his face. He arranges his hair and collar, then goes and sits down. Suddenly he looks at his hands, and continues to gaze at them silently, with a strange smile. Enter* MONIME *in a dark dress, looking drawn and unkempt.*

MONIME: Here I am.

FRANTZ: Oh! I'm glad. They haven't asked you any questions?

MONIME: No. . . .

FRANTZ: My little one. . . . You've been ill. Come and sit down. There. I'm so happy, so happy.

MONIME: Have they left you?

FRANTZ: Yes. Joseph has confessed, I don't know why. They asked him too many questions, I suppose. They must have turned his brain.

MONIME: What are they going to do to him?

FRANTZ: I don't know. I don't care. Neither of us must care. What is certain is that they won't kill him. He's too old. They'll see he's crazy and put him in an asylum. We'll go away, Monime. They won't ask us any more questions. We'll get out of this house – out of the country . . . among people who won't make us feel afraid any more. . . . I'm happy, my little one. . . .

He is sitting at her feet, clasping her knees, his eyes closed. She is very pale, and remains silent.

It's all over, Monime. Yesterday was the last time we had to hide; now we have the right to live. You can belong to me without fear and without deceit. Oh, my little one, my little one. . . . (*He strokes her legs.*) Monime, how easy it is to kill for your sake. If I managed not to tremble last night, not to slip up with my answers to their questions, if I've escaped all their traps, it was because of you. I love you, Monime. I am your lover. I've won you. What chance do they stand with their questions against that? I was stronger than they were; I shall always be stronger now. Stronger than anyone else, stronger than poverty even. . . . I've purified myself in the blood of that old woman. . . . Today, I'm a man. How could you love him, Monime, that poor little wretch that was ashamed to be poor, that lover who hadn't the heart to make love, that tender youth who was so afraid of falling a prey to his tenderness? Oh, it wasn't only her that I killed; it was that unspeakable little creature that hadn't the guts to take you. One blow of the hammer for the tender youth. One for the man that was afraid of abortionists. One for the man that wanted to be rich! Ah! The charming little greenhorn's quite dead. And with him all the sordidness – all the impurity. . . . I love you, Monime. I want you. (*Gently.*) All the time I was battering her there on her bed, I wanted you.

Silence. He buries his head in her lap. She opens her eyes and looks at him sadly. But she is hard, too.

MONIME: Frantz. Get up. You must get up. All night long I've been in agony, turning things over in my mind. You must listen to me. Frantz, get up. . . . Just now, you were talking and talking. . . . I was listening to your voice and not understanding a word you were saying. I don't know what you said, but I must tell you something now, something I discovered during the night – I felt it with the whole of my

being. Ever since you killed her, it's as if something had
been torn to pieces. We shall go away and live together
because we must, now. . . . We shall try to be as happy as
we can. Helping each other as much as possible. But I've
thought it all over – I shan't be your wife.

FRANTZ: What are you saying?

MONIME: It will be as it was before. I shall be your cousin,
your friend. We shall live together and try to forget.
Try to forget everything – our love, and the crime we
committed.

FRANTZ: But what are you saying? You're mad. I don't want to
forget anything. I want to love you. It was for that I risked
my neck.

MONIME: No, Frantz, it's not possible any more.

FRANTZ: Monime!

MONIME: Don't start shouting. You'll make both of us unhappy.

FRANTZ: Monime, you look like something out of a graveyard.
Stop it. What's the matter with you? What's happened?
What have they said to you?

MONIME: Nothing. Please stop it, Frantz, please. It's no use
talking. It's too terrible. We've got to forget.

FRANTZ (*shaking her*): But it's not possible! You're dreaming
. . . wake up. . . . It's me. It's me, Frantz; it's your lover
come to take you away to live and be happy.

MONIME: Let me go! . . .

FRANTZ: My little one . . .

MONIME: Let me go. . . . (*She pulls herself up like a Fury*.) I
don't want you to touch me with those hands – those filthy
hands. . . .

FRANTZ *looks at them and stammers in distress.*

FRANTZ: They're not filthy. They killed her, but it was for the
sake of our love.

MONIME: Leave me alone! You disgust me! You killed her
for my money.

Silence. She is breathless and panting. Suddenly she falls sobbing into the arm-chair. FRANTZ *remains rooted to the spot. He looks at his hands, bewildered, then at* MONIME, *who is weeping.*

FRANTZ: Monime. . . . Monime. . . . It isn't true! You don't think that— (*Silence. She continues to cry.*) But answer me. You can't just ignore me. . . . Other people can think that. . . . I knew they would and I don't care a damn, but you . . . it isn't possible . . . you . . . Monime?

MONIME: Think of the telegram. Bentz offered you five hundred francs a month.

FRANTZ: It meant poverty, Monime, and I thought it was impossible. You know it was so that I could love you properly that I wanted the money, so that nothing sordid could come between us and our love.

MONIME: It's not true. If you had loved me, you wouldn't have been afraid of being poor and having to hide. It was for my money you did it.

FRANTZ (*taking her head in his hands*): Look at me.

MONIME: Don't touch me.

FRANTZ: I shall hold your eyelids back by force, and then I shall have to read what is in your eyes. Don't you believe it was for you, and only for you, because I loved you? (*Silence. She does not reply. He looks at her and then suddenly recoils, frightened at what he sees in her face.*) It was horrible, but it was only for your sake, Monime . . . to protect you from poverty.

MONIME (*repeating with a faraway look*): It's not true. It was for my money.

FRANTZ: Oh! This is all too stupid!

MONIME: It was for my money! It was for my money!

FRANTZ: Why do you keep on repeating those idiotic words? I don't even believe in your money any longer. I'm a man this morning. A lover, poor and resolute. Come, let's go away without it, if it frightens you. Let's love each other, poor as we are. And when poverty and wretchedness, which of course are ennobling to people like us, have worn you out, I shall take another wife and leave you to get old by yourself. . . . What a coward I was to look for a solution, to try to protect you. I didn't love you cruelly enough. Tenderness made me want to wrap you up in money. Come then. So much the worse for you. I love you without it. Come!

MONIME: Leave me alone. I don't love you.

FRANTZ: Why are you lying? You do love me. We love each other.

MONIME: No.

FRANTZ: Yes. You can say no, because you're afraid of the corpse that's lying in there. But your mouth says yes, your body says yes.

MONIME: No.

FRANTZ: Yes. You loved me last night. You do love me, I tell you.

MONIME: Let me go! I hate touching you. I gave myself to you to make you happy.

FRANTZ: You're lying . . . you're lying. . . .

MONIME: You've chained me to you, you've dragged me down into the mud, into all these lies and all this blood, but I hated you last night. It was monstrous of you to want to come straight from her bed to mine, where there was nothing left of me for you. I feel as though the whole of me were shut up tight – dried up for ever. . . . I don't want any more of your sort of love. Soaked in blood and sweat. I want to live, to be happy like other people, and forget everything else.

Silence.

FRANTZ: I mean nothing to you any more?

MONIME: No.

Silence again.

FRANTZ: And yet you never said a word. You let me believe myself a man. You let me think I was master, let me talk like a master, and I was nothing any more. You must have had a good laugh.

MONIME: We mustn't go on hurting each other, Frantz. I assure you we can live together without doing each other any harm. We'll share my money.

FRANTZ: Why do you say 'your' money? I gave it to you, at the price of my own neck. What do you think I want with your sordid bargaining? Do you think I killed her to get half the money? Keep the lot of it. I'll make you a present of it. . . . So you don't love me any more? (*He laughs insanely.*)

MONIME: What's the matter with you?

FRANTZ: Yes. You're the strongest, the richest, the most beautiful of them all. I can tell you now that having you was my only treasure. And today you don't love me any more. Look at me, with your new woman's eyes. I'm nothing to you any more, nor to anyone else. Last night I stood up to them for six hours because I thought I was a man and that you loved me. They can come now; they shall have me. Oh! What a fool I was! God knows how long it is already since I possessed her. Perhaps I never possessed her at all. . . . The little greenhorn was still alive. I hadn't killed him after all! Look at him. Look at me. I'll help you if you can't see it all. This pout of the lips – that's my cowardice; this network of lines on my forehead – that's my laziness and indolence; the fixed expression in my eyes – that's my egotism. . . . Did you think I was tall and you were small? Look, I don't stand straight and I only look tall because I'm thin. You thought I was strong, courageous and calm, didn't you? Look at my hand – it's been trembling since yesterday. Look at me. . . . Your lover was ugly, unkind, stupid, poor and cowardly, and yet, before, you thought yourself unworthy of him and followed him into the trap that meant the end of your happiness. (*She has buried her head in her arms.*) Go on, cry! Cry! It was for your money I killed her! I wanted to go to bed with your money! It was your money I wanted to make love to! (*Both of them are panting and exhausted; there is a long silence.*) Go and be happy. You are a charming girl. You know how to take things. How not to give love more than it

deserves. You'd better marry someone else who'll help you
to become what you want to be. With the millions that will
be coming to you, you'll find a husband to your taste all
right. Later on if you think that perhaps love was worth
the name after all, you'll be able to take a lover and go to bed
with him between meals.

MONIME: You're loathsome.

FRANTZ: I shall believe that in the end. That's twice today
I've been told so. You're the salt of the earth, no doubt, both
of you. . . . I really wonder what I'm doing, loathsome as
I am, demanding friendship or love from either of you, as
though such things existed. It's ridiculous. I'm utterly ridiculous. Forgive me.

*He is crying. She watches him for a moment and then goes gently
towards him.*

MONIME: Frantz.

FRANTZ: Oh, no! Not pity. Get away from me!

MONIME: Frantz, you've been proud, and I've been foolish.
Now both of us are suffering for it. You said to me once
that God doesn't give passion to everyone. We ought to
have been content with what we had and gone on living that
way. Without that pride of yours, we might even have been
happy. It was your pride that wanted this mad, impossible
love. It was because of that that you killed her and that we've
been destroyed. I would have loved you poor; I would still
have been your mistress on the sly, bad lover though I was.
Remember, I threw myself at your feet. I clung to you and
you dragged me across the floor. I told you I should never
marry and that I would always stay with you. I even told you
to go away, that I detested you. But you would do it just the
same, out of pride.

FRANTZ (*shattered, humble*): I was all alone. Alone against the
world.

MONIME: You're proud, proud. . . . I loved you as a little
girl loves her childhood's playfellow when she meets him
again. That's all. And now I hate you for abusing that poor

love, I hate you for pinning your wild, insane dreams on me.

A long silence. They remain motionless. Two POLICEMEN *pass through on their way out, slipping on their overcoats as they go.*

THIRD POLICE OFFICER: I know the old boy confessed. But you'll never be able to convince me it wasn't the youngster that did it.

OTHER POLICE OFFICER: All right. All right. Don't get worked up about it. The boss is quite satisfied with things as they are. So am I.

He goes off; the other stays behind a moment looking silently at FRANTZ. *He is a man with a huge red moustache and a not-too-intelligent appearance. Suddenly he puts on his hat, comes up behind* FRANTZ, *and takes him by the arm.*

THE POLICE OFFICER: What did you do it with?

FRANTZ *replies immediately, without even turning round.*

FRANTZ: With a hammer wrapped in cloth.

The POLICE OFFICER *is surprised in spite of himself. He hurls himself at* FRANTZ, *who has not budged, and handcuffs him, yelling at the top of his lungs.*

POLICE OFFICER: Hey! Chief! Boys! Chief! I knew it was him . . . I knew it was him!

The POLICE *come in at all the doors.* MONIME *has looked up at first without understanding, then throws herself at* FRANTZ'S *feet.*

MONIME: I love you, Frantz!

Curtain

Thieves' Carnival

Characters

PETERBONO
HECTOR } *thieves*
GUSTAVE

LORD EDGARD

LADY HURF

EVA } *her nieces*
JULIETTE

DUPONT-DUFORT SENIOR

DUPONT-DUFORT JUNIOR

THE TOWN CRIER

THE POLICEMEN

THE NURSEMAID

THE LITTLE GIRL

THE MUSICIAN

Original Title: Le Bal des Voleurs
Translator: Lucienne Hill
First produced in 1932

Act One

The public gardens of a watering-place which saw its heyday in the 1880s. In the middle, a bandstand. The orchestra is represented by a single musician, who at the rise of the curtain is executing a solo of superlative virtuosity on the clarinet. A woman deckchair attendant goes to and fro. The summer visitors stroll up and down to the rhythm of the music. In the foreground EVA and HECTOR are locked in a dramatic screen embrace. The music stops. So does the kiss, from which HECTOR emerges, reeling a little. Applause for the musician.

HECTOR (*covered in confusion*): I say, steady. They're applauding us!

EVA (*bursts out laughing*): Of course not, it's the orchestra. I must say you appeal to me enormously.

HECTOR (*instinctively fingering his hair and moustache*): What do you like about me, specially?

EVA: Everything. (*She blows him a kiss.*) We mustn't stay here, it's too risky. I'll see you tonight at eight in the Phoenix bar. And if you should meet me with my aunt, whatever you do, pretend you don't know me.

HECTOR (*yearningly*): Your little hand, once more.

EVA: Careful. My aunt's old friend Lord Edgard is over there by the bandstand reading his paper. He'll see us. (*She holds out her hand, but turns away to watch* LORD EDGARD.)

HECTOR (*passionately*): I want to inhale the perfume of your hand!

He bends over her hand, and surreptitiously draws a jeweller's eye-glass from his pocket to take a closer look at EVA'S *rings.* EVA *withdraws her hand, unaware of the manoeuvre.*

EVA: Till tonight. (*She goes.*)

HECTOR (*weak at the knees*): My beloved . . . (*He follows her out of sight, then comes down stage again, putting away his eyeglass, and mutters with icy self-possession.*) A cool two hundred thousand. And not a flaw in the lot.

At this point the TOWN CRIER *enters with his drum and the crowd gather round to listen.*

TOWN CRIER: Townsmen of Vichy! The Municipality, anxious to preserve the well-being and security of the invalids and bathers, issues a warning for their information and protection! Numerous complaints from visitors have been lodged at the Town Hall and at the main police station, Market Street. A dangerous pack of pickle-pockets—

He has a little trouble with this word, at which the clarinet plays a little accompaniment. The TOWN CRIER *swings round on him, furious.*

– a dangerous pack of pockpickets—

Again the clarinet renders the word in music.

– is at this very hour within our gates. The local police is on the watch. Members of the Force, in plain clothes and in uniform, are ready to protect our visitors . . .

Indeed, even as he speaks policemen are threading their several ways gracefully through the crowd.

Visitors are nevertheless requested to exercise the greatest possible caution, particularly on the public highway, in public parks and in all other places of public resort. A reward in kind is offered by the Tourist Association to anyone supplying information leading to the apprehension of the felons! Tell your friends!

A roll of drums. During the proclamation HECTOR *has relieved the* TOWN CRIER *of his enormous copper watch and bulging purse. The crowd scatters, and the drum and the harangue are heard again farther off.* HECTOR *takes a seat, and the* CHAIRWOMAN *approaches.*

CHAIRWOMAN: Will you take a ticket, sir, please?
HECTOR (*largely*): Since it's customary . . .
CHAIRWOMAN: That'll be five francs, please.

While HECTOR *feels for the money, the woman steals his wallet, then the huge watch and the purse he has just taken from the* TOWN CRIER.

HECTOR (*seizing the hand on its next trip into his pocket*): Hey! What do you think you're up to?

The woman struggles to free herself, and loses her wig.

Have you gone crazy? (*He lifts his own wig and moustache a trifle.*) It's me!

The chair attendant readjusts her wig. It is PETERBONO.

PETERBONO: Sorry, old chap. It's me too. Had a good day?
HECTOR: The purse and a watch, and a cigarette lighter.
PETERBONO (*examining them*): I know that watch. It's the Town Crier's and it's made of copper. I put it back into his pocket, the poor devil, that and the purse, which you'll find if you check up contains just fifteen cents and the receipt for a registered parcel. As for the lighter, we've already got nine hundred and three, out of which only a couple work. I've known you do better, my lad!
HECTOR: I've a date tonight with a girl who'll be mine before you can say mischief, and who wears over two hundred thousand francs' worth of diamonds on her middle finger.
PETERBONO: We'll look into it. Have you noticed that little thing over there? The necklace?
HECTOR (*examining the girl through the fieldglasses he wears round his neck*): Phew! The stones are enormous!
PETERBONO: No wishful thinking. They're smaller to the naked eye. Still, off we go. Small change manoeuvre. I get offensive and you interfere.

They cross to the girl with a terrible affectation of indifference.

Ticket? Ticket?

The girl gives him a coin; PETERBONO *begins to yell.*

I've got no change! I tell you I've got no change! No change,
do you hear? No change at all, I keep on telling you!

HECTOR: What's this? No change, eh? Excuse me, Mademoiselle, allow me to put this insolent baggage in her place!

There follows a tussle under cover of which HECTOR *investigates
the clasp of the girl's necklace.*

THE GIRL (*violently freeing herself*): No, you don't!

HECTOR (*taken aback*): What do you mean, no you don't!

PETERBONO: No you don't what?

THE GIRL (*lifting her wig. It is* GUSTAVE): It's me.

HECTOR (*falling into a chair*): Charming!

PETERBONO (*exploding*): That's what comes of not working
to plan! I can't rely on anybody! Running errands, that's all
you're fit for! Errand boys! If it weren't for your poor old
mother who put you in my charge to learn the business,
you'd be out on your ear, the pair of you. Do you hear me?
Out on your ear! And without your week's pay in lieu of
notice, make no mistake! And complain to the union if you
dare! I'll tell them a thing or two, the dance you've led me,
both of you! (*To* GUSTAVE.) You! You haven't done a
stroke today, naturally!

GUSTAVE: Yes, I have. I've done two. First, there's this magnificent wallet.

PETERBONO: Let's have a look. (*He examines it, then searches
himself anxiously.*) Where did you get this? Who from?

GUSTAVE: I got it in the Boulevard Ravachol off an old
gentleman with a long white beard . . .

PETERBONO (*terrible in his anger*): – check trousers, olive-green
jacket and deer-stalker cap, am I right, pigeon-brain?

GUSTAVE (*quaking*): Yes, sir. Did you see me?

PETERBONO (*sinks into a chair, flattened by this latest blow*): That
was me, idiot, that was me! At this rate we'll be lucky if we
cover our expenses!

GUSTAVE: But I've got something else, Mr Peterbono, sir.

PETERBONO (*profoundly discouraged*): If it's something else you stole from me you can imagine my curiosity.

GUSTAVE: It isn't a thing, it's a girl. And she looks rich.

HECTOR (*jumping up*): Good God! Don't say it's the same girl. A redhead? About twenty-five? Name of Eva?

GUSTAVE: No. Dark hair, about twenty. Name of Juliette.

HECTOR: Oh, that's all right.

PETERBONO: What did you get?

GUSTAVE: Nothing yet. But I helped her fish a kid out of the Thermes Fountain. We sat in the sun to dry and we got talking. She told me she liked me.

PETERBONO: Any jewels?

GUSTAVE: One very fine pearl.

PETERBONO: Good. We must look into that. Hector, can you spare a moment this afternoon, other engagements permitting?

GUSTAVE: No! I'd like to handle this myself.

PETERBONO: What's this? What's this? Handle it yourself, would you? Well, whatever next?

GUSTAVE: It was me she took a fancy to.

PETERBONO: All the more reason. Hector will swallow her in one.

GUSTAVE: No, I tell you! Not this one!

PETERBONO (*severely*): Gustave, listen to me. Your mother put you in my care, and I took you into the firm as assistant decoy. You're young and you're ambitious. That's fine. I was ambitious myself when I was your age. But just a minute! In our profession, as in all professions, you have to work your way up from the bottom. Hector here is the finest professional seducer I know this side of Monte Carlo. There's a chap who hits the bull's eye three times out of four, and take it from me, that's a pretty handsome average. You don't mean to tell me that you, a mere apprentice, expect to turn out better work than that?

GUSTAVE: To hell with it! I'll get her for myself.

PETERBONO (*tight-lipped*): If you wish to do a job on the side in your spare time there's nothing to stop you. You'll owe me just the sixty-five per cent on what you make, that's all.

HECTOR (*who has been watching a nursemaid during this altercation*):
Peter?

PETERBONO: Hector?

HECTOR: That nursemaid over there. See the gold chain?

PETERBONO (*contemptuously*): Pooh! It's probably gilded fuse
wire.

HECTOR: Listen, it's ten to seven. We've ten minutes in hand
before supper.

PETERBONO: Very well, if you're set on it. We'll give her the
'Three Musketeers' Manoeuvre.

HECTOR: Three Musketeers Manoeuvre?

PETERBONO: It's the classic routine for nursemaids. Number
one gets off with her, number two plays ten little pigs with
the baby, and number three starts whistling bugle-calls
without a break to make her senses reel.

They go. Enter LADY HURF *and* JULIETTE.

JULIETTE: The little boy was barely five years old. He was
only in up to his waist, but he was frightened and he kept
falling over. He would have drowned, I'm sure.

LADY HURF: How dreadful! Have you noticed all these little
chimney-pot hats everywhere? How absurd they look!

JULIETTE: Fortunately this young man came to the rescue.
He was wonderful, and very sweet.

LADY HURF: All children are sweet at five. But at twelve they
begin to get silly. That's why I never wanted any.

JULIETTE: I was talking about the young man, Aunt.

LADY HURF: Oh yes, of course. There's another of those
grotesque little hats. The young man was very sweet – yes,
go on.

JULIETTE: That's all.

LADY HURF: We must invite him to dinner.

JULIETTE: He's gone. I'd never seen him before.

LADY HURF: Good. One always knows far too many people.
Besides, I can't stand stories about drowning. Your poor
uncle swam like a lump of lead. He drowned himself seven

times, I could have hit him. Ah, there's Edgard. Edgard, have you seen Eva?

LORD EDGARD (*appearing from behind his paper*): How are you, my dear?

LADY HURF: I asked if you'd seen Eva.

LORD EDGARD: Eva? No, I haven't. That's very odd. Now what can I have done with her? Perhaps she's at the Baths.

LADY HURF: At seven o'clock at night? Don't be silly.

JULIETTE: Shall we try the Phoenix bar? She often goes there.

LADY HURF: Edgard, don't stir from this spot for any reason whatsoever.

LORD EDGARD: Very good, my dear.

LADY HURF (*going*): But of course if you see her, run after her.

LORD EDGARD: Very good, my dear.

LADY HURF: Or better still, don't; you'd only lose her – just come and tell us which way she went.

LORD EDGARD: Very good, my dear.

LADY HURF: On second thoughts, no. You'd never manage to find us. Send one attendant after her, another attendant to let us know, and put a third in your place to tell us where you've gone so we can pick you up on the way home if we should happen to be passing.

LORD EDGARD: Very good, my dear.

He retires stunned behind his paper. Exit LADY HURF *with* JULIETTE. *Enter the* DUPONT-DUFORTS, *father and son, accompanied by the little jig on the clarinet, which is their signature tune.*

D.D. SENIOR: Let's follow. We'll meet them casually on the promenade, and try to tempt them to a cocktail. Didier, I don't know what's come over you. You, a hard-working, conscientious lad, brimful of initiative, and look at you. You're not paying an atom of attention to young Juliette.

D.D. JUNIOR: She snubs me.

D.D. SENIOR: What does that matter? To begin with, you aren't just anybody. You are Dupont-Dufort junior. Her aunt thinks a great deal of you. She's prepared to make any investment on your recommendation.

D.D. JUNIOR: That ought to be enough for us.

D.D. SENIOR: Son, in matters of money there's no such thing as enough. I'd far and away prefer you to pull off this marriage. Nothing short of that will put our bank fairly and squarely on its feet again. So let me see a bit of charm, a little fascination.

D.D. JUNIOR: Yes, Dad.

D.D. SENIOR: We couldn't wish for more propitious circumstances. They're bored to tears, and there's nobody here in the least presentable. So let's make ourselves agreeable, superlatively agreeable.

D.D. JUNIOR: Yes, Dad.

Exeunt the DUPONT-DUFORTS. LORD EDGARD, *who has heard every word, looks over his 'Times' to watch them go.* PETER-BONO, HECTOR *and* GUSTAVE *come in dressed as soldiers as the musician begins his second number. The policemen enter at the same time from the other side. They all perform a flirtatious little ballet round the nursemaid, the manoeuvres of the policemen seriously impeding those of the three thieves. The nursemaid finally goes; the policemen, twirling their white batons behind their backs, make gallant attempts to hinder her departure. During the ballet* LADY HURF *returns alone and goes to sit beside* LORD EDGARD. *The music stops at the exit of the policemen and the nursemaid.*

PETERBONO (*thwarted*): Lads, that's the first time I've ever known the Three Musketeers Manoeuvre to miscarry.

LADY HURF (*to* LORD EDGARD): Well, Edgard my dear, and what have you done with yourself today?

LORD EDGARD (*surprised and embarrassed as always at* LADY HURF'S *customary abruptness*): I – er – I read *The Times*.

LADY HURF (*sternly*): The same as yesterday?

LORD EDGARD (*ingenuously*): Not the same copy as yesterday.

HECTOR (*who has been watching the scene, gives a whistle of admiration*): See those pearls?

PETERBONO: Four millions!

HECTOR: How about it? What's it to be? Russian princes?

PETERBONO: No. She knows her onions by the look of her. Ruined Spanish noblemen.

GUSTAVE: That's bright of you. Whenever you masquerade as Spaniards you're rigged out like a couple of crows.

PETERBONO: Quiet, shaver! You're speaking of a trade you know nothing about.

GUSTAVE: Well, anyway, if you think I'm dressing up as your ecclesiastical secretary like the last time, it's no go. I'm not wearing a cassock in this heat.

PETERBONO: Gustave, you're trying my patience! Come along home! Hector and I will be Spanish Grandees, and you'll put on that cassock, heat or no heat.

The unwilling GUSTAVE *is borne away, to the accompaniment of a little jig on the clarinet.*

LADY HURF (*who has been deep in thought*): Edgard, the situation is grave . . .

LORD EDGARD: I know. According to *The Times*, the Empire . . .

LADY HURF: No, no, here.

LORD EDGARD (*looking round him anxiously*): Here?

LADY HURF: Listen to me. We have two tender creatures in our care. Intrigues are fermenting – marriages are brewing. Personally I can't keep track of them – it gives me the vertigo. Who is to uncover them, Edgard, who is to supervise them?

LORD EDGARD: Who?

LADY HURF: Juliette is a scatterbrain. Eva is a scatterbrain. As for me, I haven't a notion what's going on and the mere idea of it bores me to extinction. Besides, I've no more common sense than those two senseless girls. That leaves you in the midst of these three scatterbrains.

LORD EDGARD: That leaves me.

LADY HURF: Which is another way of saying nobody. I am perplexed, excessively perplexed. Anything may happen in this watering-place. Intrigues spring up under one's very feet like so much jungle vegetation. Should we do better to leave Vichy, I wonder? Ought we perhaps to bury ourselves in some rustic backwater? Edgard, for heaven's sake say something! You are the guardian of these two young things, aren't you?

LORD EDGARD: We might ask Dupont-Dufort his advice. He seems to be a man of character.

LADY HURF: A deal too much character. What a ninny you are. He's the last man from whom we want advice. The Dupont-Duforts are after our money.

LORD EDGARD: But they're rich.

LADY HURF: Exactly. That's what worries me. They're after a lot of money. An investment or a marriage settlement. Our two little ones with their millions are exceptionally tempting morsels.

LORD EDGARD: Could we not telegraph to England?

LADY HURF: What for?

LORD EDGARD: Scotland Yard might send us a detective.

LADY HURF: That would be a great help, I must say! They're crooked as corkscrews, the lot of them!

LORD EDGARD: The problem, then, is in effect insoluble.

LADY HURF: Edgard, you simply must bestir yourself. Our fate, the girls' and mine, is in your hands.

LORD EDGARD (*looks at his hands, very worried*): I don't know that I am very well equipped.

LADY HURF (*sternly*): Edgard, do you call yourself a man? And a gentleman?

LORD EDGARD: Yes.

LADY HURF: Then make a decision!

LORD EDGARD (*firmly*): Very well! I shall nevertheless summon a detective from Scotland Yard, with a special proviso that I want him honest.

LADY HURF: Over my dead body! If he's honest, he'll philander with the kitchen maids and he won't wash. It will be insufferable. And yet I don't know why I should be telling you all this. What do I want with absolute security? I'm as bored as a piece of old carpet!

LORD EDGARD: Oh, my dear . . . !

LADY HURF: That's all I am, a piece of old carpet.

LORD EDGARD: You who were once so beautiful.

LADY HURF: Yes, in the nineteen-hundreds. Oh, I could scream with rage! I want to enjoy my last few years – I want to laugh a little. Sixty years I've spent deluded into thinking life a serious business. That's sixty years too long. I am in the mood, Edgard, for a gigantic piece of folly.

LORD EDGARD: Nothing dangerous, I hope?

LADY HURF: I don't know. I'll see what occurs to me. (*She leans towards him.*) I think I should like to massacre the Dupont-Duforts.

In they come, accompanied by their particular little tune, with EVA *and* JULIETTE.

D.D. SENIOR: How are you today, milady?

D.D. JUNIOR: Milady.

D.D. SENIOR: Ah, dear Lord Edgard.

LORD EDGARD (*drawing him aside*): Take the greatest possible care.

D.D. SENIOR: But why, milord?

LORD EDGARD: Hush! I can't tell you. But take care. Leave Vichy.

D. D. JUNIOR: We ran into these ladies on the promenade.

EVA: Vichy's an impossible place. Nothing to do, nowhere to go, and all the men are hideous.

D.D. JUNIOR: Oh, how true! Quite, quite hideous, all of them!

D.D. SENIOR: All of them! (*Aside to his son.*) Excellent thing for us.

EVA: I have an engagement tonight, Aunt. I shall be late for dinner – if I'm back at all.

D.D. SENIOR (*aside to his son*): With you?

D.D. JUNIOR: No.

JULIETTE: Eva, I haven't told you. I rescued a little boy who fell into the Thermes Fountain, and I met an enchanting young man who helped me to save him.

LADY HURF: Juliette talks of nothing else.

The DUPONT-DUFORTS *look at each other anxiously.*

D.D. SENIOR: Wasn't that you?

D.D. JUNIOR: No.

JULIETTE: We sat in the sun till we were dry, and chatted. You've no idea how pleasant he was! He's slight, with dark hair and – he's not the same as yours by any chance?

EVA: No. Mine's tall, with red hair.

JULIETTE: Thank goodness!

D.D. SENIOR (*whispers*): Sonny, you have absolutely *got* to sparkle. (*Raising his voice.*) Didier, dear boy, have you been to the swimming-pool with these ladies yet? You must give them a demonstration of your impeccable crawl. You could have rescued the toddler with the greatest of ease.

JULIETTE: Oh, the crawl would have been quite useless. The Thermes Fountain is only eighteen inches deep.

Towards the end of this scene, PETERBONO, *as a very noble – all too noble – old Spanish gentleman,* HECTOR *as a Grandee, an equally spectacular achievement, and* GUSTAVE, *their ecclesiastical secretary, come in and slowly approach the others.*

PETERBONO: Careful. This is big game. Stay close, and take no risks.

HECTOR: Your monocle.

PETERBONO: The big act, 'Noblesse oblige'. Wait for the word go. Gustave, two paces behind.

The clarinet strikes up a march, heroic and ultra-Spanish. Suddenly, LADY HURF, *who has been watching this curious trio, runs to them and throws her arms round* PETERBONO'S *neck.*

LADY HURF: Why, if it isn't that dear dear Duke of Miraflores!

Music stops.

PETERBONO (*surprised and uneasy*): Uh?

LADY HURF: Don't say you've forgotten! Biarritz 1902. The luncheon parties at Pampeluna! The bull-fights! Lady Hurf.

PETERBONO: Ah . . .! Lady Hurf. Bull-fights. Lunch. Dear
friend. (*To the other two.*) I must have made up like one of her
acquaintances.

LADY HURF: I am so, so happy! I was disintegrating with
boredom. But where is the Duchess?

PETERBONO: Dead.

Tremolo from the orchestra.

LADY HURF: Oh, heavens! And your cousin the Count?

PETERBONO: Dead.

Tremolo from the orchestra.

LADY HURF: Oh, heavens! And your friend, the Admiral?

PETERBONO: Also dead.

The orchestra begins a funeral march. PETERBONO *turns to his
friends.*

Saved!

LADY HURF: My poor friend. So many funerals.

PETERBONO: Alas! However, may I present my son, Don
Hector? And my ecclesiastical secretary, Dom Petrus?

LADY HURF: Lord Edgard, whom you knew years ago. It was
he whom you beat each morning at golf, and who was always
losing his golf-balls.

PETERBONO: Ha, golf – yes. Dear friend.

LORD EDGARD (*panic-stricken, to* LADY HURF): But, my
dear—

LADY HURF (*sternly*): What's the matter? Do you mean to say
you don't remember the Duke?

LORD EDGARD: This is insane. Come now, think back—

LADY HURF: Your memory is abominable. Don't say another
word or I shall lose my temper. My nieces, Eva and Juliette,
who worry me so dreadfully because they're both very
marriageable, and their dowries are exceptionally tempting
to fortune-hunters.

The DUPONT-DUFORTS *look at each other.*

D.D. SENIOR: Dignity, lad, dignity.

D.D. JUNIOR: She can't mean us.

PETERBONO and HECTOR indulge in violent nudging.

LADY HURF: I am so delighted to have met you again. Vichy is such a dull hole. Tell me, do you remember the Ridottos on the Riviera?

PETERBONO: I should think I do!

D.D. JUNIOR (*to his father*): We're forgotten.

D.D. SENIOR: Let's introduce ourselves. Dupont-Dufort, senior.

D. D. JUNIOR: Junior.

During the introductions, EVA *stares hard at* HECTOR, *who simulates an enormous interest in the conversation.* GUSTAVE *has all but disappeared into his brief-case, and rummages feverishly among his papers to avoid* JULIETTE'S *gaze, which is fixed on him in puzzled interest.*

LADY HURF: You must be as bored as I am. It's an undreamed of stroke of fortune, our meeting, don't you think?

PETERBONO (*nudging* HECTOR): Undreamed of.

HECTOR (*nudging* PETERBONO): Yes. Undreamed of – absolutely undreamed of.

In their glee, they go much too far, but no one seems to notice.

LADY HURF: Your son is most charming. Don't you think so, Eva?

EVA: Yes.

PETERBONO: He was the most dashing officer in the entire Spanish army – before the revolution.

LADY HURF: Alas! You suffered a great deal?

PETERBONO: A great deal.

LADY HURF: Where are you staying? Not at an hotel?

PETERBONO (*vaguely*): Yes.

LADY HURF: It's out of the question, Edgard! The Duke is staying at an hotel!

LORD EDGARD: But, my dearest, I assure you—

LADY HURF: Be quiet! Dear Duke, you cannot, you simply cannot stay at an hotel. Will you do us the honour of accepting our humble hospitality? Our villa is enormous, and we shall put the west wing entirely at your disposal.

PETERBONO: Certainly, certainly, certainly, certainly—

Stupendous nudging between PETERBONO *and* HECTOR. *The* DUPONT-DUFORTS *exchange crestfallen glances.*

LADY HURF: You may, needless to say, bring your entourage. (*She looks inquiringly at* GUSTAVE.) Is he looking for something?

PETERBONO: A document, yes. Dom Petrus!

GUSTAVE (*emerging from the brief-case*): Your Grace? (*He has put on some dark glasses.*)

LADY HURF: Has he got bad eyes?

PETERBONO: Oh, very bad. His condition requires a certain amount of care. I couldn't burden you with his presence. Dom Petrus, we shall accept Lady Hurf's generous offer of hospitality. Call at the hotel, will you, and have our luggage sent on. And stay there until further notice. You will collect the mail and come to us each morning for instructions.

GUSTAVE (*furious*): But, your Grace . . .

PETERBONO: Enough!

GUSTAVE: Your Grace—

PETERBONO: Off with you!

HECTOR *gives* GUSTAVE *a push, and he wanders reluctantly away.*

LADY HURF (*moved*): Just as he used to be! That same commanding tone – the vocal magic of the Miraflores! Your cousin had it too.

PETERBONO: Alas!

LADY HURF: How did he die?

PETERBONO: Er, how he died?

LADY HURF: Yes – I was so fond of him.

PETERBONO: You want me to relate the circumstances of his passing?

LADY HURF: Yes.

PETERBONO (*turns to* HECTOR *in his panic*): Well, he died . . .

> HECTOR *mimes a motor accident, but this* PETERBONO *cannot grasp.*

He died insane.

LADY HURF: Ah, poor fellow! He always was eccentric. But your wife, the dear Duchess?

PETERBONO: Dead.

LADY HURF: Yes, I know. But how?

> HECTOR *touches his heart several times.* PETERBONO *is slow to take the suggestion, but as he has no imagination whatever himself, he gives way.*

PETERBONO: Of love.

LADY HURF (*in confusion*): Oh, I beg your pardon! And your friend the Admiral?

PETERBONO: Ah, now the Admiral . . .

> *He looks at* HECTOR, *who indicates that he has run out of ideas. He again misinterprets the pantomime.*

Drowned. But please excuse me, you are reopening wounds which time has not yet healed.

LADY HURF: Oh, forgive me, dear friend, forgive me! (*To the others.*) What breeding! What grandeur in adversity! Don't you think so, Edgard?

LORD EDGARD: My dear, I still insist that—

LADY HURF: Do stop insisting. Can't you see the Duke is suffering?

D.D. SENIOR (*to his son*): Let us join in the conversation.

D.D. JUNIOR: What an appalling avalanche of misfortunes!

D.D. SENIOR: Falling on such venerable heads!

> *No one listens.*

LADY HURF (*in a peal of laughter*): How beautiful Biarritz was in those days. Do you remember the balls?

PETERBONO: Ah, the balls . . .

LADY HURF: And Lina Veri?

PETERBONO: Lina Veri. I can't quite recall . . .

LADY HURF: Come, come. Why, you were intimate! He's aged so much. (*To the others.*)

PETERBONO: Oh, Lina Veri. Of course. The darling of Italian society.

LADY HURF: No, no, no. She was a dancer.

PETERBONO: Oh, yes, but her mother was the darling of Italian society.

LADY HURF (*to the others*): He's wandering a little. He's very tired. My dear Duke, I would like to show you your apartments right away. The villa is close by, at the end of the avenue.

PETERBONO: With pleasure.

GUSTAVE *comes running in, this time as his own charming self, but magnificently dressed.*

GUSTAVE: Good morning, Father!

PETERBONO (*off his balance*): Little basket! Allow me to present my second son, Don Pedro, whom I'd forgotten to mention.

LADY HURF: Gracious, you have another son? By whom?

PETERBONO (*panicking again*): Ah, that's a long story—

He looks at HECTOR, *who signs to him to go carefully.*

But that one also opens wounds as yet unhealed by time.

LADY HURF: Come along, Edgard.

LORD EDGARD: But, my dear—

LADY HURF: And keep quiet!

They go, HECTOR *paying elaborate attentions to* EVA, *who has continued to stare at him.*

JULIETTE (*to* GUSTAVE): Now will you kindly tell me what is going on?

GUSTAVE: Ssh! I'll explain later.

They go too. The DUPONT-DUFORTS *are left alone.*

D.D. JUNIOR: Father, they've forgotten us—!

D.D. SENIOR: All the same, we'll follow. And, Didier, twice the affability. Let's hope these young men are already attached or better still that they aren't interested in women!

They go.

Curtain

Act Two

A drawing-room in LADY HURF'S *house. It is evening, after dinner, and* JULIETTE *and* GUSTAVE *are sitting side by side; a little romantic air is heard in the distance.*

JULIETTE: It's nice here. No one is disturbing us tonight.

GUSTAVE: Yes, it is nice.

JULIETTE: For three days now you've been sad. Are you homesick for Spain?

GUSTAVE: Oh no.

JULIETTE: I'm sorry now I wouldn't work at my Spanish at school. We might have spoken it together. It would have been fun.

GUSTAVE: I only speak a few words myself.

JULIETTE: Do you? That's funny.

GUSTAVE: Yes, it is rather.

A silence.

JULIETTE: It must be amusing to be a prince.

GUSTAVE: Oh, one gets used to it, you know.

A silence.

JULIETTE: Don Pedro, what's the matter? We were much friendlier three days ago.

GUSTAVE: Nothing's the matter.

A pause. LORD EDGARD *crosses the room laden with papers.*

LORD EDGARD (*muttering*): Though I should die in the endeavour, I'll set my mind at rest.

He drops his papers. They jump up to help him, but he bars their path.

Don't touch them! Don't touch them! (*He picks up the papers himself and goes out muttering.*) This momentous discovery, if discovery there be, must be surrounded with the greatest possible precautions.

GUSTAVE: What is he looking for? He's done nothing but ferret about among those old papers since we came here.

JULIETTE: I don't know. He's a little mad. Only he's painstaking as well, you see, so sometimes the results are quite prodigious.

A little girl comes in.

Oh, here's my little friend.

CHILD: Mademoiselle Juliette, I've picked some daisies for you.

JULIETTE: Thank you, darling.

CHILD: They haven't very many petals. Daddy says they aren't the ones that lovers use.

JULIETTE: Never mind.

CHILD: Shall I get some others?

JULIETTE: No. Yes. You're very sweet. (*She kisses her.*) Run away now.

The CHILD *goes.* JULIETTE *turns to* GUSTAVE, *shamefaced.*

Do you think it's silly of me?

GUSTAVE: No.

JULIETTE: You said you loved me, Don Pedro, yet for three days now you haven't even looked at me.

GUSTAVE: I do love you, Juliette.

JULIETTE: Then why—?

GUSTAVE: I can't tell you.

JULIETTE: My father wasn't titled, I know, but my aunt is a Lady, and my grandfather was an Honourable.

GUSTAVE: How funny you are. It isn't that.

JULIETTE: Do you think the Duke of Miraflores would consent to my marrying you?

GUSTAVE (*smiling*): I'm sure he would.

JULIETTE: Why do you look so sad then, if you love me and everyone approves?

GUSTAVE: I can't tell you.

JULIETTE: But you do feel, don't you, that our lives might meet and join one day?

GUSTAVE: I would be lying if I told you I felt that.

JULIETTE (*turning away*): That's unkind of you.

GUSTAVE: Careful. Here's your cousin.

JULIETTE: Come into the garden. It's getting dark. I want you to tell me everything.

The music fades as they go. EVA *comes in, followed by* HECTOR, *in a totally different make-up from the one he wore in Act One.*

HECTOR: There, you see, they've left us the place to ourselves.

EVA: But I don't in the least need a place to myself – that's the pity of it – I could adapt myself quite easily to a great crowd around us.

HECTOR: How cruel you are!

EVA: I don't like you. I'm cruel to those I dislike. It's in my nature. But on the other hand, when someone appeals to me, there's hardly anything I wouldn't do for him.

HECTOR (*in despair*): Why, why can I not manage to appeal to you a second time?

EVA: You know perfectly well why. You're not the same now.

HECTOR: What abominable absent-mindedness! This disguise, I tell you, is the fancy of an aristocrat wearied to death of his own personality, a pastime which affords him an escape from his oppressive self. And for this accursed fancy, must I lose my love?

EVA: I remember with delight a young man who spoke to me in the park. Find him for me. I might still think him lovable.

HECTOR: This is ridiculous! Won't you even tell me if I'm getting warm? At least tell me, did I have a beard when I first appealed to you?

EVA: But it wouldn't amuse me if I were to tell you.

HECTOR (*who has turned away to change his make-up, turns back again wearing a completely new face*): It wasn't like this, I suppose?

EVA (*in a burst of laughter*): No, oh no!

HECTOR: Yet you remember my voice, my eyes?

EVA: Yes, but it isn't enough.

HECTOR: I'm the same height as I was. I'm tall, well built – I assure you I am, very well built.

EVA: I only judge by faces.

HECTOR: This is horrible! Horrible! I'll never find the face that pleased you, ever! It wasn't as a woman, by any chance?

EVA: What do you take me for?

HECTOR: Or as a Chinaman?

EVA: You're evidently out of your mind. I'll wait till you're in it again.

She goes to sit farther off; he starts to follow her and she turns on him.

No, no, no! For heaven's sake will you stop following me about and changing your beard every five minutes! You're making me giddy.

HECTOR (*stricken*): And to think that idiot Peterbono keeps on swearing it was as a test-pilot!

LORD EDGARD *crosses the room laden with papers.*

LORD EDGARD: This is unthinkable! I must find this letter, from which the truth will spring in such a curious fashion.

He sees HECTOR *in his latest make-up, drops his papers and leaps on him.*

At last! The detective from Scotland Yard.

HECTOR: No sir. (*He makes to go.*)

LORD EDGARD: Excellent! The perfect answer. I specially stipulated secrecy. But don't be afraid, I am Lord Edgard in person. You may disclose your identity.

HECTOR: I tell you I'm not the man you're expecting.

He goes.

LORD EDGARD (*following him*): I see! I see! Perfect! You're keeping word for word to my instructions! I stressed the need for caution!

LADY HURF *enters, holding a magazine.*

LADY HURF: My little Eva is bored, isn't she?

EVA *smiles and says nothing. Unseen by* LADY HURF, HECTOR *comes back in another make-up, which he silently shows* EVA. *She shakes her head and he retires, heavy-hearted.* LADY HURF *puts down her magazine with a sigh.*

My little Eva is as bored as she can be.

EVA (*with a smile*): Yes, Aunt.

LADY HURF: So am I, darling, very bored.

EVA: Only I'm twenty-five, so you see, it's rather sad.

LADY HURF: You'll see how much sadder it can be when you're sixty. For you there's always love. As you may guess, it's several years now since I officially renounced it.

EVA: Oh, love!

LADY HURF: *What* a deep sigh! Since you've been a widow, surely you've had lovers?

EVA: I never had a single one who loved me.

LADY HURF: You want the moon. If your lovers bore you, marry one of them. That will give the others an added fascination.

EVA: Marry? Whom?

LADY HURF: Needless to say these Dupont-Duforts exasperate us both. What about the Spaniards?

EVA: Prince Hector chases after me changing his moustache in the hope of rediscovering the one that first appealed to me.

LADY HURF: Truly appealed to you?

EVA (*smiling*): I don't remember.

LADY HURF: They're curious individuals.

EVA: Why?

LADY HURF: Oh, I don't know. I tell you, I'm an old carcass who doesn't know what to do with herself. I've had everything a woman could reasonably, or even unreasonably, wish for. Money, power, lovers. Now that I'm old, I feel as alone inside my skin as I did as a little girl and they made me face the wall when I'd been naughty. And here's the rub; I know that between that little girl and this old woman, there has been, under the charivari and the noise, nothing but an even greater loneliness.

EVA: I've always thought of you as happy.

LADY HURF: You don't see much, do you? I am playing a part. Only, like everything else I do, I play it well, that's all. Yours now, you play badly, little girl (*She strokes her hair.*) Child, child, you will always find yourself pursued by desires with changing beards and never have the courage to tell one of them: stay as you are – I love you. Don't think yourself a martyr now. All women are the same. My little Juliette, though, will come through because she is romantic. Her simplicity will save her. It's a favour only granted to a few.

EVA: There are some who can love.

LADY HURF: Yes. There are some who love a man. Who kill him with loving, who kill themselves for him, but they are seldom heiresses to millions. (*She strokes her hair again, with a rueful smile.*) Ah, you'll finish up like me, an old woman covered in diamonds who plays at intrigues in an effort to forget that she has never lived. And yet, I'd like to laugh a little. Here am I, playing with fire, and the fire won't even burn my fingers.

EVA: What do you mean, Aunt?

LADY HURF: Shush – here come our marionettes.

PETERBONO *and* HECTOR *appear in the doorway, preceded by the musician, and followed almost at once by the* DUPONT-DUFORTS. *They all rush towards the ladies, but it is the thieves who get there first to kiss their hands.*

(*Jumps to her feet and utters a sudden cry.*) Ah! I have an idea!

PETERBONO (*frightened, to* HECTOR): She scares the life out of me. Every time she screams like that, I think my beard's loose.

LADY HURF: Where is Juliette?

EVA: In the garden, with Prince Pedro. They're inseparable.

PETERBONO: Ah, the dear children!

LADY HURF (*calling*): Juliette!

JULIETTE (*coming in with* GUSTAVE): Did you want me, Aunt Emily?

LADY HURF (*drawing her aside*): Your eyes are red, child. Now mind, you mustn't be unhappy, or I cut the strings and the puppets will fall down.

JULIETTE: What do you mean, Aunt?

LADY HURF: If I appear to be talking through my hat, it's precisely so you won't understand me. Come along, both of you. (*She takes them by the waist and leads them into the garden.*) I have an idea to brighten up this evening; I want you to tell me what you think of it.

They go. The DUPONT-DUFORTS *look at each other.*

D.D. SENIOR: After them, sonny. And a hundred times more charm. Remember, it's our future that's at stake.

D.D. JUNIOR: Yes, Papa.

Left alone, the three thieves can unbend.

HECTOR (*offering* PETERBONO *a box of cigars*): Would you care for a cigar?

PETERBONO (*helping himself*): I'm savouring them. They're remarkably good.

HECTOR (*pouring out*): A little brandy?

PETERBONO: Thank you.

They drink.

HECTOR: Another cigar, perhaps?

PETERBONO (*grabbing a fistful without more ado*): You're too kind. No, no really, you embarrass me. (*He feels a slight remorse, and takes the box.*) But may I in return press you to a cigar?

HECTOR (*pulling them out of his pockets in handfuls*): Thank you so much. I'm all right just now.

There is a moment of beatitude and exquisite refinement. They spread themselves blissfully on the sofa. Suddenly HECTOR *indicates* GUSTAVE, *sitting sad and sombre in his corner.*

PETERBONO (*rises and goes to him*): What's wrong, laddie? Why so sad? Here you are with a wonderful room, lovely food, and a pretty little thing to flirt with, you're playing at princes, and for all that you can manage to be gloomy?

GUSTAVE: I don't want to stay here.

The other two give a start.

PETERBONO: Uh? You want to leave?

GUSTAVE: Yes.

PETERBONO: Leave here?

GUSTAVE: Yes – leave here.

PETERBONO: Hector, the boy's lost his reason.

HECTOR: What do you want to leave for?

GUSTAVE: I'm in love with Juliette.

HECTOR: Well then?

GUSTAVE: Really in love.

HECTOR: Well then?

PETERBONO: Why not? You've never been better off. She takes you for a prince, and rich at that. Go in and win, lad, she's as good as yours.

GUSTAVE: I don't want to take her, for a day, and then be forced to leave her.

PETERBONO: You'll have to leave her one day.

GUSTAVE: And – I'm ashamed of this game I have to play with her. I'd rather go away, now, and never see her again.

HECTOR: He's out of his mind.

PETERBONO: Completely.

GUSTAVE: Look, what are we here for?

PETERBONO: What are we here for? We're working, lad. It's the height of our season.

GUSTAVE: We're here to do a job. Let's do it then and go.

PETERBONO: And the preliminaries? Have you spared a single thought for the preliminaries?

GUSTAVE: They've gone on long enough, your damn preliminaries.

PETERBONO: I ask you, Hector, isn't it painful? Having to listen to an apprentice teaching us our trade!

HECTOR: Of course we'll do a job; that's what we came for, but have you even the first idea what that job's going to be?

GUSTAVE: Strip the drawing-room?

PETERBONO: With carpet-bags, eh? Like raggle-taggle gipsies! The lowness, Hector, the abysmal lowness of this youngster's mind! Understand, boy, that we haven't yet decided on the job we're going to do. And if our behaviour strikes you, a novice, as peculiar, tell yourself it's because we're in the process of investigating the possibilities of this – establishment.

GUSTAVE: You're lingering on here for the brandy and cigars, and because Hector still hopes he'll get Eva to remember him. But in actual fact you haven't the smallest inkling what you want to do. I may be an apprentice, but I'll tell you something – that's no way to work.

PETERBONO (*running to* HECTOR): Hector, hold me back!

HECTOR (*still blissfully smoking*): Gustave, don't be difficult. Try to understand.

PETERBONO: Hector, hold me back!

HECTOR: You see, we're wavering . . .

PETERBONO: Hold me back, Hector! Hold me back!

HECTOR (*takes his arm to please him*): All right, I've got you.

PETERBONO (*deflated*): Just as well.

HECTOR (*to* GUSTAVE): We're wavering between several possible courses of action . . .

GUSTAVE: Which?

HECTOR: Shall we confide in him, Pete? Is it safe to risk the indiscretion of a youth?

PETERBONO (*shrugs*): Oh, confide in him, do. Since we're answerable to him now.

HECTOR: Right. Tell him your idea first, Pete.

PETERBONO: After you, Hector, after you.

HECTOR (*embarrassed*): Aaaaaaah . . . well . . .

GUSTAVE: You haven't thought of a thing!

HECTOR (*in righteous rage*): We haven't thought of a thing?!!! We're wavering between the trick of the dud cheque given in exchange for real jewels on a Saturday, which gives us the week-end to make our getaway, or the trick of the good cheque received in exchange for dud jewels under the same conditions. We've also considered giving Lady Hurf some orchids sprayed with ether (taking good care not to smell them ourselves) so as to relieve her of her pearls as soon as she nods off.

PETERBONO (*equally incensed*): Or we might provoke the Dupont-Duforts to a duel! We wound them and then in the commotion we make off with the silver!

GUSTAVE: What if you're the ones to get wounded?

PETERBONO: Impossible!

GUSTAVE: Why?

PETERBONO (*yelling*): I don't know. But it's impossible!

HECTOR: Or again we could make out we'd been robbed and demand a colossal sum for hush-money!

PETERBONO: Pretend we found a pearl in the oysters at dinner, for instance, and swap it for a pearl of Lady Hurf's, or something.

GUSTAVE: There's no 'r' in the month.

PETERBONO: I said for instance!

GUSTAVE: In other words you just don't know. Well, I'm going to do the job tonight, and then I'm off.

PETERBONO: Tonight? And why not right away?

GUSTAVE: Yes, why not right away? I want to go away. I want to leave here as soon as possible.

PETERBONO: He'll be the ruin of us! Gustave, think of your poor old mother, who put you in my care!

GUSTAVE: No!

PETERBONO: I'll put my curse on you! Naturally you don't care a rap if I put my curse on you?

GUSTAVE: No.

PETERBONO (*bellowing*): Hector! Hold me back! (*He seizes* GUSTAVE.) Just another fortnight. We'll do the job all right, but it's nice here, and it isn't so often we're in a nice place . . .

GUSTAVE: No. I'm too unhappy.

He goes.

HECTOR (*leaps after him*): After him! We've got to stop him before he starts a scandal.

PETERBONO (*calling after him*): I've got an idea! Suppose we pretended not to know him?

HECTOR shrugs his shoulders and goes out, refusing even to consider such a solution.

Enter LORD EDGARD, *preceded by the musician playing a succession of tremolos as if he had intimations of a sudden blow of destiny. He is rummaging in his ever-present pile of papers. All of a sudden he utters a loud cry and falls in a dead faint among his scattered letters. The musician runs for help, emitting isolated notes from his instrument.*

JULIETTE (*comes in*): Uncle, Uncle, what's the matter? (*She props him up on a sofa and feels his hands.*) Ice-cold! What's this? (*She picks up a letter, reads it, and hurriedly thrusts it into her pocket. Running out.*) Aunt Emily! Aunt Emily! Come quickly!

The clarinet in great confusion multiplies his tragic tremolos. Everyone comes rushing in shouting at once.

Stroke!
At his age!
No, he's only fainted.
Stand back – give him air.
Get a doctor!
He's coming round.
He's all right now.
A sudden shock.
Perhaps he found what he was looking for.

The music stops. An enormous silence.

PETERBONO (*breathes to* HECTOR *in the silence*): The chance of a lifetime.

HECTOR: Yes. But what do we do about it?

PETERBONO: Well, nothing obviously, but it's still the chance of a lifetime.

LORD EDGARD (*sitting up slowly, says in a toneless voice*): My friends, I have a ghastly piece of news for you. The Duke of Miraflores died in Biarritz in 1904.

Everyone looks at PETERBONO, *who is very ill at ease. An impish little jig on the clarinet.*

PETERBONO: Nonsense!

HECTOR (*aside*): Talk about the chance of a lifetime!

PETERBONO: This is a fine time to be funny! Ease over to the window.

LADY HURF: Edgard, are you out of your mind?

LORD EDGARD: No, I tell you. I've found the notification. I knew I'd find it eventually. Ever since the day— (*He searches himself.*) Where is it? This is too much! Where is it? I had it a moment ago! Oh, my goodness! It's gone again.

D.D. SENIOR: Everything is coming to light!

D.D. JUNIOR: We are saved! (*To* PETERBONO, *who is imperceptibly edging towards the window.*) Aren't you staying to make sure your host is all right?

PETERBONO: Yes, oh yes!

LADY HURF: Edgard, that's a ridiculous joke to play on the dear duke.

LORD EDGARD: But, my dear, I guarantee—

LADY HURF: Come along, dear Duke, and show him you aren't dead.

PETERBONO (*uneasy*): No, no. I'm not dead.

LORD EDGARD: Yet I found the notification . . .

LADY HURF (*pinching him*): Edgard, you're making a mistake, I'm sure. You must apologize.

LORD EDGARD (*rubbing his arm*): Ouch! Why yes, now that you mention it, I think I must have been confusing him with the Duke of Orleans.

LADY HURF: Of course. Shall we call the incident closed?

PETERBONO (*in great relief*): Completely closed.

LADY HURF: Let's go outside, shall we? I've ordered coffee on the terrace. I want to tell you about my idea.

D.D. SENIOR (*in step with her*): I think it's a wonderful idea.

LADY HURF (*exasperated*): Wait a minute, my dear man, I

haven't told you yet. Listen. They're holding a Thieves' Carnival tonight at the Casino. We're all going to dress up as thieves and go to it.

D.D. SENIOR *and* JUNIOR (*immediately burst out laughing*): He! He! He! How terribly, terribly amusing!

D.D. SENIOR (*to his son as they go out*): Play up to her, son.

Exit.

PETERBONO (*furious, as he goes out with* HECTOR): I call that in very poor taste, don't you?

JULIETTE *is alone. She stands motionless a moment. The music is heard some way away, playing a romantic theme.* JULIETTE *takes out the fatal letter and reads it.*

JULIETTE: 'We regret to announce the sad death of His Serene Highness the Duke of Miraflores y Grandes, Marquis of Priola, Count of Zeste and Galba. The funeral will take place . . .' (*She stands in thought a moment.*) If his father isn't the Duke of Miraflores – then who can he be? Why has he taken the car out of the garage? Why is he hiding from me?

CHILD (*entering*): Mademoiselle Juliette, I found some. Look, daisies with lots of petals.

JULIETTE: Haven't you gone to bed yet?

CHILD: I was picking daisies for you.

JULIETTE: Thank you, you're an angel. (*She kisses her.*) His father may be an adventurer, but you see, he loves me. He does love me, doesn't he?

CHILD: Yes, of course he does.

JULIETTE: We don't care, do we, if he's an adventurer, or worse? If you were me, you'd love him, wouldn't you, just the same? Only why does that hard look come into his eyes whenever I ask him about himself? If he has designs on me, and he'd be wise to have, because I'm very rich, he should be very pleasant to me all the time – whereas – do you think he prefers Eva? That would be terrible—

CHILD: I don't know.

JULIETTE: No, of course you don't. Come along, I'll take you home. Are you afraid of the dark?

CHILD: No.

JULIETTE: That's a good girl. Nor am I. There's nothing to be afraid of, you know. Thieves won't hurt you.

They go.

Curtain

Act Three

The same set. The room is dark; a figure is seen moving about with a torch. It is GUSTAVE, *dressed in dark clothes and wearing a cap. He is silently examining the objects in the drawing-room. Suddenly he hears a noise and switches off the torch; a low whistle; two dark figures spring up, two torches flash, and focus on* GUSTAVE.

GUSTAVE: Who's that?

FIGURE: Tonight's the night.

GUSTAVE: Peterbono?

FIGURE: No. We're the new ones.

SECOND FIGURE: The new bandits.

GUSTAVE: For God's sake, what's going on? (*He draws a revolver.*) Hands up!

D.D. SENIOR (*it is no other*): Ha ha ha! That's good! Where did you get the gun? It's magnificent!

GUSTAVE: Stay where you are or I fire!

D.D. SENIOR: Come quietly! The game's up.

GUSTAVE: Stay where you are, damn you! (*He fires.*)

D.D. SENIOR (*blissfully unaware of his danger*): Oh, well done! Bravo!

GUSTAVE: What do you mean, Bravo? (*He fires again.*)

D.D. JUNIOR: It's a wonderful imitation! Where on earth did you buy those caps?

GUSTAVE: For the last time, stay where you are! (*He fires again and shatters a vase, which falls with a terrible clatter.*)

D.D. SENIOR: Didier, why do you have to be so clumsy!

D.D. JUNIOR (*protesting in the dark*): But, Dad, I didn't do it!

D.D. SENIOR: Well, it can't have been I, can it? I'm in the middle of the room.

D.D. JUNIOR: But, Dad, so am I!

D.D. SENIOR (*suddenly anxious*): Well, then, who broke the vase?

LORD EDGARD (*enters and switches on the light. He is dressed up as a policeman*): Now, now, what is all this noise? How do you like my helmet?

D.D. SENIOR (*who has got himself up, along with his son, in a terrifying apache disguise*): Superb; my lord, superb!

Exit LORD EDGARD. D.D. SENIOR *goes to* GUSTAVE.

My word, I don't think much of your costume. It doesn't come off – it's much too simple. It's the little touches that mean so much. For instance, look, this little scar here.

D.D. JUNIOR: And the black eye patch.

GUSTAVE: What are you doing dressed up like that?

D.D. SENIOR: We're going to the Casino.

D.D. JUNIOR: To the Thieves' Carnival. And so are you.

GUSTAVE: Oh? Oh yes, of course. So am I.

D.D. SENIOR: Only if I were you, I'd touch up your make-up, my boy. It's a shade too simple. You don't look a bit like a thief.

GUSTAVE: You're quite right. I'll see to it at once. (*He turns at the door.*) Tell me, is everybody going to the Thieves' Carnival?

D.D. SENIOR: Of course; everybody.

GUSTAVE: That's fine. See you later.

He goes.

D.D. SENIOR: Not an ounce of imagination in him, that boy.

D.D. JUNIOR: If the other two have rigged themselves up as absurdly as that, which they probably have, we're well on the way. The girls will have eyes for nobody but us!

D.D. SENIOR: Have you seen the latest batch of telegrams?

D.D. JUNIOR: Yes.

D.D. SENIOR: If we don't leave this house with a fat settlement, it's the colonies for us, I can tell you. Make yourself irresistible, there's a good boy.

D.D. JUNIOR: I'm doing my best, Papa.

D.D. SENIOR: I know you are. You're an honest, conscientious lad, but you mustn't slacken for one moment. The success of this evening's entertainment means a great deal to us. What's more, there's something shady about our rivals which is bound to give rise to a scandal one of these days. It was quite obviously Lady Hurf who made the old duffer keep quiet this afternoon, when he insisted the Duke of Miraflores died in 1904. Keep your eyes open, and be ready for any emergency.

D.D. JUNIOR: We have got to get rid of these gallivanters. It's a matter of life and death.

D.D. SENIOR: We'll let them dig their own graves, while we'll be more and more agreeable. Ssh! Here comes Lady Hurf.

Enter LADY HURF *and* EVA, *as thieves in petticoats. The* DUPONT-DUFORTS *cough desperately to attract attention.*

LADY HURF (*seeing them*): Oh, breathtaking! Aren't they, Eva? Breathtaking! Who would have thought they had it in them! What do you think of our guests, Eva?

EVA: What a spectacular effect! How in the world did you manage it?

D.D. SENIOR (*simpering*): We're delighted.

D.D. JUNIOR: That we delight you.

LADY HURF: They always look as though they're waiting for a tip.

EVA: Which, in a way, they are.

LADY HURF: The Duke and his sons are being very slow.

EVA: I called out to them as I went by. They can't manage to dress up as thieves, they said.

LADY HURF (*as she goes*): Go up and fetch them, gentlemen, if you would be so good, and give them a few wrinkles.

D.D. SENIOR: Certainly! Certainly! (*Aside to his son.*) Let us be pleasant.

D.D. JUNIOR: Very, very pleasant. (*They bow themselves out.*)

Exit.

JULIETTE *crosses furtively.*

EVA: Why, you're not dressed!

JULIETTE: I'm going up now.

EVA: You'll make us late.

JULIETTE: Go on ahead. I'll take the two-seater.

EVA (*unexpectedly*): Are you in love with this boy?

JULIETTE: Why do you ask me?

EVA: Yes, indeed, why does one ask people if they're in love, when one can tell at a glance, always.

JULIETTE: Can you tell?

EVA: Yes.

JULIETTE: Well, you're wrong. I'm not in love with anyone.

She turns to go, when EVA *calls her back.*

EVA: Juliette! Why do you look upon me as your enemy?

JULIETTE: You are my enemy.

EVA: No, I love you very much. Sit down.

JULIETTE (*turning on her*): You're in love with him too, that's it, isn't it? You're going to take him away from me, and you want to warn me first so that I won't be hurt too much? Why, you've even agreed on that between you, probably. You have, haven't you? Haven't you? For heaven's sake say something! Why do you smile like that?

EVA: How lucky you are to be in love as much as that.

JULIETTE: You're prettier than I am; you can get any man you want.

EVA: Oh, if I could only bring myself to want one.

JULIETTE: Don't you want him then?

EVA: No, little silly.

JULIETTE: Have you never spoken to him when I wasn't looking?

EVA: Had I ever wanted to I should have found it very difficult. He only has to come near me by accident and you can't take your eyes off us.

JULIETTE: I'm wary. I love him, you see.

EVA: Little gambler!

JULIETTE: You swear you've never set out to attract him?

EVA: I swear.

JULIETTE: Even the day you danced with him twice running?

EVA: The orchestra had struck up a second tango.

JULIETTE: Even the day you went out on the river while the Dupont-Duforts tried to teach me roulette?

EVA: Even then. He looked so sad that I suggested he should row straight back, but we couldn't find you anywhere.

JULIETTE: That day I'm not so sure. He had a strange look in his eyes that evening.

EVA: Because he'd asked me if I thought you cared for him, and I said you were an unpredictable little girl and there was no knowing what went on inside your heart.

JULIETTE: Was that truly why? (*A little pause.*) All the same, I do think you might have told him something else.

EVA: Are you satisfied now?

JULIETTE: Did you never try to attract him, not even at the beginning, not even the very first day?

EVA: Not even the first day.

JULIETTE: Yes, then, I'm satisfied.

EVA: Why will you never trust me? I feel like an old woman beside you sometimes.

JULIETTE: You're so much better-looking than I am, so much more poised, more feminine.

EVA: Do you think so?

JULIETTE: It surprises me, you know, in spite of what you say. You must admit that he's a good deal more attractive than Hector, and you don't mind *his* attentions.

EVA: Do you think I couldn't have denied myself a mere flirtation, when I could see you were so much in love?

JULIETTE: That's grand of you.

EVA: Oh no. I wish I could have wanted him so much that I'd have sacrificed you without giving you a moment's thought.

JULIETTE: When you chew your pearls, I know there's something wrong.

EVA: Yes, there's something wrong.

JULIETTE: Yet you look so lovely tonight. You'll have all the men around you at the Ball.

EVA: All of them.

JULIETTE: I'm not joking.

EVA: Nor am I. I'll have them all. And yet it's very sad.

JULIETTE: Aren't you happy?

ᵢEVA: No.

JULIETTE: Yet it's so easy. You only need to let yourself go.
Why, hardly a moment goes by that one isn't unhappy, yet
I think that must be what it means, to be happy.

EVA: You've always thought me cleverer, stronger, more
beautiful, than you because the men flocked round me. And
yet, you see, there's only you who is alive, in this house –
you're the only one perhaps in Vichy, perhaps in the whole
world.

JULIETTE (*smiling, lost in her dream*): Yes, I am alive.

EVA: And untouched, and eager to believe . . .

JULIETTE: To believe everything.

EVA: You've never had, as I have, a man without love in your
bed. You haven't even a jewel at your throat, not a ring on
your finger. You're wearing nothing but this simple linen
dress, and you're twenty years old, and you are in love.

JULIETTE *sits motionless, yielding to the unseen with a faint smile.*

(*Looking sharply at her.*) Juliette, why are you not in fancy
dress like the rest of us?

JULIETTE (*bursting with sudden joy*): Oh, I'm too happy! I
haven't the courage to stay beside you who are sad. When
I'm a little less happy, I'll think of you, I swear I will! (*She
kisses her and runs off.*) Ssh!

EVA: All this mystery! What are you trying to say?

Enter LADY HURF *with the* DUPONT-DUFORTS.

LADY HURF: We will make a truly magnificent entrance.

D.D. SENIOR: The Spanish gentlemen are ready.

LADY HURF: Do they look all right?

D.D. SENIOR: That's a matter of taste.

D.D. JUNIOR: Anyway, here they come.

Enter PETERBONO *and* HECTOR. *They have contrived to disguise themselves as absolutely ludicrous comic opera bandits. They are greeted with shrieks of laughter.*

HECTOR: What are they laughing at?

PETERBONO: What do they *think* thieves look like? Don't they ever go to the theatre?

LADY HURF: But, my dear Duke, what are you supposed to be?

PETERBONO: A thief.

HECTOR (*to* EVA): It wasn't like this, I suppose?

EVA: Heavens, no!

PETERBONO (*to* LADY HURF): Don't you like us?

LADY HURF: Enormously!

PETERBONO: Admit there's something wrong.

LADY HURF: My dear friend, one really can't expect a Spanish grandee to make much of a showing as a common thief.

PETERBONO: Well said, eh, Hector? (*Enormous nudgings.*)

LADY HURF: Come along, all of you. The car's waiting. Where is Lord Edgard? Still glued to the mirror, I suppose. Edgard!

He appears, still in his own suit, and wearing his police helmet, but he has shaved off his moustache.

LORD EDGARD: Do you think I did well to shave off my moustache?

LADY HURF (*without looking at him*): I don't know! Come along! To the Carnival!

The music immediately strikes up a lively quadrille, which the thieves dance with the ladies, without the DUPONT-DUFORTS *getting a look in. Then follows a piece of extremely vulgar jive, and the* DUPONT-DUFORTS *making the best of a bad job, finish up by dancing together with tremendous spirit. All the characters dance their way out.*

D.D. SENIOR (*bringing up the rear with his son*): Things are getting better and better and better.

D.D. JUNIOR: Let's be as witty as the very devil!

D.D. SENIOR: And, remember, Didier, twice as nice.

*The room remains empty for an instant. A servant comes in to
close the windows and turn out the lights. Another moment of silence,
and* GUSTAVE *appears, and listens. The car is heard driving off.
He goes right round the room, examining its contents one by one. All
of a sudden he flattens himself against the wall.*

JULIETTE (*enters, dressed for a journey*): Here I am.

GUSTAVE: What are you doing here? Why didn't you go with
the others?

JULIETTE: I've come to find you.

GUSTAVE: Get out of here, will you?

JULIETTE: Why are you so harsh with me?

GUSTAVE: Go on, get out!

JULIETTE: I'll go, of course, if you don't want me, only I
thought you would want me. What's the matter?

GUSTAVE: I've got a headache. I want to stay here.

JULIETTE: Why this yarn, to me?

GUSTAVE: It isn't a yarn. Get out, will you. Go on, quick
march!

JULIETTE: But – you've never spoken to me like this!

GUSTAVE: There's always a first time.

JULIETTE: What have I done?

GUSTAVE: Nothing in particular. It's too difficult to explain,
and anyway you wouldn't understand.

JULIETTE: But, Señor Pedro . . .

GUSTAVE: There isn't any Señor Pedro, for a start. My name
is Gustave. And secondly, will you please go away?

JULIETTE: And there was I thinking that you loved me—

GUSTAVE: We all make mistakes, don't we?

JULIETTE: But you used to tell me so.

GUSTAVE: I was lying.

JULIETTE: Oh, no! I don't believe it!

GUSTAVE (*going to her purposefully*): Listen, my little pet, I'm
telling you to get out of here, double quick.

JULIETTE: Why?

GUSTAVE: You'll see why later on. In the meantime go up to
your room and weep over your lost illusions. (*He takes her*

arm to lead her to the door.) What are you dressed up in this coat for? What kind of a costume is that meant to be?

JULIETTE: Travelling costume.

GUSTAVE: Travelling costume? You're mad.

JULIETTE: Please don't be angry. I came to find you so we could go away. You told me once we'd go away together.

GUSTAVE: I was joking. Anyway, how do you know I mean to go away?

JULIETTE: I know.

GUSTAVE: You look as though you know a lot of things. Come along with me.

JULIETTE: We might meet one of the servants in the passage.

He looks at her.

We'd better not move from here. We'll be quite safe in this room.

GUSTAVE: The Dupont-Duforts must be waiting for you. Go and dress up as a pickpocket like the rest of them.

JULIETTE: Don't pickpockets ever wear travelling clothes?

GUSTAVE: You're not going to travel. You're going to a carnival.

JULIETTE: Once they've stolen thieves go away as a rule. Why won't you let me come with you, since you're going away?

GUSTAVE (*seizes her*): You know too much, my girl!

JULIETTE: Oh, please, don't hurt me!

GUSTAVE: Don't be afraid. Just a precaution.

He ties her to a chair, and searches in her handbag.

JULIETTE: Oh, don't rob my bag. There's nothing in it. Anyway, I give it to you.

GUSTAVE: Thank you. All I want is a handkerchief.

JULIETTE: What for?

GUSTAVE: To gag you with. (*He finds her handkerchief, which is microscopic.*) I ask you, what's the point of a handkerchief that size? Never mind, mine's clean.

JULIETTE: I'm not going to scream – I swear I won't scream –
Señor Pedro! Gustave – Gusta . . .

He gags her.

GUSTAVE: There. If you think this a Thieves' Carnival, my
lass, you'll have to think again. I'm a real thief, I am. So is
Hector, and so is the Duke of Miraflores. Except that those
two are imbeciles as well. You've built yourself a castle
in the air, that's all, and your aunt, who's got bats in her belfry,
has built herself a dozen. But let me tell you *I* came to do a
job, and I intend to do it.

She struggles.

All right. All right. It's no good trying to soften me. I'm used
to girls.

*He begins to fill his sacks with the most unlikely objects in the room.
After a while he looks at her with misgiving.*

It's not too tight, is it?

She shakes her head.

That's a good girl. You see, old girl, I did a bit of billing
and cooing, I know, but to be frank I didn't mean a word of
it. I had to do it for the job.

She struggles again.

Does that upset you? Yes, I know, it isn't very pretty. But
then in every trade there's always a little bit like that which
isn't very pretty. Apart from that, I'm an honest sort of
chap in my own way. I follow my trade, simply, without
frills and fancies. Not like Hector and Peterbono. Peterbono
has to be the Duke of Miraflores. One must be honest in
one's own particular line. Life's not worth living otherwise.
(*He takes a furtive look at her.*) You sure it's not too tight? (*He
gives her a smile.*) It worries me a bit, playing a trick like that
on you, because you know, I lied just now. I am fond of you
really. (*He goes back to his work.*) After all, when God invented

thieves he had to deprive them of a thing or two, so he took away from them the esteem of honest folk. When you come to think of it, it's not so terrible. It could have been much worse. (*He shrugs, and laughs, without daring to meet her eyes.*) In a little while, you'll see, we'll have forgotten all about it.

He goes on collecting objects. She struggles again, and he looks at her.

If there's anything you care for specially, you must tell me. I'll leave it for you, as a souvenir. I mean, I'd *like* to give you a little present.

She looks at him and he stops in embarrassment.

Please, don't look at me like that! You're breaking my heart! Can't you see I've got to do this? So just let me get quietly on with my job.

She moves.

Are you uncomfortable? You're not choking, are you? Look, Juliette, if you swear not to call out, I'll take the gag off. Do you swear?

She nods.

All right then, I trust you. (*He removes the handkerchief.*) What are you going to say to me, now that you know I'm a real thief? (*He sits down, resigned.*)

JULIETTE (*the moment she is ungagged*): This is absurd! Absolutely absurd. Untie me at once!

GUSTAVE: *Oh*, no! I'm a good sort, but business is business.

JULIETTE: At least listen to me!

GUSTAVE: What do you want to say?

JULIETTE: You don't imagine I came to find you, wearing my travelling coat, merely in order to sit here like a nincompoop bound and gagged in a chair? Of course I know you're a thief. If you weren't a real thief, I wouldn't have thought you were planning to leave in the middle of the night, would I, seeing you're a guest of my aunt's?

GUSTAVE: What are you talking about?

JULIETTE: I've been telling you over and over again for the last hour. I love you. I saw you take a car out of the garage, I guessed you really were a thief, and that tonight was the night. As I supposed you'd go the moment the job was done, I dressed and got ready to go with you. You don't intend to stay, do you?

GUSTAVE: That's no question to ask a thief.

JULIETTE: Well then, take me with you.

GUSTAVE: But I'm a thief.

JULIETTE (*crying out in exasperation*): I tell you I know you're a thief! There's no need to go on and on about it. I wonder you don't draw attention to yourself. Come along, untie my hands.

GUSTAVE: But, Juliette—

JULIETTE: Untie my hands. They're terribly painful.

GUSTAVE: Do you swear not to run away and raise the alarm?

JULIETTE: Yes, yes, I swear. Oh, how stupid you are!

GUSTAVE: I trust you of course, but I just don't understand.

He unties her. She immediately powders her face, and then gets up with determination.

JULIETTE: We've wasted at least a quarter of an hour. Make haste. It wouldn't do to get caught now. Have you enough with this lot? (*She indicates the sacks with her foot.*)

GUSTAVE: What are you doing?

JULIETTE: Really, I shall begin to wonder if you're all there soon. Yes, or no, do I appeal to you?

GUSTAVE: Oh yes, but—

JULIETTE: Good. That's the main thing. Now, listen to me. Gustave, if you like me, I love you and I want to be your wife – oh, don't worry, if you're afraid of awkward questions at the Registry Office, we won't get properly married. There. Now then— (*She picks up one of the sacks.*) Is this all we're taking with us?

GUSTAVE (*snatching the sack from her*): Juliette, no! You don't know what you're doing! You mustn't come with me. What would become of you?

JULIETTE: I'd help you. I'd keep a look-out, and I'd whistle when I saw someone coming. I can whistle beautifully. Listen— (*She gives an earsplitting whistle.*)

GUSTAVE (*terrified*): Ssssh! For heaven's sake!

They listen for a moment.

JULIETTE (*humbly*): I'm sorry. What a fool I am. Take me away. I'll whistle very quietly, I promise you, and then only when it's absolutely necessary.

GUSTAVE: Juliette, this is only a whim. You're playing with me. It's unkind of you.

JULIETTE: Oh no, you mustn't think that! Never think that! I love you.

GUSTAVE: But do you know the dangers of this kind of life?

JULIETTE: Yes. Kiss me.

GUSTAVE: Juliette, it's good-bye to your peace of mind.

JULIETTE: It was on the way to killing me, my peace of mind. Kiss me.

GUSTAVE: But you're happy here, Juliette. You don't know what it means to be on the run, to be afraid. You're used to luxury.

JULIETTE: Why, we're rich! Look at this! If it worries you, we won't steal so long as the police are out looking for me.

GUSTAVE: Thieves aren't wealthy folk. You get precious little for what you sell.

JULIETTE: Well, we'll be poor then. Kiss me.

They join in a long kiss.

(*Radiantly.*) I am so happy. Now, hurry. (*She stops.*) Why, you haven't taken the little Fragonards. You're mad, my darling, they're the most valuable things in the house. (*She runs to take them down.*) And the little enamels. (*She rummages in the sack.*) Leave the candlesticks. They're imitation bronze. You see how useful I am to you. I shall be such a help, you'll see. Kiss me.

GUSTAVE (*taking her in his arms again*): My little robber girl.

They go.

Curtain

Act Four

In the conservatory, an hour later. The clarinet, which has begun by playing the Carnival theme, takes it up again in a nostalgic manner. The characters wander in in single file, heads hanging, and sit down, vexed and dejected.

LADY HURF: It's positively absurd.

HECTOR: I do think they might have let us in.

LADY HURF: Too absurd. Fancy writing the title of the Carnival in microscopic lettering. Economy is an absolute obsession with the French.

LORD EDGARD: We were turned away in the most humiliating fashion.

EVA: What do you expect, Uncle? I can quite see that our attire alarmed them.

LADY HURF: A Carnival of Leaves! The idiocy of it!! A Carnival of Leaves!

D.D. SENIOR: What puzzles me is how you could confuse a Carnival of Leaves with a Carnival of Thieves.

LADY HURF: You should have consulted the notices yourself then, my good friend, if your eyesight is so sharp.

D.D. SENIOR: But dammit . . .

D.D. JUNIOR: Don't be rash, Papa.

LADY HURF: To begin with, it's thanks to your disguises that our party was shown the door.

PETERBONO: I should definitely have got in, for one. It's a funny thing. They quite thought I was going as a palm tree.

LADY HURF: Of course, but for them we should all have been admitted. What abominable taste! Look at them, will you? They might be a couple of pantomime buccaneers.

D.D. SENIOR: I should have thought for a Carnival of Thieves . . .

LADY HURF: Leaves! Leaves! Leaves! Are you going to spend the rest of the evening calling it a Carnival of Thieves?

D.D. JUNIOR: Keep calm, Father. (*To* LADY HURF.) We are dreadfully sorry.

D.D. SENIOR (*abjectly*): We'll never do it again.

LADY HURF: A fine time to say so!

LORD EDGARD: Could we not perhaps spend the evening as we are, among ourselves, so as not to waste our efforts altogether?

LADY HURF: Edgard, what an insane idea. Let us go up and change. We'll play yet one more stupefying game of bridge.

She sighs and the guests sigh with her.

LORD EDGARD: If I'd known we were going to play bridge I would have preferred to keep my moustache.

LADY HURF (*distractedly*): So would I! (*To* PETERBONO, *on her way out.*) My dear Duke, can you forgive me for this wasted evening?

PETERBONO (*nudging* HECTOR): No evening is ever really wasted.

LADY HURF: Another time I'll be more careful when I read the posters, and more discriminating in my choice of company.

She goes with EVA *and* LORD EDGARD.

PETERBONO: Ring. Pearls.

HECTOR: Pocket-book.

PETERBONO: Perfect.

The DUPONT-DUFORTS *find themselves alone.*

D.D. SENIOR: Things are going badly.

D.D. JUNIOR: Very badly.

D.D. SENIOR: These gay dogs are here on the same errand as we are, that's quite obvious, but everything is going their way and nothing is coming ours.

D.D. JUNIOR (*looking in a mirror*): Yet we achieved a really lovely make-up.

D.D. SENIOR: Not for a Carnival of Leaves.

D.D. JUNIOR: Fancy organizing a Carnival of Leaves!

D.D. SENIOR: Fancy, what's more, reading 'Carnival of Thieves' when it's down in black and white on all the posters 'Carnival of Leaves'. The old goose!

D.D. JUNIOR (*catching sight of the drawing-room through the open window*): Daddy!

D.D. SENIOR: What is it?

D.D. JUNIOR: Look at the wall!

D.D. SENIOR: What about the wall?

D.D. JUNIOR: The Fragonards!

D.D. SENIOR: If you think at a time like this I feel like going into ecstasies over a lot of paintings!

D.D. JUNIOR: Daddy, the Fragonards aren't on the wall. (*He rushes into the room.*)

D.D. SENIOR: Well?

D.D. JUNIOR (*from the room*): Nor are the enamels! The bronze candlesticks are missing! And the snuff-boxes! All the drawers are open! (*Rushing out again.*) Daddy, there's been a burglary!

D.D. SENIOR: Let's go. They'll think we did it.

D.D. JUNIOR: Don't be ridiculous! We were at the carnival with everybody else! Daddy! There's been a robbery here!

D.D. SENIOR (*who has been to make sure*): You're absolutely right. There's been a robbery. But what are you so pleased about? That won't set our affairs to rights.

D.D. JUNIOR: Don't you understand? There's been a robbery while we were at the Casino. Don't you see suspicion can only fall on the one person who made himself conspicuous by his absence? Now then, who, I ask you, made himself conspicuous by his absence?

D.D. SENIOR: Young Pedro?

D.D. JUNIOR: Of course! Young Pedro.

D.D. SENIOR: In that case, surely the others would be his accomplices.

D.D. JUNIOR: They are his accomplices. They came with us

to allay suspicion, that's quite clear. But now you may be sure they're gone, or will have before very long.

D.D. SENIOR: Didier, you're magnificent! You do my old heart good. Kiss me, son! At last they are unmasked. They're done for, laddie, and our affairs have never looked so promising.

D.D. JUNIOR: We must clinch matters. There's to be no escape and no denial. We must telephone the police at once. (*He picks up the receiver.*) Give me the police please. And hurry!

D.D. SENIOR (*trundling round the drawing-room and bellowing*): The Fragonards! The enamels! The candlesticks! The snuff-boxes! Two drawers burst open! Magnificent!

D.D. JUNIOR: Hallo? Is that the police station? This is the Villa des Boyards. A serious robbery has just taken place. Yes, the thieves are still on the premises. You'll catch them red-handed if you hurry. Hurry!

D.D. SENIOR (*coming back radiant*): Come to your father, laddie!

They embrace.

D.D. JUNIOR: Let's call the company and confront the rascals! Hey there! Come quickly, everybody!

D.D. SENIOR: Hey there! Hey!

LORD EDGARD (*entering. He, and likewise the others when they come down, have all changed back into their usual clothes*): What's the matter?

D.D. JUNIOR: There's been a burglary!

LORD EDGARD: That's no surprise to anybody in these troubled times. Where?

D.D. JUNIOR: Here!

LORD EDGARD: Here!

D.D. SENIOR (*breathless with excitement*): Here! Here in this very room!

LORD EDGARD: In the drawing-room? What did they take?

D.D. SENIOR (*like a street hawker*): Fragonards! Enamels! Snuff-boxes! Candlesticks! Drawers! Come in and see! Come and see!

LORD EDGARD *goes into the room, comes back and staggers into an arm-chair.*

LORD EDGARD: Terrible! Terrible! I had an idea this would happen.

D.D. SENIOR ⎫
D.D. JUNIOR ⎭ So had we!

LORD EDGARD: Do you know who did it?

D.D. SENIOR: We have an idea!

LORD EDGARD: So have I!

Enter EVA.

My child, we've just been burgled!

EVA: What?

D.D. SENIOR (*off again*): The Fragonards! The enamels! The candlesticks! The snuff-boxes!

EVA: I'm glad about the candlesticks, they were appalling. But it's a shame about the Fragonards.

HECTOR *enters triumphantly in a new make-up.*

HECTOR: Eva, this time I've got it!

EVA: No.

LORD EDGARD (*leaping on him*): At last! The detective! My dear fellow, you're in the nick of time. A serious robbery has just been committed. We suspect some impostors whom we are entertaining at the moment, owing to a curious fancy of my cousin's. Kindly arrest them at once, my dear fellow.

EVA: What's come over you, Uncle? That's Prince Hector. Hector, do take off that beard.

HECTOR (*modestly, as he reveals himself*): Yes, sir, it's me.

LORD EDGARD (*in a sudden rage*): How much longer do you intend to make a fool of me, young man?

HECTOR (*backing imperceptibly towards the door*): But, your lordship, I'm not making a fool of you, really.

LORD EDGARD: I can take a joke, in doubtful taste though it is with a man of my years, but don't repeat it a dozen times a day!

HECTOR (*nearing the door*): But I'm not making a fool . . .

He bumps into the DUPONT-DUFORTS, *who have cut off his retreat.*

D.D. JUNIOR: Oh no.
D.D. SENIOR: Of course you're not making a fool of him.
  Don't go. Everything will be all right.
HECTOR: Look here, what's going on? Am I under suspicion?
EVA: Gentlemen, will you please leave His Highness alone?
HECTOR: I should think so. Why, it's absurd, isn't it, Eva?
LADY HURF (*entering with* PETERBONO): What is all this
  shouting? I've never heard such a commotion!
PETERBONO: We simply can't hear ourselves speak!
LORD EDGARD: It's terrible! There's been a dreadful robbery!
  I had my suspicions all along. I told you he died in 1904! I
  told you they were all impostors!
D.D. SENIOR (*at the same time*): The Fragonards! The enamels!
  The snuff-boxes! The candlesticks! The drawers!
LADY HURF: One at a time, please! I don't know what you're
  talking about. First of all I must sit down. I'm worn out.

During the ejaculations of the others, and the silence which follows,
HECTOR *is desperately indicating to* PETERBONO *that they must
be off.* PETERBONO *thinks his cuff-links are undone, his tie crooked
or that something is hanging down. He brushes himself, looks in
the mirror, still fails to understand, and finally shrugs his shoulders
and gives up.*

Now. Tell me all about it.
PETERBONO (*engagingly*): Splendid idea. Tell us all about it.
LORD EDGARD (*before they stop him*): Didn't I tell you he
  died in—
D.D. SENIOR (*at the same time*): Everything! Everything! The
  Fragonards! The . . .

They look at each other and stop dead.

EVA: There's been a burglary.
LADY HURF: A burglary?
  JACP—K

EVA: Yes. While we were out the enamels were stolen, and the Fragonards, and believe it or not, the candlesticks.

LADY HURF: Oh good. They were imitation.

LORD EDGARD: I told you so! I told you so!

LADY HURF: One of the servants, I expect. Are they all here?

EVA: I don't know.

D.D. SENIOR: We must inform the police.

LADY HURF: No.

D.D. SENIOR: What do you mean, no?

LADY HURF: No, I tell you. I will not have policemen in my house.

D.D. JUNIOR: But we've already telephoned, your ladyship.

LADY HURF: My good sirs, have you completely forgotten your manners? I beg you to remember that this is my house. You appear to have abandoned every vestige of constraint these last few days.

D.D. JUNIOR: But we—

D.D. SENIOR: You see, we—

LADY HURF: Eva, ring through at once and tell them not to come.

D.D. SENIOR: Too late. They're bound to be on the way.

All this time PETERBONO *and* HECTOR *have been quietly edging towards the door. When* LADY HURF *tells* EVA *to call off the police, they stop, still hopeful. At these last words, they make a frenzied dash for it.*

Look! They're getting away!

D.D. JUNIOR: This is too much! We'll save you, whether you like it or not! Hands up!

D.D. SENIOR: Hands up!

They cover the thieves with their revolvers.

LADY HURF: Gentlemen, I am mistress in this house! I order you to put away those firearms!

D.D. JUNIOR: No!

D.D. SENIOR: No. You'll thank us for it later on.

LADY HURF: Eva, I'm going to have hysterics! Call the servants! Emile! Here, quickly! Joseph! Help!

Enter police, during her cries.

POLICEMAN: Here we are! Horace, you take the fat one!

They have seen these two horrible bandits pointing their guns at the gentry. Without a moment's indecision, they hurl themselves on the DUPONT-DUFORTS.

Aha, me beauties! We've got you!

D.D. SENIOR *and* JUNIOR (*backing away*): But – but—We didn't do anything! No, no, not us! Not us! Quite the reverse! We're the ones who telephoned! This is preposterous! It's them!

They collide as they retreat, try to escape the other way and collide again, in the course of a droll little ballet which culminates in their capture.

POLICEMEN (*hoisting them on to their shoulders with the showmanship of circus acrobats*): Upsadaisy! (*To* HECTOR.) If you'd like to give us a hand, sir, by taking the trouble to open the door, sir, it'd be much appreciated.

HECTOR: No trouble. Absolutely no trouble at all.

The POLICEMEN *carry off the* DUPONT-DUFORTS *despite their agonizing protestations.*

LORD EDGARD (*wildly*): But, my dear . . .

LADY HURF (*sternly*): Edgard! Be quiet.

D.D. SENIOR (*yelling in vain as he is borne away*): For God's sake say something! Tell them! Tell them!

D.D. JUNIOR (*as he whirls past her*): Mademoiselle Eva!

They have gone, played out by their own little melody.

LADY HURF (*calmly*): There! That's a relief. Three whole weeks those folk have been here, and I hadn't a notion how to get rid of them.

LORD EDGARD (*overcome by so many emotions, falls semiconscious into an arm-chair*): When I think I came here to cure my liver trouble!

LADY HURF: Eva dear, run up and get your uncle his smelling-salts.

EVA *goes*. LADY HURF *looks at* PETERBONO, *who ever since the arrest of the* DUPONT-DUFORTS *has been choking in the grip of irrepressible hysteria.*

My dear man, save your laughter. I know perfectly well you are the real thief.

He stops dead. She feels in his pocket.

Give me back my pearls. You haven't been very clever.

PETERBONO: What do you mean?

LADY HURF: Have you a lot of luggage? How long will it take you to pack?

PETERBONO (*piteously*): Not long.

LADY HURF: Then I advise you to make the greatest possible haste upstairs.

PETERBONO: Yes.

Enter HECTOR.

HECTOR (*superbly*): There. The rascals are in good hands, your Ladyship.

PETERBONO *coughs*.

Father dear, are you not feeling well?

LADY HURF: No, he's not feeling at all well. I think you had better both go up to your rooms.

HECTOR: Really, Father? Where's the trouble exactly?

LORD EDGARD (*himself once more*): I told you the Duke of Miraflores died in 1904!

LADY HURF: I knew it long ago, my dear.

HECTOR (*still not understanding* PETERBONO'S *desperate dumbshow, says waggishly*): Ha! ha! ha! Still the same old joke, eh?

LADY HURF: The duke died in my arms, or near enough. So

that I knew quite well whom we were dealing with. Only you
see, my poor old Edgard, I was so very, very bored.

HECTOR (*finally going to* PETERBONO): What's the matter, for
heaven's sake?

PETERBONO: Idiot! I've been trying to tell you for the last
half-hour. The game's up, but she's letting us go free.

HECTOR: Uh? Don't be silly, they've arrested the others.

LADY HURF (*going to them with a smile*): You don't, I'm sure,
want to await the visit of the inspector of police, gentlemen.

HECTOR: This is unthinkable! What are we accused of? We
were with you the whole evening!

PETERBONO: Don't be canny. Come on.

HECTOR: My dear father, I don't know what you're talking
about. Madam, we are here as your guests, and this robbery
is no reason to treat us, the Miraflores y Grandes, in this
cavalier fashion.

PETERBONO (*unable to suppress a giggle, despite the tragic situation*):
Miraflores y Grandes! Oh, my Lord! You're off your head,
old chap. Come on.

LADY HURF: Go along, sir, do, as everyone advises you.

HECTOR: I will not tolerate this attitude. (*To* PETERBONO.)
Play up, will you?

EVA (*coming back*): Here are the salts.

HECTOR: I will not tolerate this attitude. Because if you consider our presence undesirable, I laugh to scorn – do you
hear, to scorn, your utterly unfounded and insulting allega-
tions. There's someone here, I know, who will think my
presence far from undesirable. Eva, Eva my darling, I've
found my face at last! (*He turns away and rapidly re-creates the
appearance he had in the first scene.*)

PETERBONO: Hector, stop playing about. The police are on
their way.

HECTOR (*making up*): Let me alone. We're saved, I tell you!

LADY HURF (*sits down dispirited*): Edgard, if this headstrong
child falls in love with him again, the situation is absolutely
hopeless.

LORD EDGARD: I have not the faintest idea of what is going

on. What is he doing? Is this another piece of comicality? He goes very much too far, that boy.

HECTOR (*turning round triumphantly*): Eva beloved! It *was* like this, wasn't it?

A silence. EVA *looks at him. The others hold their breath.*

EVA (*calmly breaking the tension*): Yes, that's how you were. Only I must have looked at you too hastily, I think, because now you don't appeal to me at all.

LADY HURF (*leaping up*): Heaven be praised! Now, off with you! Quickly, off with you!

HECTOR: But, Eva, listen! Eva, I can't believe . . .

PETERBONO (*in a whisper*): Hurry, idiot, hurry! She's taken back the necklace, but I've still got the ring.

They go with great dignity. A gay little tune signals their departure.

LADY HURF (*watching them go with a tender little smile*): Poor old fellow. I let him keep the ring. They stayed here a full fortnight after all, because of me. We haven't any right to make them waste their time. I imagine it's a trade which can't bring in all that much.

LORD EDGARD: What I don't fathom is where the boy comes in.

The two women look at him in sudden anguish.

The boy, the young one, who was so pleasant, you remember?

EVA: Juliette! Where's Juliette?

LADY HURF: Juliette! She didn't come to the Carnival. Isn't she upstairs? Perhaps in the morning-room? Or in the garden?

EVA: I'll run and see. Oh, it's inconceivable.

LORD EDGARD: What is inconceivable? I don't understand, quite.

LADY HURF *drops on to the sofa, and plays nervously with her pearls.*

Why do you look so tragic? It's all over now, isn't it?

LADY HURF: No, stupid, it is not all over. This boy has carried off Juliette along with the pictures in the drawing-room. How many times did I tell you to bestir yourself and take precautions if we didn't want disaster?

EVA (*coming back*): She's not upstairs. The servants are combing the grounds.

LADY HURF: It's horrible!

LORD EDGARD: Juliette, our little Juliette. Is it possible? Can she have been stolen?

EVA: Yes.

LORD EDGARD: But she's a big girl now. She could have defended herself. Or called for help. The house is overrun with staff.

LADY HURF: Can't you understand? She's in his power! He's bewitched her. He'll make her steal for him, or walk the streets!

LORD EDGARD: The streets. (*It dawns on him.*) The streets!

He staggers under the blow. The clarinet plays an air heavy with tragedy. The three of them lapse into pensive and painful silence. The clarinet resumes its tragic theme with an overtone of mockery, and then leads into the romance which is indeed altogether fitting at this moment, for GUSTAVE *enters on tiptoe, laden with so many things that he cannot see where he is going. He is carrying* JULIETTE, *who is asleep, and his various sacks. He crosses the drawing-room, unseen by anybody; suddenly he bumps into an arm-chair. He drops his sacks with a clatter, and startles the others, who see him and cry out.*

He's killed her!

GUSTAVE, *terrified, makes to put* JULIETTE *down on the sofa, but at the cries she wakens and clings to him.*

JULIETTE: No, no, no! Why did you bring me back? No, he's not to go! If he goes I'm going with him!

LADY HURF: Juliette!

LORD EDGARD: My child.

JULIETTE (*screaming through a flood of tears*): Yes, you despise him, I know, but I love him! Don't try to tell me anything – I want to go with him because I love him! Don't say a word, I'd only hate you for it! Gustave, Gustave, why did you bring me back?

He struggles and tries to run away, but she clutches him.

No. Stay here, or let me come with you. Why did you bring me back? Was I too stupid for you? Too naïve? Is it because I fell asleep beside you in the car that you don't want me? It's true one doesn't as a rule doze off the night of one's elopement, but I was tired, my darling. I'm not used to staying up so late. (*She hides her head in his arms.*)

LORD EDGARD: What is she saying?

LADY HURF (*moved*): Do be quiet! It's very lovely what she's saying.

JULIETTE (*turning to them like a little fury, without letting go of* GUSTAVE): No, no, I'm not ashamed! I'm not ashamed! You can say anything you like, I'll never be ashamed! I love him. I want him for my lover, since you will never let him be my husband. Look. I'm going to kiss him now in front of you.

She throws her arms round his neck. He holds back for a second, then as he sees her tousled hair and her radiant tear-stained face, he too forgets the others.

GUSTAVE: I love you, Juliette.

JULIETTE: You see, we're kissing here, in front of them.

They kiss.

LORD EDGARD (*adjusting his pince-nez*): Why, they're kissing.

LADY HURF: That's right. They're kissing. What about it? Did you never do as much? (*She contemplates them, entranced.*) How enchanting they are!

LORD EDGARD: Aren't they? Do you remember, Emily?

LADY HURF: They make a delightful couple, don't they?

LORD EDGARD (*lost in his memories*): Delightful. Do you remember? The Crystal Palace?

LADY HURF: She's nearly as tall as he is. He is adorable. Look at the breeding in that profile. The exquisite shyness and yet the strength of it. He will make a fairy-tale husband for our terrible, gentle little Juliette. (*She stops.*) Edgard, what are you talking me into? He's a thief!

LORD EDGARD (*smiling*): Ah yes, a thief.

LADY HURF: Well then, it's out of the question. He must go at once.

The clarinet stops from shock.

LORD EDGARD (*crestfallen*): But – but they love each other.

LADY HURF: I know they love each other. But it's the only thing to do. Absolutely the only thing. She simply cannot marry a boy who has neither a father nor a mother.

LORD EDGARD: Ah! (*He thinks furiously for a moment, then cries suddenly.*) Wait a minute! Wait a minute!

GUSTAVE *and* JULIETTE, *startled by his cry, come out of their embrace.* LORD EDGARD *runs out like one demented.*

LADY HURF: Where do you suppose he's going?

JULIETTE: I'll never leave him, never, never, never.

GUSTAVE (*holding her to him, says by way of explanation*): We love each other.

The clarinet plays a little supplication.

LADY HURF: I gather so. But there it is. You're nothing but a nobody, if not worse. I'm afraid you'll have to go.

Another entreaty from the clarinet.

JULIETTE: If he goes I go with him.

LADY HURF: This time we will be here to stop you.

The clarinet screams in heart-rending imploration. LADY HURF *turns furiously on the musician.*

As for you, my good sir, you're beginning to get on my nerves! Go away!

The clarinet attempts a musical protest.

Get out of here this instant!

She drives him out. Pathetically the musician goes, expressing his despair on his instrument. LORD EDGARD *returns like a meteor, carrying ribbons, medals and a photograph. He marches threateningly over to* GUSTAVE.

LORD EDGARD: You are twenty years old, are you not?
GUSTAVE: Yes.
LORD EDGARD: Right (*He looks at the photograph, looks at it a second time, backs, screwing up his eyes in the manner of a painter scrutinizing a picture.*) Hold your head up. Fine. Open your shirt. Fine. Now for the mark behind the ear. (*He turns back his ear.*) Fine. (*He shows him the medal.*) Do you recognize this medal?
GUSTAVE: No.
LORD EDGARD (*throwing it away*): Never mind. You are my son! My son who was stolen from me at a tender age.

He falls into his arms.

LADY HURF: Edgard, have you taken leave of your senses?
GUSTAVE (*furiously*): Let me go, sir. I don't know what you're talking about. (*To* JULIETTE.) What's the matter with him?
LORD EDGARD (*to* LADY HURF): Do you deny that a son was stolen from me at a tender age? (*To* GUSTAVE.) Do you deny that you are uncertain of your paternal origins? Yes, yes, you are my son, my own son, my beloved son!

He falls on his neck again.

JULIETTE: Isn't that lucky! Gustave, isn't that lucky!
GUSTAVE (*freeing himself roughly*): No, it won't work.
LORD EDGARD: What won't work?
GUSTAVE: I'm quite sure I'm not your son.
LORD EDGARD: So I shall have waited twenty years for Heaven

to give me back my child, and now when Heaven at last sees fit to give him back to me, it is this very child who refuses to acknowledge his own father!

GUSTAVE: No. It's all a scheme because you can see your little girl is in love with me, but I'm sorry, I can't accept.

LADY HURF: That's very honourable of him.

LORD EDGARD: This is horrible! Horrible! My son denies me! (*He prances with rage.*)

GUSTAVE: No, I can't accept. It's nice of you to do it, very nice of you. But I can't. I'm not one of your sort.

LADY HURF: It is really unfortunate that this boy should be the only one amongst us to suffer from class-consciousness.

LORD EDGARD: I am abominably humiliated. Such contempt from my own son! I shall crumple up with sorrow. (*He does in fact crumple up with sorrow on the nearest sofa.*) Here I am, crumpled up. How much longer do I have to stay crumpled?

LADY HURF: Couldn't you see your way to accepting? You're making your father very unhappy.

GUSTAVE: How can I! I haven't any reason—

JULIETTE: Oh, but you have! Come into the garden as you did before. I'm going to explain all your reasons to you. Do come, please. Come anyway. You haven't anything to lose after all, by coming into the garden.

She drags him out.

LADY HURF (*as soon as they're gone*): Edgard, it's not true! You never had a son stolen from you at a tender age!

LORD EDGARD: No, it isn't true. It's a picture I cut out of a magazine.

LADY HURF: So you've acted like an imbecile for over fifty years and yet you had it in you to think of that all by yourself.

EVA: How happy they are going to be.

LADY HURF (*dreamily*): Yes.

EVA: And I shall continue to play the young and charming widow who is always such a great success.

LADY HURF: My poor Eva, faith is a gift, alas, and there's no learning it. It's over, our fine escapade. Here we are alone again, like bobbing corks. It's only for those who have played it with all the zest of youth that the comedy is a success, and only then because they were playing their youth, a thing which succeeds always. They were not even conscious of the comedy.

Enter a bearded gentleman.

BEARDED GENT: I am from Scotland Yard.

LORD EDGARD (*lets out a roar, leaps on to him and pulls his beard*): Oh no, it won't work this time!

DETECTIVE: Stop it! You're hurting me!

LORD EDGARD (*greatly astonished*): What! Do you mean it's your own?

DETECTIVE: Of course it's my own!

LORD EDGARD: Then you really are the detective I sent for?

DETECTIVE: I've just said so, haven't I?

LORD EDGARD: Well we don't need you any more. The entertainment is over.

DETECTIVE (*blithely*): In that case . . .

He pulls his clarinet out of his pocket – for it is none other than the musician – and strikes up a quick-step which does duty as a finale. The characters come in through all the doors, dancing and exchanging beards.

Curtain

Restless Heart

Characters

THÉRÈSE TARDE
MONSIEUR TARDE
MADAME TARDE } *Orchestra at the Café Lebonze*
GOSTA
JEANNETTE

MONSIEUR LEBONZE

WAITER

FLORENT FRANCE

HARTMANN

MADAME BAZIN

MARIE FRANCE

THE FITTER

HER ASSISTANT

THE HEAD HOUSEMAID

SCULLERY MAID

CUSTOMERS AT THE CAFÉ LEBONZE

Original Title: La Sauvage
Translator: Lucienne Hill
First produced in 1934

Act One

The interior of a café in a seaside resort. The greater part of the stage is taken up by the bandstand. Service door, left, through which the waiters come and go, with their loaded trays. Two tables, both unoccupied, one of them reserved. The rest of the café is not seen. The orchestra consists of GOSTA, *pianist,* TARDE, *double-bass,* MME TARDE, *cellist,* THÉRÈSE *and* JEANNETTE, *violins. When the curtain goes up, the orchestra is just finishing a very spirited piece. The waiter is by the bandstand, listening. A customer calls him and he dashes forward, dusting a table as he passes.*

WAITER: Yes, sir!

The musicians lay down their instruments. A little half-hearted applause.

JEANNETTE (*glancing at the unoccupied table beside the platform*): He's late today.

THÉRÈSE (*laying down her violin*): He said he might be. He's meeting his manager on the ten-thirty train.

JEANNETTE: Aren't you afraid he might not come again, sometimes?

THÉRÈSE: Some evenings I'm afraid, yes.

JEANNETTE: I've had men promise to marry me too, you know. Getting to that altar rail though, that's the thing.

THÉRÈSE: I'm so happy as we are, that even if we didn't get as far as that . . .

JEANNETTE: Now, now, careful! Don't you ever give him the idea that you're resigned to only being his mistress! And another thing. When you go out with him, watch your manners. In your position a girl can never be too ladylike.

THÉRÈSE *bursts out laughing.*

(*Imperturbably.*) As far as the rest goes, leave it alone. Don't harp on it, it only irritates them. But the trimmings now, you want to talk about *those* – your trousseau, the loose covers . . .

THÉRÈSE (*still laughing*): Just think how I should bore him if I did!

JEANNETTE: There's no way round it, my child. Ask any girl who's been through it. Take fat Louisa now. She had a good dodge when she managed to land her gasworks engineer. She used to pat the heads of kids in the street and sigh that she'd do anything to have one of her own. Him with his worship of children, he'd blubber into his moustache. That's the way *she* hooked him. It didn't commit her to anything. After they were married, she refused to have any.

THÉRÈSE (*laughing*): Jeannette, you're wasting your time. If he wants to marry me, good! If he doesn't . . .

TARDE *goes round with the music sheets.*

TARDE: Come along, look lively! It's gone midnight. Time for the finale.

He hangs up a card bearing the figure 12, and writes the title of the number on a slate.

GOSTA (*looking at the clock and going to* THÉRÈSE): It's midnight, Thérèse.

THÉRÈSE (*blankly*): Yes . . .

GOSTA (*giving her something*): There. Don't let anybody see.

THÉRÈSE: What is it?

GOSTA: Open it.

THÉRÈSE (*unwrapping the parcel*): A bottle of scent? But – why?

GOSTA: You're twenty years old tonight, Thérèse. Nobody but me remembered.

THÉRÈSE: My birthday – today? But . . .

GOSTA (*with a smile*): Tomorrow really, but it's midnight.

THÉRÈSE: Oh, Gosta, it's sweet of you! Gosta . . . There's something I've been meaning to tell you . . .

TARDE: Gosta, what have you done with your music? I can't
find it anywhere. Hurry. Monsieur Lebonze has just come in.

He hustles him away.

JEANNETTE: What did he give you?
THÉRÈSE: A bottle of scent. It's sweet of him . . . I haven't
dared to tell him yet. I still think I ought to tell him myself . . .
JEANNETTE: But your father said he would do it!
THÉRÈSE: He'll do it so clumsily.
JEANNETTE: Well, you can't expect everyone to know how he
feels! He hasn't told a soul that he's in love with you, you
know!
THÉRÈSE: No, poor thing.
JEANNETTE: What does your mother say about it?
THÉRÈSE: Oh, you know my mother. She'd go to any lengths
to keep him. I daren't turn round. Are they talking to him?
JEANNETTE (*glancing round*): No. They're putting their heads
together. Gosta's at the back. He's looking for his music.
THÉRÈSE: I can't face it. (*Calling.*) Father, I'm going out for a
minute. (*She beckons to him.*) Are you going to tell him?
TARDE: It's my duty! Don't stay out too long. The boss is in
the house.

He goes back to his wife as THÉRÈSE *slips out.*

Do you think he suspects something? There's a nasty glint
in his eye.
MME TARDE: No. But we must tell him before Monsieur
Florent calls for Thérèse. You never know, he might turn
ugly.
TARDE: What – here, in public?
MME TARDE: Yes.
TARDE: I never heard of such a thing!
MME TARDE: Suppose we waited till we've played the finale?
TARDE: No. I'd rather tell him straight out and then give the
signal to strike up. It's the march from *Tannhäuser*. He can
work it off on the piano. Right. Here goes.

He takes a step towards GOSTA, *but turns back again.*

Was he in a good mood at supper-time?

MME TARDE: Not very.

TARDE: Oh. (*Squaring his shoulders.*) Dammit, I really don't see why we should be scared to tell him! Who's the master here?

MME TARDE: I couldn't say, I'm sure.

TARDE: What do you mean, you couldn't say? Who is your husband, who's the leader of this orchestra, who's Thérèse's father, tell me that?

MME TARDE: You are. In theory.

TARDE: What do you mean in theory? I shall be firm!

MME TARDE: Please yourself. But if he blacks your eye don't say I didn't warn you.

TARDE: Blacks my eye! Blacks my—! Good grief, woman, let's be logical about this! Do we have to consult him before we give our girl in marriage? What business is it of his anyway?

MME TARDE: None at all. But that may not stop him knocking you down.

TARDE: Knocking me down! Knocking me—! He doesn't know when to stop, that chap! I've been closing my eyes for thirteen years to his fun and games with you. What more does he want?

MME TARDE: You know as well as I do how fond he is of the child.

TARDE: Keeping it in the family, eh? I'm within my rights! I shall put my foot down!

MME TARDE: I dare say, but you know his temper. Just take care, that's all.

GOSTA (*coming downstage with his music*): I've found it. Shall we start?

TARDE (*sighing*): Yes, off we go. (*Going to* MME TARDE.) How many drinks has he had?

MME TARDE: One.

TARDE: Good. (*He walks resolutely over to* GOSTA.) Now then, have you found that music yet?

GOSTA: Yes.

TARDE *clears his throat, then begins nervously to lay the music sheets on to the stands.*

TARDE: Did you read about that Sicilian fellow in the papers?

GOSTA: Yes.

TARDE: Shot twelve! Terrible business. (MME TARDE *gives him a nudge.*) Oh, yes! That reminds me. You've heard about Thérèse, have you?

GOSTA (*looking up*): Thérèse? No, what about her?

TARDE (*to* MME TARDE): Didn't you tell him?

MME TARDE: No.

TARDE: But gracious me, he should have been told! You tell him! I'll fetch Thérèse. I see Monsieur Lebonze getting impatient over there.

MME TARDE (*catching hold of his arm*): Oh, no, you don't!

GOSTA *has risen, anxiously.*

GOSTA (*going to them*): What was it you wanted to tell me about Thérèse?

TARDE: Well now – um, it's like this . . .

MME TARDE: Oh, it's nothing very serious, you know!

GOSTA (*looking at them*): You're going to lie to me, the pair of you. (*To* MME TARDE.) Your mouth is all crooked like when you know you've got a clout coming.

MME TARDE: What are you raving about?

TARDE (*laughing on the wrong side of his face*): He's mad! Absolutely mad! A clout coming! I ask you! Why, the very idea!

GOSTA: Well, what about Thérèse? What do you want with her?

TARDE (*inanely*): Me? Why, nothing – nothing at all! (*Solemnly.*) Ah yes, I was forgetting. The best, that's what I want for my little girl. You know the famous Monsieur France – the composer – the one who gave a recital last month at the Casino?

GOSTA: Yes. What about him?

MME TARDE: That dark gentleman who's been here several times and who spoke to Thérèse? That's him.

GOSTA: Does she know him?

TARDE: Yes. You know how quickly young people get together in these seaside towns. . . .

MME TARDE: He's very nice you know, Gosta. . . .

TARDE: Besides, there's no getting away from it, he's a genius! The undisputed king of his profession!

GOSTA: What are you trying to tell me? I don't like that look on your faces. We'd got to Florent France. Go on from there.

TARDE (*backing*): Fine musician.

GOSTA: I know that.

TARDE: It's men of that calibre who've made our country what it is!

GOSTA (*seizing his tie*): Will you talk, damn you!

TARDE (*backing*): Now, now – not on the bandstand, Gosta!

MME TARDE (*hanging on to* GOSTA'S *arm*): It's the child's happiness, Gosta! It's her future that matters! He's going to marry her, don't you see! He's going to marry her! It's too good to be true!

GOSTA (*shaking her off without letting go of* TARDE): I might have known it! Take your hands off me, you! You've been trying long enough to sell her off to somebody! How much are you making on the deal, eh? Answer me! (*He shakes him.*)

TARDE: Gosta, you're mad! On the bandstand! Suppose Monsieur Lebonze came along!

GOSTA: I'd tell him what a slimy rat you are and tan the hide off you in front of him!

TARDE (*struggling to keep upright*): But this is insane! After all, who's the master here?

MME TARDE: She's in love this time, Gosta, I swear she is!

GOSTA: She's a baby! You've dazzled her with the thought of the money she might have – money she doesn't even want! Because she's worth a hundred of you put together! And it's you, you greasy old ruin, who—

TARDE (*as* GOSTA *shakes him*): Who's the master here?

JEANNETTE *has run to the cloakroom door.*

JEANNETTE: Thérèse! Thérèse! Quick!

GOSTA (*holding* TARDE *at arm's length*): You scum! I'd like to squash you under my shoe, like the piece of dirt you are! That's right, try and look dignified. Straighten your tie, go on!

TARDE (*whimpering*): Godstrewth, who's the master here?

THÉRÈSE *has come running in.*

THÉRÈSE: Gosta! Let him alone! You don't know what you're talking about. Nobody drove me to it! I love him!

GOSTA *has released* TARDE. *He looks at her.*

GOSTA: Why didn't you tell me?

THÉRÈSE: I didn't tell you because . . . (*She stops short, in embarrassment.*) I don't know why I didn't tell you.

M. LEBONZE *comes bustling in with his napkin under his arm.*

M. LEBONZE: When are we going to have that finale, this evening or next week?

TARDE: Very sorry, Monsieur Lebonze, I'm sure! Right away! Gosta, to your stool! (*Yelping.*) Come along! Come along! Business before pleasure!

GOSTA (*pale, his fists clenched*): Will you shut your mouth?

TARDE (*faltering under the other's gaze*): Business before pleasure – I mean . . . that's all I said.

THÉRÈSE (*gently*): Go to the piano, Gosta, please. I'll explain everything later.

GOSTA *turns on his heel and goes to the piano.*

M. LEBONZE: My word, but you're acting as if you owned the place, the pack of you!

TARDE: We're all set, Monsieur Lebonze! Ready everybody? One, two, three!

The music strikes up.

M. LEBONZE: And about time! Now don't let me hear another word out of any of you about anything! Otherwise there'll be trouble!

He stalks majestically away, pushing a chair into position and flicking a table with his napkin as he goes. The following lines are rapidly exchanged during the music.

MME TARDE: You fool! I knew you'd make a mess of it!

TARDE: He didn't make a mess of me, though! (*He heaves at his little joke, then says sternly.*) If he starts again, he'll be sorry. I shall be ruthless!

Music.

MME TARDE (*sighing*): Let's hope he doesn't leave me! You don't think he'll leave me, do you?

TARDE: Now look here! I've closed my eyes to your fancy man for thirteen years, but if he's tired of thumbing his nose at me, you don't imagine I'm going to go running after him, do you?

MME TARDE: You're a coward!

TARDE: You said so before.

MME TARDE: I despise you, do you hear me? I despise you!

TARDE: You'd do better to play in tune. Meet you at the next rest!

MME TARDE: Coward! Coward!

TARDE: When do we get those sharps then, tomorrow?

MME TARDE: Cuckold! Daft old cuckold!

TARDE: Whose fault's that? (*Suddenly beaming.*) Look out. Here he comes!

FLORENT *comes in with* HARTMANN. TARDE *bows over his double-bass.*

Maestro!

MME TARDE *simpers.* THÉRÈSE *gives a little smile but does not move.* HARTMANN *and* FLORENT *sit down, facing the orchestra.*

FLORENT: Well, Hartmann?

HARTMANN: Well.

FLORENT: What do you think of her?

HARTMANN: Not the dark one?

FLORENT (*with a little laugh*): No, of course not.

A pause.

HARTMANN: Is that the father, the old fellow with the double-bass? He's unbelievable!

FLORENT: The mother is the cellist.

HARTMANN (*studying them with a smile*): Florent, you're an extraordinary fellow! You seriously intend to marry that little thing in spite of those two characters? She didn't insist on it, I presume?

FLORENT: She is my mistress.

HARTMANN: You're in love with her, then?

FLORENT (*laughing*): That seems a good enough explanation.

HARTMANN *puts on his thick tortoiseshell glasses and carefully scrutinizes* THÉRÈSE.

HARTMANN: She's very pretty, of course, but . . . I've always been a sort of father confessor to you, Florent. Are you sure it isn't a mistake?

FLORENT: Sure? I who am never sure of anything, I feel for the first time absolutely certain. I can't tell you how wonderful it is!

HARTMANN: What about your work?

FLORENT: It's just as well you came to fetch me. For the last month I've done nothing, needless to say.

HARTMANN: Oh, yes, you have. You've lost a lot of money. I've already paid six hundred thousand francs in compensation money.

FLORENT: Suppose I told you that I haven't touched my piano once?

HARTMANN: The devil you haven't! (*Looking at* THÉRÈSE *again.*) She *is* very pretty.

FLORENT (*softly*): I love her, Hartmann.

HARTMANN: I'm beginning to believe you do.

He listens to the music a moment, and pulls a face.

I'll tell you one thing. She's a terrible violinist.

FLORENT (*smiling*): I know. But I don't care. I'm not taking her away for her to play the fiddle. I'm taking her away so I'll be happy, all my life, with her.

HARTMANN: Is that true?

FLORENT: Those are the very words I say to myself each morning when I wake. Is it true? And I answer myself very quickly: Yes, it's true.

HARTMANN (*smiling*): And is it?

FLORENT: I couldn't lie to myself every morning.

A pause.

HARTMANN (*with a sigh*): Lord, but she plays badly.

FLORENT: She plays badly, Hartmann, but she loves me well.

HARTMANN: Does she tell you so?

FLORENT: Never. But when we're alone, she rubs her head against me like a little fawn. She looks at me, deep down into my eyes. With me, she says, there's no need to be an especially good diver – you reach the bottom in no time at all. Is she right, Hartmann?

HARTMANN (*after looking at* THÉRÈSE *for a while*): How lucky for you that the girl you love should be as open and straight-forward as yourself, Florent.

FLORENT: Why?

HARTMANN: No reason. You are a charming man, Florent, and I'm sure you'll make her very happy.

FLORENT: Hartmann, you're hiding something! I feel you're about to tell me that I'm a monster without knowing it!

HARTMANN (*smiling*): Maybe.

FLORENT (*lightly*): Have I some hidden vice? Speak now, for tomorrow is my wedding day!

HARTMANN: A kind of vice, yes.

FLORENT: Its name?

HARTMANN: It has several. Brilliance, intelligence, effort-lessness – luck too.

FLORENT (*laughing*): Why, that sounds perfectly charming to me!

HARTMANN: It is. But I trembled to think you might fall in love with a suspicious, demanding, tormented sort of girl. How fortunate that she should be a child of light like you!

M. *and* MME TARDE *throw ingratiating nods and smiles to* FLORENT *as they play.*

The parents are superb! The rest of the band aren't so bad either! What has it done to her, I wonder, rubbing shoulders with them all?

FLORENT: Nothing can soil her. She is immune. It could have made her lewd and cheap. It has merely decked her in strength and candour, in a sort of virility. Do you know that she refuses to take a penny from me? She makes her own clothes and uses cheap face powder and she won't even let me buy her a present!

HARTMANN: But if you marry her, she'll let you feed and clothe her, surely?

FLORENT (*smiling*): I hope so. I'm none too sure. Yesterday, for the first time, she accepted some money to buy herself some suitcases. But I had to bully her into it. She would have come away quite happily with her two dresses in a cardboard box. That must appeal to you, I'm sure!

HARTMANN (*looking at him with a good-natured grin now*): Well now, I'll forgive her for her wrong notes. (*Sighing.*) To think you'll have made a success of everything, Florent, even falling in love.

FLORENT: I'm lucky.

HARTMANN: Almost too lucky.

FLORENT: You can never be too lucky.

HARTMANN: You can – sometimes.

The number is over. THÉRÈSE *comes quickly down the platform and runs to* FLORENT, *who rises and goes to meet her.*

THÉRÈSE: How late you were today!

FLORENT: Hullo, my little wild thing.

THÉRÈSE (*indicating the café and laughing*): Did you hear that pathetic applause? Look, they're all slinking out! They don't do that when *you* play, do they?

FLORENT (*laughing with her*): They're philistines. Music is wasted on them. (*Taking her by the shoulders.*) Quick. Now for my questionnaire. Have you thought about me today?

THÉRÈSE: Every minute.

FLORENT: Are you sure you haven't told anyone that you love me?

THÉRÉSE: Yes, I have. I told my friend.

FLORENT: Thérèse! And you never say it to me!

THÉRÈSE (*in his ear*): I never want to say it to you. But if I didn't say it to other people now and then I think it would choke me.

FLORENT: And no after thoughts?

THÉRÈSE: My thoughts are all before you. In my eyes – and on my lips. (*She lifts her face up to him to be kissed.*)

FLORENT (*murmuring*): In front of everyone?

THÉRÈSE: Who are *they*?

He leans towards her. She pushes him gently away with a glance at GOSTA.

No, not yet.

FLORENT: Why not?

THÉRÈSE: I'll tell you later.

GOSTA *has come down off the rostrum. He picks up his hat, crosses them and goes out without a glance in their direction.*
FLORENT *takes* THÉRÈSE'S *arm as she stands looking after* GOSTA *and guides her over to* HARTMANN.

FLORENT: Thérèse, this is Hartmann. He's only my friend really, but when we meet businessmen, he pretends to be my manager, because he talks bigger than I do.

THÉRÈSE: How sternly he's looking at me! Perhaps he isn't going to like me?

FLORENT: Yes, he will. I'm sure he will. Well, Hartmann, what's the verdict?

HARTMANN: Nine out of ten. She's passed with honours.

FLORENT: You look thoughtful. Was I lying?

HARTMANN (*taking* THÉRÈSE'S *hand*): Florent, you never lie.
Thérèse is perfect. Thérèse is the one girl on earth who
deserved you. But those eyes are very bright, that little forehead is very wise. She will need a lot of loving.

THÉRÈSE (*withdrawing her hand*): Why do you say that?

FLORENT: He thinks I'm a monster. He thinks I'm incapable
of making anybody happy.

THÉRÈSE: Then he can't know you very well.

FLORENT: He does. He's known me for years. That's what's
so serious.

THÉRÈSE: Not the way I know you. (*To* HARTMANN.) I've
looked at him asleep beside me; I've listened to him talking
in his dreams as he turns over. Well, even in his night-time
kingdom, I am sure of him.

HARTMANN: And are you sure of yourself?

THÉRÈSE (*like a child answering a question*): Yes, sir.

HARTMANN: Do you believe that he will never hurt you?

THÉRÈSE: He is the soul of kindness.

HARTMANN: And doesn't it frighten you to meet the soul of
kindness, the soul of intelligence and joy? You're a brave
girl.

FLORENT: Hartmann is a silly old woman. Promise me you'll
never listen to him, Thérèse.

M. *and* MME TARDE, *who, with much winking and nudging, have
stayed up on the rostrum all this time, putting away their instruments, venture forward, obsequiously rubbing their hands.*

MME TARDE: Good evening, Monsieur Florent! So it's
tomorrow morning that you plan to take my little girl away,
is it?

FLORENT: Yes, madame.

TARDE: Doesn't it just show you! Life's a funny thing. I'm
only a poor man, maestro, and yet I'm giving you a treasure!

MME TARDE: A precious treasure that it breaks our hearts to
part with, believe you me!

M. LEBONZE *comes in, shouting over his shoulder.*

M. LEBONZE: Certainly, sir, certainly, certainly! Anything you care to name! (*Sotto voce to* TARDE.) The customer over in the corner has just ordered two more bottles – one for the band. Don't pack up yet. I'll go and ask him what he wants you to play.

He goes out again.

JEANNETTE (*sitting down again crossly*): This is another two in the morning lark!
TARDE (*taking out his music, highly excited*): Yes, but champagne!
JEANNETTE: Oh, we all know that old dodge! They'll charge him for vintage and give us moussec!

M. LEBONZE *reappears.*

M. LEBONZE: Change of plan. You can all go except Gosta. He doesn't want the band now, he just wants the piano. He wants to hear the Moonlight Rhapsody on the piano. He's crying. He says it'll remind him of his wife.
TARDE: Well now, er – the thing is, Gosta . . . We had a slight tiff. I think he's gone.
M. LEBONZE: Have you finished making a fool of me? I said nobody was to move from here! (*To the waiter.*) You there! Go and fetch him back. He must have gone up to his room.
WAITER: Very good, Monsieur Lebonze. But do you think you could calm the customer down? He says if we don't play the Moonlight Rhapsody at once, he'll get it played elsewhere. He says he's tired of waiting.
M. LEBONZE (*going out, apoplectic*): Give me strength! If Gosta isn't here in one minute, I swear I'll throw you all out, bag and baggage!

He storms out.

TARDE (*sinking into a chair*): It's the finish of us! I'm ashamed, maestro, that you should see such lack of discipline in this orchestra. We meet with acclaim everywhere we go! But he's a brute of a man! A fiendish temper to him – always flaring up over nothing!

The WAITER *comes back at the same time as* LEBONZE.

M. LEBONZE: Well?

WAITER: His door's locked. He doesn't answer.

THÉRÈSE (*to* FLORENT): I'm the only one who can persuade him. I shan't be long. Come with me, Jeannette.

The girls go out.

M. LEBONZE: Right: I'm not going on my knees to any third-rate piano-thumper! Take my car and fetch me the pianist from the Royal. (*To* TARDE.) As for you, you can pack your traps and clear out. I'm getting another band tomorrow.

TARDE: Monsieur Lebonze, Monsieur Lebonze, I've a wife and child to support!

M. LEBONZE: That's your worry!

FLORENT (*stepping forward*): Look, I think I could solve the problem. I'll play the piece if you like.

M. LEBONZE (*grunting*): Yes, but can you play?

FLORENT: A little. (*To* TARDE.) Do you have the music of the Moonlight Rhapsody?

M. LEBONZE (*grumbling*): H'm! Calls himself a pianist and can't play the Moonlight Rhapsody by heart! All right then, do your worst. It's you or nothing. (*To* TARDE.) But I'm warning you, if the customer isn't satisfied, you can start packing!

He goes out.

TARDE: Oh, maestro, I don't know how to thank you! Condescending – in this establishment – in my orchestra . . .!

MME TARDE (*who has gone to fetch the music*): Here's the music, Monsieur Florent. Oh, they don't make many like you and that's a fact!

HARTMANN *goes up on the platform with* FLORENT.

HARTMANN (*over his shoulder to* TARDE *as he goes*): Normally it's two hundred thousand francs, old chap.

TARDE (*weak at the knees*): Two hundred thousand francs! On my bandstand!

THÉRÈSE *comes back with* JEANNETTE.

THÉRÈSE: He isn't in his room. The doorman says he saw him go towards the beach. Why, who's that playing?

TARDE (*drawing himself up to his full height*): Maestro Florent France! In my orchestra!

THÉRÈSE: Father, are you out of your mind! You let him—

TARDE: He insisted. And do you know how much this is costing me? – at least how much it could cost me. Two hundred thousand francs!

THÉRÈSE: Oh, I'm so ashamed.

TARDE: What?

THÉRÈSE: For that drunken sot – in this cheap saloon! You shouldn't have let him!

TARDE: Don't be silly. I'm going to see if Monsieur Lebonze is pleased.

He trots out, rubbing his hands.

THÉRÈSE *watches* FLORENT *playing for a moment or two.*

THÉRÈSE (*murmuring*): Florent . . . It's odd to see him playing up there. . . . (*A pause. She goes on dreamily.*) Come to think of it, I should have liked it if he'd been a member of the band and I'd grown to love him as we worked together. . . .

JEANNETTE (*putting her violin into its case*): You're joking, I hope?

THÉRÈSE: No. Oh, I know I'll learn to forget about his money if I try. But it isn't always very easy.

JEANNETTE (*with a short laugh*): You're making me cry.

THÉRÈSE: If he were poor and unhappy, it's funny but I feel he would belong to me more . . . It would be rather as if he were a little boy again. I could hold him close to me, and stroke his hair and say, 'There, don't be sad, I'm here, I'll help you.'

JEANNETTE (*tucking her violin under her arm*): You'll find all the unhappy men you want, I shouldn't worry. Meanwhile,

make the most of this one now you've got him. (*Giving*
THÉRÈSE *a kiss.*) Good-bye, Thérèse. I hope I'll see you
tomorrow morning before you go. But in case I shouldn't,
here's a tip. Get him to buy you diamonds, dear, all the
diamonds you can. They're still the easiest things to sell.

THÉRÈSE: What do you mean?

JEANNETTE (*going out*): Nothing, nothing. Good luck, anyway.

She goes.

MME TARDE: What was she talking about? Be careful of her,
she's no good. And don't go out with her and Florent
whatever you do. She'd pinch him soon as look at you.

THÉRÈSE (*shrugging*): You're talking nonsense.

MME TARDE: Ah, my child, you don't know the male sex!
When a woman who knows what's what offers herself to a
man . . . (*Eyeing* FLORENT.) Especially a lovely lad like
him. What a nice gesture, offering to play like that! Oh,
you're going to be so happy, and cosseted and spoilt! (*She
sighs.*) That's the kind of man I should have liked. Gosta has
been a big disappointment to me, by and large. With you
gone, who's to say that he won't leave me? Ah well, your
happiness comes first! (*With another deep sigh, she comes nearer
to* THÉRÈSE *and says impulsively.*) Give me a kiss! This may
be the last time we're alone together. You are my little girl,
after all. The eve of a wedding, that's when a mother feels
these things.

THÉRÈSE (*freeing herself slightly*): In the first place, there isn't
any wedding yet. And you know as well as I do that we've
never been exactly loving.

MME TARDE: That's what I mean! This evening it's all come
to a head! It's welling up inside me! My girl, my little girl!

THÉRÈSE (*pushing her away*): No. No theatricals, please.

MME TARDE: Oh, you are a hard little bitch! But blood's
thicker than water, I don't care what you say. Besides, a
mother has her duty. On a night like this, there's a certain
little talk we ought to have with the bride-to-be! (*Putting on*

JACP–M

a suitable expression.) Be sweet and docile, dear. Just lie back. Don't be afraid.

THÉRÈSE: Don't be absurd. I'm not a little girl, and well you know it.

MME TARDE (*frantic*): Shush! You didn't tell him so, I hope?

THÉRÈSE: Of course I did.

MME TARDE (*furious*): You fool! Suppose he threw you over?

THÉRÈSE (*smiling*): At last. That sounds more like you.

MME TARDE: You don't know your luck! I don't mind telling you I never thought he'd marry you. Oh, let me kiss you!

THÉRÈSE: Not again! What is all this leading up to?

MME TARDE: With his connexions, you must see to it he does the very best for you. Don't give up your art. This time next year you must be a star!

THÉRÈSE (*softly*): I think he thinks I play badly.

MME TARDE: Never mind, never mind! He'll coach you! Either way, don't you give him a moment's peace until he's started you on your career. Make your hay while the sun shines, my girl. Take it from me, it doesn't shine long.

THÉRÈSE (*trying to break away*): Please! Leave me alone now, will you?

MME TARDE (*catching her*): No, no, wait, wait! Gracious me, you *are* jumpy! Listen a minute. . . . You know how difficult things are just now. And I needn't tell you how mean your father is with his money. You might see your way to doing a little something for me – on the quiet, of course—

THÉRÈSE (*shaking slightly*): What do you mean?

MME TARDE: Oh, nothing, bless me – nothing at all! I waited till tonight because there was no point in bothering you before. And anyway, I had to come to terms regarding the commission. Well, now, it's like this. I went to see Vinteuil – you know, the big jewellers on the Avenue de la Plage. Very high-class establishment; branch in London, two in Paris. To cut a long story short, I told him everything.

THÉRÈSE: What? What did you tell him?

MME TARDE: Well, I told him you were getting married – to a very rich man!

THÉRÈSE: But you shouldn't have! I told you you weren't to tell anybody!

MME TARDE: Now be sensible, what difference does it make? People will have to know some time. So, anyway, as I was saying. He'll be buying you a ring, obviously. Now, what would it cost you to say, 'I've seen just what I want in Vinteuil's window'? Wait, wait . . .! There's a square cut diamond, platinum setting; a beauty— No, wait! Let me finish do! Vinteuil wants eight hundred thousand for it. I told him that if you were to say you'd set your heart on it, he could certainly ask nine hundred. If your fiancé argues about the price, of course he'll come down. But he's promised me the difference.

THÉRÈSE (*recoiling*): Oh, you make me sick!

MME TARDE (*changing her tone*): Make you sick? Make you sick, do I? Oh, stop acting the dainty miss. You were never that particular before. What can a hundred thousand more or less mean to him with his millions? And for me, it's a windfall!

THÉRÈSE: And did you think I would agree to deceive him?

MME TARDE: But I tell you he'd never know!

THÉRÈSE: Even if he never knew! Especially if he never knew! (*She buries her head in her hands.*) What do you take me for, all of you?

TARDE *hustles in, very excited.*

TARDE: I've a stupendous proposition to make to you! Old Pa Lebonze can't contain himself at the thought of who he's got strumming away there on his old piano!

MME TARDE (*with a conspiratorial look at* THÉRÈSE). Think it over, Thérèse. Remember all I sacrificed for you. But mind, it's between ourselves, eh?

She goes out.

TARDE (*anxiously*): What was she saying to you? You want to watch out for her. She isn't a bad old girl, as they go – but she has a small mind. Listen, chick. Something Pa Lebonze

said gave me a brilliant idea. All you have to do is postpone
your going away for a couple of days. That won't kill you,
will it? Now don't interrupt till you've heard what I've got
to say. Well, now . . . You know we're giving a benefit
performance at the end of the season. Right. To mark the
occasion of your leaving us, Monsieur Lebonze has agreed
to bring it forward a week. You follow me?

THÉRÈSE: Yes, Father.

TARDE (*on unsure ground*): That's my girlie! Well now. This is
a proposition that might bring us both in quite a bit of
money. (I'd see you got your fair share, that goes without
saying.) Right. Now then. The idea came to me in a flash
when I saw your fiancé at the piano up there. Now, I ask
you, couldn't you, on the occasion of this farewell concert –
you could say it brought back memories, that you'd love to
see him up on that platform where you'd been working for so
long . . . It's perfectly natural – you're such a sentimental
little thing! (Just like me, soft as putty.) Couldn't you, I say,
persuade him – on an honorary basis, of course – to come and
play one or two little pieces with us? As one of the family!
It would be so nice!

THÉRÈSE (*stammering*): You too, you too . . .

TARDE: What do you mean, me too? Don't tell me your
mother had the same idea?

THÉRÈSE: Do you think he's a machine for making money for
you? Can't you forget that wretched money for one second?

TARDE: We'd like to, but it's mighty difficult. Oh, come on,
don't be such a little prig. You're as mercenary as I am.

THÉRÈSE: That's not true! You tried to teach me to be, but
I'm not with *him*!

TARDE: Oh, be quiet! You prefer your mother's little scheme
because you think you'll make more out of it. How much
is she offering you?

THÉRÈSE: Go away!

TARDE: Not before we've come to terms.

THÉRÈSE (*on the verge of tears*): Oh, leave me alone! Please,
please, leave me alone!

TARDE (*lumbering after her*): How much did your Ma offer you? I'll give you seventy-five per cent. There! You can't call me mean, now can you?

THÉRÈSE *runs up on to the bandstand, interrupts* FLORENT'S *playing and throws herself into his arms.*

THÉRÈSE: Florent! Florent! Take me away from here!
FLORENT: Thérèse, what's the matter?
THÉRÈSE (*clinging to him*): Let's go, please, please! Let's go quickly so I shan't see them any more!

The WAITER *comes in, pushing* GOSTA *in front of him.*

WAITER: Here he is. I'll give you three guesses where I found him. On the beach, at the end of the jetty!

M. LEBONZE *comes running in.*

M. LEBONZE (*bawling*): So you've shown up at last! All right, all right! Don't give me any excuses! I'll deal with you in the morning! (*To* FLORENT.) My dear sir, I can't thank you enough. I may not be much of an expert, but I know talent when I see it. Did Thérèse mention the little proposition we—
THÉRÈSE (*quickly*): Yes – yes, I did.
M. LEBONZE: Think it over. It might do us both a bit of good. (*Holding out his hand.*) Now, if you'll excuse me . . . In the catering trade, morning's at six, as they say. I'm off to bed. (*To the* WAITER *as he goes out.*) You! Look sharp and stack your chairs! And switch off those centre lights while you're about it. No point in burning money.

He goes. The end of the Act is played in softer lighting among the chairs which the WAITER *stacks round the bandstand, in readiness for the sweepers.*

THÉRÈSE (*gently to* GOSTA, *who is staring at her, motionless*): Gosta, you're fond of me, aren't you? I'm happy tonight. I should like everybody to be happy too. This is Monsieur

Florent France – you know, the composer. Florent, this is Gosta, an old friend of mine, whom I'm very fond of.

FLORENT: Then I'm very happy to know him.

He holds out his hand. GOSTA *does not take it.*

Won't you shake hands with me?

GOSTA (*roughly*): What do you want with her? (*He advances on* FLORENT.)

MME TARDE (*screaming*): Gosta!

GOSTA: What do you want with her?

He seizes FLORENT *by the lapels.*

FLORENT (*freeing himself and pushing him away*): Are you out of your mind? Who are you?

GOSTA: Nothing! That's what I am! Nothing! Nothing but a poor wretch who watched her grow up and who wouldn't want to see her turn into a whore!

MME TARDE (*screeching*): Gosta! Gosta darling!

THÉRÈSE (*quietly*): Oh, Gosta, how could you? He's rich, I know, but that isn't my fault.

GOSTA: No, of course it isn't your fault! Still, it's a funny thing, isn't it? You never fell in love with mortal man before, yet he's the one you love!

THÉRÈSE: But I can't help it if I love him!

GOSTA: Of course not! That's your instinct! And there you were, sniffing after money with your dirty little snout, just like all the others!

THÉRÈSE (*in a small, broken voice*): Oh, you're vile! Go away!

GOSTA: All right, all right, we'll clear the floor for you, don't worry! We're none of us good enough for you now! Oh God, I never thought it of you! I never thought you'd be like all the rest!

THÉRÈSE (*in a murmur*): It's too silly . . .

MME TARDE (*to* GOSTA): Hush now, darling, be quiet. You know what happens when you get excited. You'll have an upset stomach for a week.

THÉRÈSE: Take him away, Mother. Gosta, go away, please go away. You're not yourself.

GOSTA (*as the* TARDES *try to drag him away*): That's right, I'm mad! That's the easiest way round it, isn't it? I'm mad . . .

MME TARDE: There, there, my poor old dear! Don't take on so! (*She kisses him.*) It hurts, I know, I know . . . Come along now, lovey.

They manage to drag him out.

FLORENT: But – who is this man?

TARDE *comes back.*

TARDE: In my capacity as conductor of this orchestra, may I apologize for any—

THÉRÈSE: Go away.

TARDE (*hastily*): Right! You make my excuses for me!

He scuttles out.

THÉRÈSE (*quickly, without looking at* FLORENT): He's one of our musicians. He's known me since I was a little girl. He's a simple, violent man. He thought they'd driven me into it. He thought I was giving myself to you for your money.

FLORENT: But your mother . . .?

THÉRÈSE: Yes. That's another thing I hoped I shouldn't have to tell you yet. She called him darling. He's her lover – has been for a long time.

FLORENT: Thérèse, I'm very sorry.

THÉRÈSE (*quickly*): No, don't!

MME TARDE *comes in simpering.*

MME TARDE: Back I come, disturbing the lovebirds again! He's quietened down now. I came back for my bag. I've some tablets that will help him sleep. Ah, men, men! You're all the same, dear maestro, demons every one of you! There's a song I used to sing, when I was Thérèse's age – in my early cabaret days, you know.

Singing, with gestures, while continuing to hunt for her bag.

Someone's lost her ocarino
Poor Nana
Nana's lost her nono
With his ocarino
Nono's lost his nana with his ocarino.
Where *did* I put that bag? In the cloakroom, maybe. . . .

She goes out. THÉRÈSE *stands frozen.*

FLORENT: I can't wait to take you away from here, Thérèse.
THÉRÈSE (*tonelessly*): Yes.
FLORENT: You'll like it in my house.
THÉRÈSE: Yes, I'm sure I will . . .
FLORENT: My sister is innocent and sweet like you. You'll be
great friends. And my aunt is the most enchanting old lady
in the world.

The song is heard next door. Then MME TARDE *crosses the stage,
and goes out again with an arch little smile and a nodded good night,
singing as she goes.*
THÉRÈSE *runs to the open door, pushes it to and leans against it.*

THÉRÈSE: Get out. Get out. If I could only shut her out of
my sight. She's ugly, isn't she? Ugly and crude and vulgar
when she sings those dirty songs! And that lover of hers. . . .
FLORENT: I know, darling, but what does it matter? We'll
wipe out all that.
THÉRÈSE: Do you think you can?
FLORENT (*firmly*): Yes, my darling.
THÉRÈSE (*with a sudden cry*): Oh don't be so proud of your
strength, so certain of yourself! (*A pause.*) Forgive me, Florent.
But if you knew how horrible she is! And my father too. If
I told you all the things I know, the things I've seen!
FLORENT (*taking her in his arms*): Thérèse, you're trembling!
Yet you've let me see them quite happily for the last month?
You weren't ashamed before.

THÉRÈSE: Until just now – it's funny – I didn't know. That's another thing they have just taught me.

FLORENT: Taught you? What have they taught you?

THÉRÈSE: What I am. What you are.

FLORENT (*kneels beside her and clasps her knees*): Oh, my foolish darling! But I'm only your lover! And you are more of a miracle, I promise you, than money and expensive education. Did nobody ever tell you that you were the wealthy one?

THÉRÈSE: How sweet and clever you are. . . . Earlier on, yes, I thought I was somebody despite your money. I said so to the girl who plays in the orchestra with me. She laughed her head off. I see what she meant now.

FLORENT: My sweet silly! How could a girl as free and proud as you be affected, for one second, by a mere matter of money?

THÉRÈSE (*shaking her head with a sad little smile*): Not only money. No, Florent. A while ago you could have comforted me, I'm sure. Now, your very way of doing it, so sensitive, so right, wounds me a little.

FLORENT: You mystify me, darling.

THÉRÈSE: Yes, it's funny, I hardly understand myself any more. Just now, when poor Gosta wanted to fight you, I knew you were the stronger of the two. I ought to have been proud of you. I almost hated you for being stronger in that way too. For being the strongest, always.

FLORENT (*smiling*): Sweet nitwit. Now you're blaming me because I'm strong! I'll pick a quarrel with that waiter, shall I – and have him lay me flat so that you'll love me?

THÉRÈSE (*trembling slightly*): You're quite right to laugh at me. I *am* being silly, aren't I, Florent? I do deserve you, I am like you, aren't I? Aren't I? Florent, tell me I'm not like them?

FLORENT: No, Thérèse, I swear you're not.

THÉRÈSE: But they do make you ashamed though, don't they?

FLORENT: Not the slightest bit. They make me laugh.

THÉRÈSE: What's wrong with me, then, tell me? Why do I feel like this? I'm not happy in the way I was.

FLORENT (*holding her*): My love, my little love. Why, everything hurts you!

They kiss. Enter the TARDES.

TARDE: Delicious pair!

MME TARDE (*beaming*): It takes me back to my giddy young days!

FLORENT *breaks away from* THÉRÈSE *in slight embarrassment.*

TARDE: Kiss her, my boy, go ahead and kiss her! She's all yours!

MME TARDE: Don't mind us, dear maestro. We're all artistes here. I'm as hot-blooded as they come myself!

THÉRÈSE (*with a sharp cry*): Mother!

TARDE: Her happiness! That's all we've ever thought about – our little girl's happiness! We're not like other parents . . . (*With a glance at* MME TARDE.) Yes, well . . . hrrm. The only thing that bothers us, I'm bound to say, is Thérèse leaving at such short notice. From the professional point of view . . .

FLORENT: But you can find a violinist to take her place, surely?

TARDE: Oh, of course, of course, but that isn't the point, I'm afraid. She was very popular here, you know, and . . . The fact of the matter is, Monsieur Lebonze has given us notice to quit the day that Thérèse leaves. Financially speaking, it's a disaster.

FLORENT (*taking out his wallet*): But I must compensate you for that, of course! It's the least I can do. After all, if it hadn't been for me—

THÉRÈSE *leaps forward.*

THÉRÈSE: No!

TARDE: What do you mean, no? Whyever not, girlie?

MME TARDE: Come now, Thérèse, your fiancé says himself that it's the least he can do!

THÉRÈSE: No! Not that eternal money again! You've done me enough harm already, you've made me lose enough happiness as it is, today! You're not to touch his money! And I won't have you going into ecstasies because he's good enough to want to marry me! I'm beautiful, I'm young, I love him – that's worth his riches and his fame! I won't hear another word about that money! (*To* FLORENT.) You gave me some to buy myself some luggage yesterday. I don't even want that! (*She runs to fetch her bag.*)

TARDE (*wildly*): Don't listen to her! Don't listen to her!

MME TARDE *follows after her, whimpering.*

MME TARDE: Thérèse! Thérèse, baby, be reasonable!
THÉRÈSE: There! There! There! Take it!

She throws the notes at FLORENT'S *feet. The* TARDES *make to dash forward.*

Stay where you are! Don't you dare move, either of you!
TARDE: But you're crazy! He *gave* it to you, stupid!
THÉRÈSE: Yes, I'm crazy! (*She looks at* FLORENT, *panting.*) There!
FLORENT (*bursts out laughing*): My darling! What a wonderful girl you are! But what does money matter? We'll never mention the dirty word again! We won't even have any if you'd rather. We can manage perfectly well without.

He pulls his money out of his pockets.

THÉRÈSE (*murmuring*): How simple it all is for you. I'm cold with shame and you're playing a pretty little game.
FLORENT (*laughing as he throws away all the money he has on him*): Away it goes! There! All gone! So much for money! From now on we won't even know what the word means!
TARDE (*incoherently*): Oh, but you're too kind! Oh, it's too much! (*To his wife.*) Lock the doors!
FLORENT (*throwing down his last coin*): There, my darling. Now will you let me kiss you? I haven't a single cent left on me.

THÉRÈSE *stands passively as he kisses her. She looks at the* TARDES, *who are quivering with thwarted greed.*

THÉRÈSE: Look at them both! It gives them a pain to see those banknotes on the floor. How gracefully you threw them down, Florent. People like us don't have that talent. Just look at their faces, will you? (*A pause. She cries suddenly.*) I was a fool to start this. It hurts me too, despite myself, to see that money on the floor. I've pricked my finger too often with my needle, I've stayed too long bent over my sewing for my paltry wage! I wanted to act proud, but I was lying. (*She drops to her knees.*) Down on my knees! I must go down on my knees and pick it up so I'll not act a lie! I belong to the same breed.

FLORENT: Thérèse! Don't!

He lifts her to her feet. She stands stiffly, with tightly shut eyes and clenched teeth.

My mad darling!

TARDE (*exploding*): That's right! Mad, that's what she is, mad! You see to her! We'll pick it all up for you – and give it you back . . . You can trust us!

The TARDES *scramble forward.*
HARTMANN, *who has watched the whole scene without moving, comes over to* FLORENT, *who is holding* THÉRÈSE, *in tears, in his arms.*

HARTMANN (*quietly*): You will have to tread very carefully, Florent.

The other two are still busily picking up the money.

Curtain

Act Two

A panelled room lined with books, large french windows looking out on to the grorunds. Family portraits on the walls. It is afternoon. THÉRÈSE *stands watching* TARDE, *who is trying all the arm-chairs in the room in turn.*

TARDE: I wish I could remember which chair it was I fell asleep in last night. It was sensational. Not that they aren't all pretty good. Must be worth quite a bit, a chair like that. (*He starts all over again.*) No. I've tried that one. Come to think of it, that particular sensation of well-being was more likely due to the dinner. Marvellous, that stuffed grouse we had last night. The trout this lunchtime wasn't so dusty either. (*He helps himself to a cigar and sniffs it.*) Man of taste, your fiancé.

On second thoughts, he takes another and puts it in his pocket.

THÉRÈSE: You'll leave one or two, won't you?
TARDE: What do you take me for? I'm a gay old dog, but I know my manners. (*Settling himself comfortably.*) Aren't you going to sit down? That little one over by the fireplace is quite cosy. (*A pause.*) You'd pay about five hundred francs for a cigar this size. That's the equivalent of twenty whiffs! If Lady Tarde could see me now! You've written to her, I hope?
THÉRÈSE: Have you?
TARDE (*with a nonchalant wave of his cigar*): That's different. She's your mother. I've been so booked up lately, what with my morning constitutional and my afternoon nap . . . We're having chicken milanese tonight.
THÉRÈSE: How do you know?

TARDE: I asked the cook. (*Dreamily.*) Chicken milanese . . . Have you any idea what that is? (*No answer. He turns round.*) Can't you answer me? You're not very nice to your old father. On our own, fair enough. I'm used to it. But it must look jolly odd to strangers. After all, I can't think what you've got against me. I'm a neat dresser. I know how to behave. I've plenty of small talk. You just try and think, out of the fathers of the girls you know, which one could wear a dinner jacket with my ease and smoke a five-hundred-franc cigar? (*Pause.*) Naturally, you won't say. You love making me feel small. But I defy you to mention *one*.

Another pause. He stares absorbedly at a small cabinet beside him. He begins to look worried.

What's happened to your young man today? He doesn't leave us after lunch as a rule.

THÉRÈSE: I don't know. He's talking with Hartmann.

TARDE (*very worried now*): I say, if they're working, he won't be back for quite some time. Maybe you could serve the drinks yourself? After all, you're the young lady of the house, eh, girlie?

THÉRÈSE: No.

TARDE (*rising*): It isn't quite the thing for me to help myself, I suppose. Still, we *are* in the country . . .

THÉRÈSE (*catching his arm*): I forbid you to touch that cupboard!

TARDE: Well! Bless me, whyever not?

THÉRÈSE: I'm tired of seeing you ferret about in all the cupboards in this house.

TARDE: I hope you aren't calling your father a thief!

THÉRÈSE: I wouldn't put it past you to help yourself to the odd ornament.

TARDE: Oh, you are unfair to me! Can't you understand that I merely take an artistic interest in the *objets d'art* of this mansion!

A pause. He sits down, suddenly deflated.

You shouldn't have brought me here, Thérèse. Your old father has felt the kiss of luxury and gracious living. You know, I never should have consecrated my life to that thankless muse of music. I was meant for better things. Because your mother, don't forget, was a woman of the people – 'was' – hark at me! I feel so good here that I keep imagining she's dead. Your mother, I should say, *is* a woman of the people, but my parents gave me the best middle-class blood. And willy nilly, under the old bohemian, the solid burgher stock will out.

He has risen as he speaks, and tried without success to open the cocktail cabinet. He now takes out a penknife and tries to pick the lock.

THÉRÈSE: Which is it – the solid burgher or the old bohemian, who's busy tinkering with the cocktail cabinet?

TARDE *shuts his penknife, peeved, and goes back to his chair, picking up another cigar on his way, which he puts in his pocket.*

TARDE: What's got into you? You've been on edge all morning. I can't think why you insisted on bringing me here if all you wanted was to make my life a misery. And do you know why, even? I'm going to surprise you, girlie. You don't.

THÉRÈSE, *tired of this, leans her head against the window pane.*

Oh, of course, your father's a silly old fool, we all know that! But then, would you mind explaining something to the old fool, which he can't quite grasp? You're ashamed of me, aren't you? Right. Since this morning, as a matter of fact, you haven't missed a chance of rubbing it in. Don't tinker with the cocktail cabinet, don't ferret about, don't smoke all the cigars. Your fingernails are dirty, there's dandruff on your collar – and so on and so on. (Dandruff, I may say, is common to all artists – it's an occupational disease.) So you're ashamed of me. Right. You've always gone on at me about my nails and my dandruff. You've a nasty nature, nothing new in that. But now, this is where it all becomes peculiar.

How many days have we been here, girlie? (*She says nothing.*)
I'll tell you. Six. One, two, three, four, five, six. So there were
five days – the first five of our stay here – when you weren't
ashamed of me. Now you may say you're not obliged to feel
ashamed of me every day of the week. Well, I'll tell you
something, girlie, in all honesty. If there was one time –
which Heaven forbid! – when my conduct might have given
you cause to blush, it was during the first two or three days
of our stay here. Yes, I won't deny it, the first day I lost my
head. Those magnificent dinners, those unlimited cigars, the
brandy that used to come round, regular as clockwork, after
every meal . . . (*He heaves a sigh and eyes the drinks cupboard
again.*) Dinner-time that first evening, I'll admit it, I behaved
disgracefully. I had five helpings of chocolate mousse. I
dropped an anchovy into my wineglass. I burped. I may say
it didn't matter a scrap. Each time, I came out with just the
right little witticism to turn the merriment on to my side.
Still, that day – you see, your old father admits it, very
humbly – that day, I might – conceivably – taken all in all –
I might, I repeat, have given you cause to feel ashamed of me.

THÉRÈSE: You needn't go round and round the point. You
did.

TARDE: Ah, I did! I did – did I? And how did you behave at
table that first evening, pray? You roared with laughter every
time I put my foot in it. It was you who pressed me to that
fifth helping of chocolate mousse. Not content with that, you
deliberately misled me as to the function of that little bowl
of warm water we were presented with after the pudding.
If your young man hadn't intervened, you'd have stood by
and watched me drink it, you wicked girl! And when I let
out that unfortunate little noise, your fiancé, who knows
how to behave, looked the other way. Not you. You laughed
out loud, you applauded, very ostentatiously, and you
shouted 'Good luck, Father!' Do you deny that you cried
'Good luck, Father'?

THÉRÈSE (*wearily*): Yes, I did.

TARDE: Do you deny that after we'd retired to the lounge you played on the understandable weakness of an old man who never tasted the good things of life and made me smoke four cigars; you filled my brandy glass seven times so I'd get drunk and make an exhibition of myself. Which I did, naturally. When I've had a drop in, I'm apt to break into song. But even so, there are songs and songs. Left to myself I might have warbled La Madelon. But no. You insisted on a rendering of Fifi the Fan Dancer with gestures. And you laughed like an inebriated barmaid. Why, I blush for you when I think of it. Do you deny your behaviour that first evening?

THÉRÈSE: No, Father.

TARDE: You will therefore admit that it is in complete contradiction to the way you're criticizing me today over nothing at all?

THÉRÈSE: Yes, Father.

TARDE: Can you tell me, in that case, the meaning of this sudden change of attitude?

THÉRÈSE: That's for you to find out, isn't it?

The MAID *comes in with the coffee.*

MAID: Monsieur Florent begs Mademoiselle to excuse him for a moment longer. He said not to wait for coffee.

TARDE (*calling out as she goes*): I say. Miss – ma'am! Is the drinks cupboard locked?

MAID: No, sir. It's never locked. (*She opens it.*)

TARDE (*to* THÉRÈSE): I told you! (*With a gracious smile.*) Very many thanks, ma'am.

MAID: Thank you, sir.

TARDE: You're welcome, ma'am.

The MAID *goes out.* TARDE *walks purposefully to the cocktail cabinet.*

Mine's a brandy. What about you, girlie?

THÉRÈSE: No, nothing.

TARDE: I'll give you a little armagnac. (*He fills a second glass.*) Flush with the brim, the way you like it! (*He drinks, sinking*

JACP–N

comfortably into his chair.) You know, girlie, I've a confession
to make. I've been thinking things over. I was wrong to want
your young man to play in that shoddy joint of old man
Lebonze's, for a paltry hundred or so profit. (*He empties his
glass and sets it down.*) There, I'm making a clean breast of it.
I'm even wondering whether I won't give him back a part
of what he lent me.

THÉRÈSE: You must be out of your mind!

TARDE: No, no. I'm quite sane. (*He pours himself another drink.*)
Yes, I'm not sure that I won't give him back part of the
money. (*He takes a swallow.*) Mind you, I haven't the slightest
doubt that he meant it as a gift. (*A swallow.*) I'm even wondering whether a gesture of that sort wouldn't be the tiniest bit
rude. . . . (*The glass is empty.*) A touch more armagnac?

*She does not answer. He pours himself another drink and settles
back in his chair.*

In short, there's a lot to be said for and against. However,
I'm wondering if I shouldn't make at least a symbolic
gesture – a few hundred francs, a thousand maybe. . . . (*He
drinks dreamily.*) If it's a symbolic gesture, you might say that
five hundred francs would meet the case. (*A pause.*) Four
hundred, come to that. (*He takes another swallow.*) On the
other hand, I wouldn't for the world have anybody think
me mean. . . .

THÉRÈSE: You want to make a symbolic gesture – you of all
people? You – afraid of looking mean?

TARDE: Well, there we are.

THÉRÈSE: Who would have thought it? Who would have
guessed that deep down all you wanted was respectability!

TARDE: I've always been respectable. It was your mother who
rubbed off on me.

THÉRÈSE: Yes, there you are, you, who've had egg on your
waistcoat for sixty years, wearing a neat white collar every
day! (*She starts forward.*) Where did you pick up that tie?
It isn't yours.

TARDE: I did not 'pick it up'! Your fiancé gave it to me.

THÉRÈSE: Did you ask him for it?

TARDE (*genuinely indignant*): What do you take me for? He was wearing it. I merely said it was very smart and pointed out that it had the same purple thread in it as my country suit. Which is perfectly true, you can check up. So then – I don't know what came over him – he burst out laughing, took it off his neck and gave it me. The dear, impulsive fellow . . .!

He pulls out a little pocket mirror and arranges his tie, humming gaily.

Pom . . . pom . . . pom . . . You'd pay a good two thousand francs for a tie like this.

He tucks away his mirror and continues to smoke nobly.

THÉRÈSE (*smiling despite herself*): How happy you are here!

TARDE: So much so that I daren't even admit it to myself.

THÉRÈSE: Why not?

TARDE (*humbly*): I'm afraid you'll send me away. (*He touches wood.*)

THÉRÈSE: And I, would you say I was happy?

TARDE: Oh, you're such a funny girl. It's so hard to tell with you. Aren't you?

THÉRÈSE: Do you think, if I'd come here with the idea of being happy, I'd have insisted on bringing you with me, Father?

TARDE: Why shouldn't you like the joys of family life, just like any other girl, lass?

THÉRÈSE: Don't talk like a fool. You aren't one. Doesn't it strike you as odd that I should bring you here? Don't you ever ask yourself questions, at night, after your last glass of brandy, in your handsome quilted bed?

TARDE: Oh, you know me, I'm not very inquisitive. You want me, here I am. Besides, I fall asleep so soon after my dinner.

THÉRÈSE: Doesn't it seem strange to you that I should encourage you to be vulgar, obscene?

TARDE: Now, now – let's not exaggerate. I wasn't obscene.

THÉRÈSE: Yes, Father, you were. And I wanted to scream – I

dug my nails into the palms of my hands so as not to cry.

TARDE: But you should have told me, girlie! You know me.
Once I get going, I don't realize—

THÉRÈSE (*her eyes closed*): No. I wanted you to go even further.
I'd have liked you to prance about in your underwear to
make us laugh – to go on drinking until you were sick in
front of everybody.

TARDE (*appalled at the very thought*): Thérèse, you're frightening
me! (*Going to her.*) Thérèse, look at me!

THÉRÈSE: Well?

TARDE: What would your young man have said if I'd been
sick all over his carpets?

THÉRÈSE: You would have disgusted him so much, and so
would I too, probably, that he'd have thrown us both down
the front steps.

TARDE: But this is dreadful! You tried to wreck your future
marriage – on purpose? But why? Dammit, I am your father,
I insist on knowing why! I feel I'm going mad! I've got to
understand why!

THÉRÈSE (*kindly*): That would really be beyond you, Father.

TARDE (*dropping into a chair*): I've given birth to a monster!
A monster of pride!

THÉRÈSE: Would you call me especially proud?

TARDE: On your mother's side, they're as spineless as jellyfish.
But with the Tarde family, pride is unconquerable! And it's
me you take after, girlie.

THÉRÈSE: It would be lucky, Father, if it were only pride.

TARDE: I ask you, what is it, if it isn't pride? Why else should
you feel so strongly about a man that you don't love?

THÉRÈSE: But who said I didn't love him?

TARDE: If you did, do you think you'd amuse yourself getting
your father drunk so that he'd be disgusted?

THÉRÈSE: It's true though, Father.

TARDE: Oh, no, no, no! I simply won't believe it! I've been in
love, too, lass – not your mother – later . . . (you're a big
girl now, I can tell you these things). She was a harpist we
had in the orchestra for a time. A tall, slender creature she

was, and real style with it. Lovely girl . . . Well, I swear
to you nothing so far-fetched would ever have entered my
head. And yet, in some ways, I'm more passionate than you.

THÉRÈSE (*her eyes closed*): And it wouldn't have entered your
head to be purposely nasty, purposely coarse? To cling
tooth and nail to your right to rebel?

TARDE: Rebel? Good grief, girl, explain yourself! What are
you rebelling against? Come along now, girlie, calm down
and tell me all about it.

THÉRÈSE: Against him and all that's like him here.

TARDE: All that's like him? What pray?

THÉRÈSE: His house, that looks so bright and welcoming the
first day the better to show you that you don't belong in it.
Father, I run when I have to cross the drawing-room alone!
Every chair reproaches me for wanting to install myself here!
And all those old ladies in their great gilt frames!

TARDE: Pretty handsome some of them are too, I must say.

THÉRÈSE: And his books! Look, those rows of books that
made him what he is, that know him better than I'll ever
know him! His books that I don't know at all and can't
defend myself against!

TARDE: Well, bless me, it's simple enough! Read them, girlie!

THÉRÈSE (*pitifully*): I've tried. But they don't speak to me the
way they speak to him. He'd have to explain to me, and I
don't want that. Oh, but I won't have them think they
frighten me! (*She tumbles the books out on to the floor.*) There,
that's for the one that makes him melancholy! There, that's
for the one that makes him dream! There! There! There!
That's for all the ones that make him laugh and not me!

TARDE (*picking them up after her*): Thérèse, girlie! Thérèse,
you're mad! You'll spoil them! Thérèse, stop it now!

*The books are falling faster than he can pick them up. He struggles
with an armful of them.* THÉRÈSE *snatches them out of his hands,
and throws them down again.*

THÉRÈSE: You're not to pick them up! I want him to find
them on the floor when he comes in!

TARDE *drops the last book he was holding and flops into a chair, discouraged.*

TARDE: Your behaviour leaves me speechless, my child. I fail to see how a few harmless books . . .

THÉRÈSE: Everything here is for him, and against me! (*Pointing at the picture.*) Look, his mother. She's dead and gone, couldn't she have stayed in her frame up there and let me be? But even the dead are in league with him! I know they are!

TARDE: Oh well, of course, if you're going to start invoking the dead! . . .

THÉRÈSE: Have they told you about his mother yet?

TARDE: Delightful woman, I believe, sweet, distinguished, every inch a lady.

THÉRÈSE (*with a dry laugh*): And can you see me up in a frame like that, all sweetness and distinction? Tell me, Father, can you?

TARDE: Ah, now wait a minute! In the first place, you can't deny that none of your friends are half as ladylike as you. And as for sweetness – well, I wouldn't call you any less sweet than the next girl, really . . .

THÉRÈSE: Wouldn't you? Do you remember how sweet I was the day you wanted me to be 'nice' to old father Lebonze?

TARDE (*rising outraged*): This is a fine time to rake all that up! Oh, you've really surpassed yourself, you have! Talk about tact! (*He storms up and down the room, furious.*) Anyway, we're artists! Artists can be as eccentric as they like in any company, you ask anybody!

THÉRÈSE: Artists! Why I do believe you really mean that! Have you ever listened to your efforts on the double-bass? Have you heard me play the violin? And then have you listened to him play, even with one finger – without its breaking your heart?

TARDE: Ah, now I won't have that. You're a very nice little performer, chick. And as for me, you mustn't forget that I won the bronze medal at the Arcachon Academy of Music.

There are quite a few folk we could hold a candle to, you know.

THÉRÈSE (*with a little, hopeless smile*): Well, we'd better hurry up and find them, hadn't we, and hold our candle to them. Because, with the rest of the world . . . (*She stops in front of the mother's portrait.*) She can smile away there, in her fine frame. It must be good to come into a house as a real bride, without shame, without defiance -- to be clear and gentle – and have people love you . . .

FLORENT *comes hurrying in, followed by* HARTMANN.

FLORENT: Darling, do forgive me. Have you had coffee?

TARDE: Oh, yes, thanks very much. And we had a message to say Monsieur Florent said to have the brandy without him. So naturally, we started to have it . . .

FLORENT: Good. My dear Monsieur Tarde, you asked if I could lend you a morning coat.

THÉRÈSE *looks up.*

TARDE (*ill at ease*): Yes, chick. You see, your fiancé told me he had two. So I thought – a wedding only lasts one day after all. Silly to go to all that expense . . . And a morning coat doesn't need to fit all that well . . .

FLORENT: The coat is on your bed. Would you like to go up and try it on?

TARDE: Why, certainly, certainly, my dear son-in-law to be – and thank you, thank you, thank you . . .

Everybody is waiting for him to go. He sits down timidly.

As soon as we've had the liqueurs, I shall be only too delighted to – er . . .

FLORENT (*going to the cocktail cabinet*): What will you have?

TARDE: I was just comparing cognac and armagnac before you came in and I'm bound to say I was in two minds about which I—

FLORENT: Here's the cognac, and here's the armagnac. (*He puts them into his arms.*) Which is your glass?

TARDE: Oh, any one will do, I'm not fussy.

FLORENT: There you are. Do you think you could go up to your room right away and have your brandy without us?

TARDE (*rising with dignity*): And what, may I ask, am I to understand by that?

FLORENT (*smiling*): Why, just what I said.

TARDE: This is a sort of dismissal, unless I'm much mistaken?

FLORENT: In a way, but not for long. And with two full bottles to keep you company.

TARDE (*with a very noble gesture*): No need to labour the point. I quite understand. (*He takes a step.*) I'm not obliged to stay in my room though, am I? If I get tired of waiting, is it all right to go for a walk?

FLORENT (*seeing him to the door*): Of course.

TARDE: In that case – since you were so civil about the suit, would it be agreeable if I asked for the loan of a walking-stick? I feel very odd walking without a cane and – in all the rush, I forgot to bring mine . . .

FLORENT: You'll find several in the hall. Take whichever one you like.

He pushes him.

TARDE: Well then, if you don't mind, I'll take the one with the gold and ivory knob. That's the one I like the feel of best – that is to say, the – er – look of.

FLORENT: It's yours. I'll get it for you.

He goes out.

TARDE (*dashing after him and shouting*): Please don't trouble! Please don't trouble!

FLORENT *has already gone. His voice drops.*

Please don't trouble . . . Oh, it's too silly, he really shouldn't have troubled . . . (*He calls timidly through the half-open door.*) Don't bother to look . . . there's no rush . . .

FLORENT *comes back with another cane.*

FLORENT: Odd. I could have sworn I'd seen it there yesterday. Would you like this one instead?

TARDE (*waffling*): I was meaning to tell you . . . I thought you'd say yes . . . It's up in my room . . .

FLORENT (*laughing as he pushes him out*): Splendid! Off you go!

TARDE *goes out.*

THÉRÈSE: What's the matter? Why did you send him away?

FLORENT: Thérèse, I received an anonymous letter this morning. Do you recognize the style? (*Reading the letter.*) 'I take up my pen because there is something important you ought to know about the party to whom you are proposing to give your name.'

THÉRÈSE: Well?

FLORENT: The letter was brought by the waiter from the Station Café, where the sender was waiting to see me. I need hardly tell you that I treated the whole thing as a joke. But I didn't want to give anyone a chance to pester you, so I sent Hartmann along. He found your friend from the orchestra and for reasons best known to himself he's brought her back here. Do you want to see her, or shall I send her away?

THÉRÈSE: I want to see her.

FLORENT: Very well. I'll fetch her.

He goes out. HARTMANN *goes to* THÉRÈSE.

HARTMANN: I'm afraid I've been rather indiscreet. I met your friend and instead of sending her away as Florent had said, I bought her a drink and asked her one or two questions. (THÉRÈSE *looks at him.*) She didn't say much, but I got the impression that the anonymous letter wasn't her idea. She was sent for by – a certain person. (*He looks at* THÉRÈSE *with a smile, then takes her suddenly by the shoulders.*) My child, are you sure you aren't doing something silly?

THÉRÈSE (*freeing herself*): I don't know what you mean.

HARTMANN: Thérèse my dear, look me in the eye. I'm not sure what evil genie it is you're grappling with. I can vaguely guess. No, don't shrug like that. One day you may realize

that I'm the only person in this house who can talk to you
like this.

THÉRÈSE *has broken away from him. He catches her, takes her
by the arms and says gently, but firmly:*

You love Florent. That is something solid, something real.
Why not forget all this tedious nonsense?

THÉRÈSE: It isn't tedious nonsense.

HARTMANN: Yes, it is. Listen to me. In this house, every time
you feel pain when you haven't cut your finger – every time
you cry when nothing has hurt you, that will be a piece of
tedious nonsense. You forget you are in the house of happiness where pain and sorrow have no place. The owner has
held the door open for you. Don't hesitate. Make haste and
come in.

THÉRÈSE: I won't listen to you and your fine talk. What
business is it of yours anyway? Why can't you leave me in
peace?

HARTMANN: I'm an old egoist, Thérèse, and I've let a good
few people cut their own throats in my time. But it looks as
though I must care for you a great deal. This time it seems
to me too silly to let you run away from happiness.

THÉRÈSE (*tearing herself away*): Happiness! Anyone would
think happiness was the only thing on earth! Yes, I do want
to run away from it! I won't let it swallow me whole! I have
a right to go on suffering and crying with the pain of it.
Extraordinary, isn't it? You can't understand that, can you?

HARTMANN (*quietly*): How do you know, Thérèse?

FLORENT *comes in with* JEANNETTE.

FLORENT: Thérèse, here is your friend. We'll leave you
together.

THÉRÈSE: No. Don't go.

The GIRLS *look intensely at each other.*

Well? Say what you have to say. Go on then, talk. You sent
an anonymous letter. You've something to say, say it.

JEANNETTE *says nothing.*

You're ashamed to talk in front of me, is that it? All right, I'll go.

FLORENT (*restraining her*): No, Thérèse. I won't listen to a word unless you're here.

THÉRÈSE: But can't you see she's afraid? She won't talk if I'm here.

FLORENT: Then she won't talk at all.

THÉRÈSE: Yes! I want her to tell you what she's come to say. Go on, you, talk! What's the matter, have you lost your tongue?

JEANNETTE: Talk – talk – what do you mean, talk? What do you want me to do – say what you told me to say or say what you told me not to say?

FLORENT: What?

JEANNETTE: I've changed my mind. Get someone else to do your dirty work. I'm going. (*She turns to* FLORENT.) Can somebody drive me back to the station?

THÉRÈSE: Oh, no, you don't! You came here to say something, my girl, and say it you will!

JEANNETTE: Thérèse, you're mad! Let me go!

FLORENT: I think we ought to let her leave, Thérèse.

THÉRÈSE: No I want her to speak. I want her to say the dirty thing she's brought with her. Look at her, with her flashy clothes and her cheap jewellery. She doesn't even need to say anything. She's brought her wretched little bit of filth in here, along with her cheap scent and the fag end in the corner of her mouth! Come on, Jeannette, come on, my old girl friend, talk! Talk, can't you? (*She shakes her.*) For God's sake what are you waiting for? That's what you came for, isn't it? You're scared!

JEANNETTE: No, but if you want to know, it makes me sick. I don't want to look like what I'm not. (*She turns abruptly to* FLORENT.) I don't say I wasn't envious of her luck, as who wouldn't be? But as for coming and throwing muck all over everything, that's not my way. It was she wrote and asked me to come.

THÉRÈSE: Fool! Fool!

JEANNETTE: I was to get my train fare and an extra ten thousand francs.

A pause. FLORENT *turns to* THÉRÈSE.

FLORENT: Why did you send for this girl? What did you want her to tell me?

THÉRÈSE *says nothing. He turns to* JEANNETTE *and takes her by the arm.*

What was it you had to say to me?

JEANNETTE (*freeing herself*): All right! There's no need to break my arm! I'll tell you and glad to, since you're that keen to know. She wrote and asked me to come and tell you she had been Gosta's mistress.

FLORENT: Gosta . . .

JEANNETTE: Yes, her mother's lover. Sorry it isn't more exciting!

FLORENT (*to* THÉRÈSE): But this is insane! Why did you want to make me believe that?

THÉRÈSE: Did you hear? Did you hear? Sorry it isn't more exciting, she says! There's no point now that you know I sent for her. But I made her say it just the same so that you would hear those words ringing in here, so that your mother should hear them in her gold frame – and your old gardener whom I loathe and your prim old housemaids and your books too, your foul, foul books!

JEANNETTE (*picking one up*): Talking of books, you've quite an overflow, haven't you?

FLORENT *sees all the books on the floor, and looks at* THÉRÈSE.

THÉRÈSE: I threw them on the floor.

FLORENT: Why?

THÉRÈSE: No reason.

FLORENT (*taking her by the shoulders*): Thérèse, I want you to tell me why.

THÉRÈSE: Go on, dig your great hands into me, I shan't tell

you why! I wanted you to know what I'd have tried to make
you believe if that fool hadn't made such a mess of it. I want
you to know that I threw your books about, that I brought
my father here and let you give him money and got him
drunk and made him sing his dirty songs – on purpose! But
why I did those things, why I hate you all, that I'll never tell
you, because you hadn't the wit to find out for yourself!

FLORENT (*stunned*): But . . . Thérèse, I can't believe it . . .
Only an hour ago we were so happy!

THÉRÈSE: You were happy, not me.

FLORENT: You're trembling!

THÉRÈSE: Yes, I'm trembling. I'm trembling at being the only
one here who can't smile, the only one who's poor and dirty
and ashamed!

*She flings herself down on the settee. He looks at her helplessly, not
daring to go near her.*

HARTMANN (*taking* JEANNETTE *aside*): Come with me, I told
the taxi to wait.

JEANNETTE: No. I'm not leaving without talking to Thérèse
in private. I don't mind coming on a four-hour train journey
and being made to look a damn fool at the end of it, but I
don't intend to be out of pocket into the bargain.

HARTMANN: I have full authority to settle that side of the
matter.

JEANNETTE: Have you? That's different. (*Turning to her.*)
Good-bye, Thérèse – and act sensible, girl, I should. You've
got yourself a good place here, keep it. (*To* HARTMANN *as
she goes out.*) If I were in her shoes . . .!

HARTMANN: Ah, but then you aren't.

They go out. THÉRÈSE *is on the sofa, her head buried in the
cushions.* FLORENT *stands beside her.*

FLORENT (*murmuring*): You were unhappy, my darling, and I
never guessed. My little silly, trying to make me believe she
was her mother's lover's mistress! What a complicated thing
to think of! Her mother's lover's mistress! It seems to me

that if I had been a little goose who was set on pretending to be as black as pitch, I still think I should have thought of something less far-fetched.

She lifts her head, looks at him, opens her mouth to speak, then drops wearily back again.

(*Sitting beside her.*) Do you think I'm going to let a single sorrow live in you? (*He raises her and holds her facing him. She turns her head away.*) Don't I look stronger than all the heartache in the world? Look into my eyes.

She has not moved. He shakes her, tries to see her face.

Now, what was it you said about my house? You feel poor in it, do you? You feel alone? My foul books. Why foul? It's by reading these books that I learnt to wait for you and love you ever since I was nineteen years old. When you get to know them, you'll love them too. (*He picks them up.*) Come, let's tidy the place up a bit. All this bad feeling because you don't know each other very well. I'll introduce you. Give me your hand. (*He tries to lift her to her feet, but she clings to the settee.*) Won't you stand up? It's not very polite to shake hands sitting down. Still, I'm sure the house will excuse you. These old country places are very easy-going. (*He begins, half laughing, half moved, as if he were talking to a child, while he sits stroking her hair.*) Well now, you trees, and old panelled walls, and arm-chairs, I must ask you to excuse this young lady, who is a tiny bit sad still because she hasn't learnt how to make friends with you. You're a bit pleased with yourselves, anyway, all of you. You should have taken more care not to frighten her. You chairs over there, you should have told her you weren't as fearsome as all that, in spite of your grand airs, and anyway, you've none of you any style to boast of. You, grandfathers and great-uncles, why did you look so superior? You none of you set the world on fire when you were in it. And as for you, Mother, I'm surprised at you. She was unhappy, and you never said a word to her!

Why couldn't you sing her the lullaby you used to sing to
me when I was small and couldn't sleep?

Suddenly THÉRÈSE *begins to sing, in a voice harsh with tears, her
face hidden in the sofa cushions.*

THÉRÈSE: Someone's lost her ocarino
Poor Nana
Nana's lost her nono
With his ocarino
Nono's lost his nana with his ocarino.

She stops, choked by a sob.

FLORENT: What were you singing?
THÉRÈSE (*her head in her arms*): That's the song *my* mother
used to sing to me!
FLORENT: Thérèse!

*He lifts her forcibly to her feet. Her face is bathed in tears. She
reels slightly – he shakes her, and cries, frightened.*

Thérèse, look at me! Thérèse, you're crying. I thought this
was only a little girl's tantrum, like the other day, because
they all thought you were marrying me for my money.
Thérèse, it isn't only that, is it?
THÉRÈSE (*softly*): Listen. You will have to let me go. (*He is
about to speak, but she stops him with a gesture.*) You see, I'm not
shouting. I'm not making a scene. You are going to have to
let me go.
FLORENT: Thérèse, you're mad!
THÉRÈSE (*backing away as if she were afraid of him*): Don't touch
me.
FLORENT: I want to take you in my arms. I must hold you
close to me, now, and make you well again.
THÉRÈSE: No. Everything hurts too much now. You don't
know how it feels, you'll never know. It seethes and swells
and bursts inside . . . You must let me go away, without
scenes, without tears, while I still can. Please. I'm asking you.
Because if I stayed a little longer, I'd go mad . . .

FLORENT: At least tell me when it was I hurt you, if you don't want me to go mad too.

THÉRÈSE (*with a helpless gesture, like a little girl*): I can't.

FLORENT: You must. I won't let you leave this room until you do.

THÉRÈSE (*shaking her head*): No, please. Let me go. (*She looks squarely at him and adds in a hard voice.*) If you love me.

FLORENT (*calm and sure of himself*): I shan't let you go because I love you and because you love me, I know you do. I don't know what pride or evil spirit it is that's twisting your face at this moment. But I do know that they are only weeds growing inside you and not the real you at all. Struggle as you may, I'll pull those weeds out one by one.

THÉRÈSE (*crying out suddenly*): For pity's sake, can't you be quiet! I'm ashamed, I'm ashamed of being like this, but I always will be. Can't you leave me alone, all of you!

She sinks into an arm-chair, trembling.

FLORENT: I'm going to hurt you. Forgive me, darling, but I must save you from yourself. Something is driving you away just now from this house and from me. But I know that something just as strong is keeping you here too. You're weeping and you're trembling because those two forces are at war in you. So don't think I'm going to stand by and do nothing. I told you once that I liked fighting. Look at me and speak if you dare. After that I may let you go. (*He forces her head up. She looks at him, panting.*) Look at me. You can feel, can't you, that I'm stronger than you and all the pain in you?

Her head is pressed back against the chair. Fearfully she looks into those clear eyes, which are searching her own. She is about to yield when her father comes in. He is wearing morning dress and a silk hat.

TARDE: I know you said not to come in, but I couldn't resist it. What do you think of your father now, eh, girlie?

FLORENT (*striding over to him*): Will you get out of here?

THÉRÈSE *runs to her father and clings to his arm.*

THÉRÈSE: No, Father! Stay here! I need you!

FLORENT: Thérèse, let go of him.

THÉRÈSE: No, I shan't, I shan't! Oh I'm so glad you came down, Father! I'm saved now! You're here! You're here!

FLORENT (*shaking his other arm*): Will you clear out!

THÉRÈSE: Father, stay where you are!

TARDE: Well, but, girlie, I'm beginning to wonder if I'm not rather 'de trop'.

FLORENT: Yes, you certainly are! Get out!

THÉRÈSE: No. Father! I need you! (*She puts her arms round him.*) Father, dear little Father! Oh I'm glad, glad that you're so scruffy and ridiculous, and vulgar!

TARDE: Hey, hey, hey, girlie! I know you're joking, but even so, I'm your father, don't you forget that!

THÉRÈSE (*with a sort of horrible joy*): Oh, I'm not forgetting it! I'm your daughter, all right! I'm the daughter of the little gent with the black nails and the dandruff on his collar; the little gent who talks so grand, but who tried to sell me, here, there and everywhere, as soon as I was of an age for men to fancy me!

TARDE (*with dignity*): What are you talking about? I simply do not understand. (*To* FLORENT.) She doesn't know what she's saying.

THÉRÈSE: Oh, no, I'm not forgetting you're my father! I'm not forgetting any of the sordid secrets that tie me to you more surely than if I loved you! Oh, we make a good pair, Father! We don't need to blush for each other, we're the same breed, aren't we, you and I?

TARDE: Of course, child, of course. (*To* FLORENT.) I don't know what's got into her, I don't really.

THÉRÈSE (*to* FLORENT): Have you nothing to say now? You can feel, can't you, that I'm a long way away, now that I'm clinging to him! Oh, you'd pulled me over to your side, you know, with that great strength of yours. But I've escaped you. You'll never reach me now.

FLORENT: No, Thérèse, you're struggling to get away, but you haven't escaped me.

THÉRÈSE: Yes, now that I've lost all hope I have escaped you, Florent. I'm in a country now where you've never set foot, and you would never know the way to follow me and bring me back. Because you don't know what it's like to feel the ground give way under you. You don't know what it's like to fight for air and flounder in the mud and sink. You know nothing about anything that's human, Florent. (*She looks at him.*) You never had a real pain – a hurt that's as shameful as an oozing, secret wound. You never hated anyone, one can tell from your eyes – even those who've done you harm.

FLORENT: No, Thérèse. But I can teach you how not to hate either, I know I can.

THÉRÈSE: How sure of yourself you are . . .

FLORENT: Yes. And I'm sure I can make you happy too.

THÉRÈSE: How strong you are . . .

FLORENT: Yes.

THÉRÈSE: You've never been ashamed or poor. I've gone miles out of my way so as not to go up some steps because I had holes in my stockings. I've run dirty errands for people and I was a big girl and I smiled and said thank you for the tip and bit back my shame at it. Did you never run errands, Florent – did you never break the bottle of milk and linger in the dark hallway, not daring to go up the stairs again?

TARDE: Must you relate all that silly rubbish!

THÉRÈSE: Yes, Father, I must.

FLORENT: No, I've never been poor, Thérèse, but that isn't my fault.

THÉRÈSE: Nothing is your fault! You've never been ill, either, I'm sure. I've had ringworm and scabies and nits – all the diseases of the poor. The teacher used to part my hair with a ruler when she'd noticed it.

TARDE (*outraged*): Nits, I ask you!

FLORENT (*shaking his head*): I'll fight, Thérèse, and I'll be stronger than everything that poverty did to you.

THÉRÈSE (*with a mirthless laugh*): Did you hear that. He'll fight! You fight blithely against other people's suffering because you don't know that it drops on you like a cloak that sticks to your skin. If you'd ever been weak or cowardly, you would take infinite precautions before you touched that bleeding cloak. You must take great care not to hurt the feelings of the poor. (*She takes her father's hand.*) Come, Father. Put on your topper and let's go. (*Turning to face* FLORENT.) Let us pass, please.

FLORENT (*barring the way*): No, Thérèse.

THÉRÈSE (*shivering as she looks into his eyes*): 'She is adorable.' I heard you saying that to Hartmann. You didn't expect this, did you? This hatred that ploughs up my face, this shrill voice, these squalid details. I must be as hideous as poverty just now. You're as white as a sheet. The conquered are frightening, aren't they?

FLORENT: Why do you use such silly words? You aren't conquered. And the last thing I could ever be is a conqueror.

THÉRÈSE: You are a rich man. That's worse. A conqueror who never fought a battle.

FLORENT: But you can't go on for ever blaming me for my money! What do you expect me to do with it?

THÉRÈSE: Oh, nothing, Florent. You could throw it all to the winds, laughing, the way you did the other day, but my pain wouldn't vanish with it . . . You aren't only rich in money, you see, you're rich in the house where you grew up, rich in your life's deep peace and the age-old tranquillity of your forefathers. You are rich in your joy of living, that never had to attack or to defend itself, and in your talent too. You see, there really are too many things to be thrown overboard. And you mustn't think that you're a monster. You've tortured me, but you're kind, you know, and it isn't your fault, because you know nothing.

She looks at him for a second, then suddenly anger floods her. She advances on him.

You know nothing! That's what hurts the most! It's your privilege to know nothing! Oh, I feel heavy tonight with all the pain that must have seared the hearts of the poor when they found out that rich people knew nothing, and that there was no hope that one day they'd find out. But tonight, you will know, you'll know about me if nothing else! Go on, Father, you tell him, if you have the courage! Tell him all the shabby little details he can never have known and which have given me this sorry knowledge, I who am younger than he . . . Go on, tell him! Tell him about when I was eleven, and that dear old gentleman who was so kind—

TARDE: She's mad! He was a friend of the family! She doesn't know what she's saying!

THÉRÈSE: Tell him about all the times when Mother came home drunk and sick and I had to undress her and put her to bed!

TARDE: Stop it, for mercy's sake!

THÉRÈSE: And he wanted me to love his mother, did I tell you? He wanted me to shed tears over this gracious lady here, with her lullabies and her rose garden. But that's not all! Tell him some more, so we'll make a really graceful exit. Tell him it wasn't so far-fetched what I wanted Jeannette to tell him about this afternoon. Tell him that Mother nagged me often enough to give in to Gosta so she wouldn't lose him!

TARDE (*sincerely*): Oh no, that I should never have stood for!

THÉRÈSE: Tell him that at fourteen I had a lover!

TARDE: I forbid you to say any more! Don't listen to her!

THÉRÈSE (*pushing past him*): I had a lover at fourteen, do you hear? A boy I didn't even know! He took me and I let him have his way, without love – and not from viciousness either, from a sort of apathy, a resignation you could never understand. I only saw him once. I became pregnant. When I found out, he'd been gone a long time. I got rid of it myself, alone in my room.

TARDE: Girlie!

THÉRÈSE: All alone. And I lay bleeding on the floor . . .

TARDE: I forbid you . . .

THÉRÈSE: . . . and bit everything in sight so that I shouldn't scream! There. I never told it to a living soul. And now it's out. Now I'll never have the courage to look you in the face again. (*She flings herself down exhausted, and hides her head in her arms.*)

TARDE (*exploding, sincerely outraged*): This time you've gone too far! I'm an old scoundrel and life hasn't always been too easy. And I've often let myself sink lower than you'd believe. But to talk about it, for all the world to hear, to be proud of it almost, never – never, do you hear me – never would your father have done that!

A pause.

FLORENT (*in a strange voice*): What do you want me to do, Thérèse?

THÉRÈSE: Let me go without looking at me, if you still love me a little. (*She gets up and goes to the door without looking round.*) Come, Father.

TARDE (*as he goes*): I must ask you once again to excuse this outburst, which offends and humiliates me and for which I am not responsible. After all, speaking man to man – one does a lot of things, but to shout them from the roof-tops! – no, there I draw the line!

He bows and goes out after THÉRÈSE. HARTMANN *comes hurrying in.*

HARTMANN: What happened? I've just met her running up to her room!

FLORENT (*quietly*): She's lost.

HARTMANN: You must do something, Florent!

FLORENT: I don't know what to do. I feel so helpless, Hartmann.

HARTMANN: You, helpless? What in the world can she have said to you?

FLORENT: I don't understand her. She blames me for never having been poor, for not knowing how to hate or be unhappy. She's ashamed of her father and she brings him here on purpose! She's ashamed of her past life and she sends for that girl to tell this dirty lie!

HARTMANN: Do you remember what I told you the night I

met her? I said how lucky you were that she wasn't a hard, demanding, tormented sort of girl.

FLORENT: Why, do you think I haven't enough love in me to give a girl like that?

HARTMANN: You are like all very rich folk, Florent, who never have enough small change to give to beggars. You said once that one can never be too lucky. You've just had proof that one can. You are like the kings of old. You have been given, in profusion, and for nothing, what the rest of us have to pay very dearly for. So resign yourself, like royalty, to being a little bit of an outsider on this earth.

FLORENT: But I love her, Hartmann . . .

HARTMANN: That's where you broke the rules. Kings must never love anything but their delight.

FLORENT: It isn't only that. We don't understand her, Hartmann. That can't be the only thing that has hurt her so much.

HARTMANN (*quietly*): Yes, Florent, it is. You can believe me. I who really know her.

FLORENT *looks up and meets his eye. Instinctively, he steps back.*

FLORENT: What are you trying to say to me?

HARTMANN: When I met you I was an old man trying, with fumbling fingers, to wrest harmonies out of unresponding matter – a man lost in the hopeless quest for those celestial voices which you had already found, unaided, on the day you were born. (*A pause. He smiles.*) I didn't weep, I didn't scream in protest – I wasn't your sweetheart. But it had something of the same effect on me. I hated you.

FLORENT (*haltingly*): But what have you all got against me? I can't help it.

HARTMANN (*picking up his unlit pipe*): No. You can't help it. And now I'm only an old businessman who knows the exact measure of his musical potentialities and who is very fond of you. (*He knocks out his pipe to hide his emotion.*) It's funny, I never thought I should ever tell you that. But at least let it

help you not to leave her upstairs, packing her shabby little
suitcase, and sinking, deeper and deeper, all alone.

FLORENT: I'm afraid of seeing her look at me the way she
did just now. In five minutes I know it will be too late. But
what am I to do? Tell me. Tell me what to do . . .

HARTMANN looks away evasively. FLORENT *turns to him, his
face ravaged with grief, and murmurs:*

Oh God, help me.

HARTMANN: That may be the answer. To suffer and need help,
if you know how to learn.

He has moved to the doorway. He bumps into THÉRÈSE, *who is
wearing her outdoor clothes.*

THÉRÈSE (*in a small, level voice. She goes to* FLORENT): Good-bye,
Florent. (*She holds out her hand.*) I didn't want to slink away
like a coward. I can still look you in the face, you see. Don't
keep too sad a memory of me.

FLORENT (*mutters, without moving*): Good-bye, Thérèse . . .
Forgive me. I didn't know . . .

A pause. She looks at him.

THÉRÈSE (*quietly*): Why, you're crying.

He does not answer.

You know how to cry, then?

FLORENT (*mechanically wiping his cheek*): Am I? I'm sorry.

THÉRÈSE *looks at him for a little while.*

THÉRÈSE: So you aren't always sure of yourself, sure of the
happiness you spread, sure that all the policemen in heaven
and on earth are on your side?

FLORENT: I feel as ignorant and helpless as a father whose child
is dying of an unknown illness. You're in pain, and it's my
love that hurts you. You're in pain, and my love can't make
you well again. You talked of sufferings that I could never
know. Can you imagine this one?

THÉRÈSE (*gently*): If only you could try, just once, to be like everybody else – cowardly, petty, selfish, mean. Just once – couldn't you?

FLORENT: I can't.

THÉRÈSE: If you could try, instead of succeeding always, in everything you do, to carve out your niche painfully like other people, making a mess of it, and starting again – with sweat and pain and shame. If you could try, I might perhaps be set free?

FLORENT: I can't. It isn't easy, you know, to unlearn how to be happy. Before, I did feel sometimes that I was more privileged than other men, that I should never have to pay for anything with a tear or a cry. It suited me. Tonight, I've come to see that suffering too is a privilege that isn't given to all.

THÉRÈSE (*weeping for joy*): Oh, my dearest, you're unsure too! You're ashamed, you're unhappy. Why, then you aren't one of the truly rich! (*She picks a tear from* FLORENT'S *face.*) There. Look at it, all shining on my fingertip. What do I care about anything else now that you've paid me with a tear. Oh, why didn't you cry out and tell me you were weeping so I should feel less lonely!

FLORENT: I was afraid you wouldn't understand.

THÉRÈSE: Honestly? So you need to be understood – you need to be helped, then, too? And I was going away like a fool, without knowing it! (*She throws herself into his arms.*) Oh, need me, need me, if only for your meals and for your walks, the way a child does, if you don't need me like a man! Need me so that I shan't suffer too much!

FLORENT: I need you.

THÉRÈSE: That was another thing that hurt. You have so many things around you that watch over you and clothe you and keep you warm.

FLORENT: I need you, Thérèse.

THÉRÈSE: More than all your other joys?

FLORENT: More than all my other joys.

THÉRÈSE (*smiling*): Then call them back quickly! They don't

scare me now! (*Hiding her head on his breast.*) I lied, you know –
I love you. I love you as you are. Don't try to be like other
people. I don't care any more about not having friends or a
family, or a home. Ask your sister and your aunt to come
here. I know I shall love them. I'm clear, I'm crystal clear
too and rich! You are my home and my family and the air I
breathe and the sun that keeps me warm.

TARDE *comes in, carrying his overcoat and his two decrepit suitcases.*

TARDE: As God is my judge, I never wanted this. It broke my
heart to shut these two bags.

THÉRÈSE: Father! I'm happy! I'm happy, happy, happy,
Father!

TARDE: Good God! After a shindy like that I'd like to know
how you can manage to be happy!

THÉRÈSE: I'm happy because you're going away, Father, with
your two battered suitcases – and because I'm free of you at
last!

TARDE: Going away? Where to?

THÉRÈSE: Anywhere you like, Father! The farther away the
better!

TARDE (*pitifully*): But I'll come back for the wedding, won't I?

THÉRÈSE (*ringingly*): No, Father!

TARDE: But I say, girlie – your old dad . . .!

THÉRÈSE (*pitiless*): No, Father.

TARDE: Well . . . You'll be staying, will you?

THÉRÈSE: Yes, I'm staying! And I'm strong and I'm proud
and I'm young and I have all my life ahead of me in which to
be happy!

She is in FLORENT'S *arms, transfigured.* TARDE *has pathetically
picked up his two suitcases.*

Curtain

Act Three

Same set. Evening, but it is still fairly light outside. The sound of the piano is heard from time to time. THÉRÈSE *is standing in the middle of the room, being fitted for her wedding dress. The two workgirls are on their knees beside her.* MME BAZIN, *Florent's aunt, a sweet old lady in lace and ribbons and brooches, is sitting knitting on the veranda upstage.*

HARTMANN *is sitting in a far corner of the room, smoking his pipe. Outside, on the terrace behind* MME BAZIN, *three servants, among them the little scullery maid, are staring wide-eyed at* THÉRÈSE.

MME BAZIN (*to the servants*): Now, be off with you. You've seen enough for one evening. You can gaze your fill on the day of the wedding.

THE HEAD HOUSEMAID (*to the scullery maid, who is still standing entranced*): Come along, you! Don't stand there, gawping! You shouldn't be here in the first place. You know you're not allowed into the master's garden. Now then, back to your kitchen and look sharp about it. (*To* MME BAZIN.) I do apologize, madam. She followed me in without my noticing.

MME BAZIN: I can't understand it. She always knew her place before.

MAID: Madam is right. I don't know what's got into her lately. She's always nosing about where she shouldn't. I'm very sorry, madam, I'll see it doesn't occur again.

She goes.

MME BAZIN: The evenings are drawing in already.

A pause.

FITTER (*to the girls*): Spread the train right out. (*To* THÉRÈSE.) We can see the whole effect so much better down here than in your room, mademoiselle. Now, we must hurry if we don't want to miss the train back.

MARIE (*yawning*): You've been at it for hours! I wanted to teach you to play tennis. I do think it's eccentric of you not to play.

THÉRÈSE: Yes.

MARIE: If only there were a river anywhere near. I'm simply dying to get on to the water again. I haven't done any rowing since I left England in May.

Another pause.

FITTER: Give me those pins.

MARIE: Have you ever been to England?

THÉRÈSE: No.

MARIE: I've just spent three years there. I went to an absolutely marvellous school. You can't imagine how different it is! What a shame your parents didn't send you there. There's nothing like it for teaching a girl about life.

THÉRÈSE (*gently*): There are one or two other ways, you know.

MARIE: Oh, of course. But in France we're so strictly brought up, we're dumbbells until the day we get married. There is one way, of course, if your parents aren't too old-fashioned – and that's to go out to work. But that's easier said than done.

FITTER: Mademoiselle is unfortunately right. Another fifty girls were dismissed this season from Monsieur Lapérouse's.

MARIE: Oh, it isn't that so much. With a little influence one can always get some sort of job. I meant family objections. There are still some parents who look on work as degrading for a girl. I can't think why! I think working is absolutely marvellous, don't you?

THÉRÈSE (*with a faint smile*): It depends. One should always work at something one likes very much, like Florent.

MARIE: Oh, no, artists don't count! I meant proper work. A well-paid job in a bank, say, or an insurance company.

MME BAZIN: Well, all my life I've never stopped working –
knitting, tapestry, crochet work or whatever it happened to
be – and I must say, I've thrived on it. It's funny, but I'm
not happy unless I'm doing something. Now, I pay two
gardeners, but do you know, I often cut my own flowers in
the morning.

MARIE: The main thing about working, though, is that it gives
a girl complete independence.

THÉRÈSE: You do a lot of clockwatching, you know, in an
office or a workroom.

FITTER: Mademoiselle is so right! Monsieur Lapérouse has
quite a novel way of solving that problem. He's had all the
clocks in the establishment removed and none of the girls
is allowed to wear a watch.

THÉRÈSE (*lifting the chin of the little workgirl kneeling at her feet*):
Tell her that one doesn't have fun every day of the week at
Lapérouse's.

FITTER: Oh, I can assure you, all our girls are very contented
with their lot, mademoiselle – very contented indeed!

THÉRÈSE (*smiling gently at the little workgirl*): I'm sure they are.

MME BAZIN: When I was a girl, seamstresses used to work
sixteen hours a day. They were worse off than they are now,
of course, but on the other hand, one felt much more inclined
to give them things. Many's the dress I've given to the
women who used to come and work at home, and very good,
wearable dresses they were too. Nowadays, it wouldn't occur
to one. The working classes are better off than we are these days.

MARIE: Darling Thérèse! You really are terribly old-fashioned!
I suppose you think a young lady's place is in the home!
Didn't it ever bore you, sitting at home all day?

THÉRÈSE (*smiling*): Oh, mine was rather an unusual home, you
know.

MME BAZIN: You're quite right, Thérèse. Stand up to her.
Marie's nothing but a little socialist!

MARIE: Of course I am! I think every girl should go out to
work. It's good for the soul. One must move with the times,
Aunt Caroline!

MME BAZIN: That's what we used to say in my day too. But that was mostly so Mamma would let us ride a bicycle.

MARIE: But those days are over! The upper classes aren't the salt of the earth now. All men were created equal, and man's lot is to earn his bread by the sweat of his brow!

FITTER: I'm inclined to agree. The modern girl should earn her own living. Unfortunately, far too few of them have given the matter sufficient thought.

THÉRÈSE (*to the girl*): I hope you gave the matter sufficient thought before you went to work at Monsieur Lapérouse's?

FITTER (*with a polite little laugh*): Mademoiselle will have her little joke . . . Besides, I quite see that in your case our little controversy doesn't apply. A married lady has a house to run, social engagements to fulfil. But in Mademoiselle France's circumstances, I do definitely think a young lady should have a job. As a matter of fact, Monsieur Lapérouse has made a special study of outfits exclusively for the working girl. He is bringing out two models this season, one of sea-green broadcloth trimmed with mink, called 'Forty Hour Week', and the other, rather more formal in heavy midnight blue faille, worn with just the one, utterly simple diamond clip, which he has christened 'Miss Trade Unionist'.

MME BAZIN: Odd how the language changes. In my day trade unionists were people who blew up railway trains.

FITTER: Because, of course, it *is* quite a problem. The young lady who goes out to work in the afternoon simply hasn't time to change for the odd cocktail party or informal dinner. The problem was to create a model which would be equally suitable for office, restaurant, cinema – or, at a pinch, one of the smaller theatres. I'm sure Monsieur Lapérouse would be delighted to send someone along with the two models, should you proceed with your plans.

MARIE: Thank you. But I don't aim to start work before next season. During the summer months, with invitations literally flooding in, it really can't be managed. In October, if he has anything interesting, I'll be glad to have a look at it.

FITTER: I'll tell Monsieur Lapérouse. Leontine – take that

thread out, will you? (*To* THÉRÈSE.) Would you like a rest, mademoiselle?

THÉRÈSE: No.

FITTER: We've nearly finished; one has to be so careful of the hem, it is so very tricky . . . (*To* MARIE.) I do hope your decision doesn't mean that you will give up the idea of that delicious little skiing outfit I was telling you about.

MARIE: Oh, I shall still take a month's holiday in January. I don't believe in being too rigid.

FITTER: I'm so glad! It would break my heart to see anybody else wear it! It might have been designed for you!

MARIE: Another advantage of having a job is that I can pay for it myself. There won't be any recriminations over what I spend this time. I shall pay my hotel bills and buy my clothes out of my own money.

FITTER: That is the working girl's great strength.

MARIE: Of course! Shopgirls and typists envy us, but they don't know their luck. Think of the freedom your own money gives you, money you've actually earned yourself! If they only knew the cheese-paring that goes on in the best French families!

THÉRÈSE (*to the girl*): You see, I bet you never guessed how lucky you were.

MARIE: But it's obvious! Look, I know a girl who's been working as a secretary in a bank for the last year. I've never been allowed to have my own car. She's just brought herself a little two-seater!

THÉRÈSE: And she's a secretary? She must have a wonderful job.

MARIE: Well, to tell the truth, her father is paying half.

THÉRÈSE: Ah, I see.

MARIE: She and a girl friend are going on a motor tour through Italy and Greece.

THÉRÈSE: But what about the bank? Will she have a long enough holiday?

MARIE: Of course. It's her uncle's bank.

THÉRÈSE: Ah, that's all right, then.

MME BAZIN: I don't care what you say, dear, I just don't see the fun of working for other people. I simply don't understand how any self-respecting person can take orders from strangers. I've been my own mistress all my life and very proud of it I am too!

FITTER: There. If you could bear to wait five minutes, mademoiselle, we must just put the finishing touches to the little jacket. Then you can see the whole effect. Come along, you two. We must hurry if we want to catch that train.

She makes for the door, followed by her two girls. THÉRÈSE *runs after the little workgirl and takes hold of her arm.*

THÉRÈSE: Wait a minute. . . . (*To the* FITTER.) Do you mind? I should like a word with this child.

FITTER: Certainly, mademoiselle. Leontine, join us in the linen room, will you?

She goes.

THÉRÈSE (*drawing the girl into a corner*): Leontine – that is your name, isn't it?

GIRL: Yes.

THÉRÈSE: How old are you?

GIRL: Fourteen, I'm small for my age. There are five of us at home. I'm the smallest.

THÉRÈSE: I'm making you work late tonight, for my dress.

GIRL: It won't be the first time, don't you worry. This time it's rather fun, coming out into the country.

THÉRÈSE: Listen, Leontine – I only wanted to say . . . I know it isn't true what they were saying. It's tiring, having to work, and it's dull and it goes on day in day out. So . . . I don't quite know how to say this – I expect you'll think it's silly. That dress costs so much, and I'll only wear it once. A whole year of your wages at Lapérouse . . . Listen . . . (*She leans over and whispers.*) Leontine, forgive me for the dress. (*She pushes her out.*) Run along now, quick. And don't look at me like that! It's nothing to laugh at . . .

The girl runs out. MME BAZIN *peers at her over her spectacles.*

MME BAZIN: It's frightening, how thin those little things are. But there, what can you expect? I've seen them in Paris, lunching off coffee and a roll. They would rather buy a lipstick than a good thick steak. Most foolish. I'm old now and I have to watch my diet, but when I was young, I couldn't for the life of me have gone without red meat.

THÉRÈSE *turns abruptly as if to say something. She meets* HART-MANN'S *eye, as he sits smiling behind his pipe. She stops and smiles too.*

(*Gathering up her things.*) There. That's done. It takes me weeks to make these woollies. I was never a very good knitter. I keep dropping stitches, oh dear! But the poor are so grateful when they know that one has knitted them one-self! (*To* MARIE.) All this talk about earning your own pocket money! You know perfectly well that if you would knit for my slum comforts fund I would give you three thousand francs for each woolly.

MARIE *shrugs. This is evidently an old argument.*

Ah, these modern girls don't bother their heads about charity the way we old ones do. We were brought up to worry a great deal about the poor. But they? All they think of is clothes and motor-cars. (*She gets up.*) I'm going to look at those new rose bushes before it gets quite dark. I don't trust that gardener of Florent's. They need constant attention. You'll call me in when they bring the jacket, Thérèse, won't you? (*To* MARIE.) Will you keep me company, child?

MARIE (*rising*): If you like, Aunt.

MME BAZIN (*leaning on her shoulder as she goes out*): Those poor wretches are always so short of winter woollies. If you'd agreed to join my knitting party, I'd have given you as much as four thousand francs a garment. You'll never earn as much as that in a bank.

They go.

HARTMANN (*smiling*): H'm. I think we came very near to a little righteous intervention then, eh?

THÉRÈSE (*smiling too*): I don't mind for myself any more. Only I was ashamed, because of that little girl. I'm a fool.

HARTMANN: You're never a fool, Thérèse.

A pause. They listen. FLORENT *is heard playing next door.*

THÉRÈSE (*murmuring, with a smile full of tenderness*): How well he plays . . . He's happy, isn't he? I *am* trying.

HARTMANN: Yes, he's happy.

THÉRÈSE: I want to believe in him, Hartmann. I want to believe in them. I want to understand. Before, I never even tried. I used to say, I'm too young. I'll understand when I'm old. I wanted to rebel with all my might. Now . . .

HARTMANN: Now?

THÉRÈSE: (*smiling*): I'm trying.

A pause.

But why are they so charming, so open, and yet so heartless without knowing it? I try, often, to chat with Marie. We're the same age. It's funny, we have nothing to say to each other. Madame Bazin gives me little talks about life, sometimes. I feel like an old woman beside her. I'm the one who's chary of teaching her too much.

HARTMANN (*taking her hand*): How calmly you say that now.

THÉRÈSE (*smiling*): I've stormed so much. . . . Oh, those six days, those six horrible days! Sometimes, it was as if a great horse were rearing up inside me. (*A pause. She says dreamily.*) He's run away. He's a long, long way off now. I mustn't be sorry he's gone. He was an evil beast.

HARTMANN: Don't say that, Thérèse. He was a good horse, noble and black and proud. Letting him go was the price you paid for your happiness. That damned happiness he fought so shy of, do you remember? I'm sure it has begun to wrap itself around you, hasn't it – that damned happiness?

THÉRÈSE: It's true. I need their warmth now that they've taken away my own. But what a strange game it is, that happiness of theirs . . .

HARTMANN: You must learn to play your part in it, Thérèse.

THÉRÈSE: I am learning. Already I feel bathed in ease and sweetness. I feel less hard. Less pure too. I can feel quietude making its steady inroads in me day by day. I don't seek into the heart of things any more. I understand, I explain, I make few demands . . . I'm growing less vulnerable too, I'm sure. Soon, all the little tongues of pain in me will have slithered away like lizards under stones, and I'll have nothing but small birdlike sorrows, just like them.

HARTMANN: Soon? Aren't they all gone yet?

THÉRÈSE (*still smiling*): Hush! Listen . . . How easy everything is when he plays . . . Every note sets something back into its ideal place. Oh, it's a wonderful feat of organization, that happiness of theirs! Evil becomes a wicked angel you grapple gaily with for practice and which you always crush. Poverty, a chance to prove your goodness by being charitable. Work a pleasant pastime for the leisurely. And love . . . this smooth delight, without fears, or doubts, or heartache. Listen to the way he plays, Hartmann, without asking himself anything, ever. I am only one joy among his other joys. As soon as he thought he'd shut me up inside his happiness – having shed his little tear – he never felt another pang of doubt about any mortal thing. He is as sure of me as he is of everything . . . (*She adds in a murmur.*) I who am so unsure.

HARTMANN: He loves you, Thérèse.

THÉRÈSE: I want to believe it, Hartmann, I do, I do! But that tear he shed for my sake – oh, I wish I could have kept it in a little box . . . It dried and now I've nothing.

HARTMANN: You have your anxiety and your love . . . That's the best part.

THÉRÈSE: Hartmann, he doesn't even need my love, he's much too rich . . . (*She stiffens suddenly.*) Oh, but I'm not tamed yet! There are still some things that I refuse to understand!

She stops short. The little SCULLERY MAID *is creeping along the terrace, gazing hungrily at* THÉRÈSE. *One can feel that she is afraid of being caught in the forbidden stretch of garden. As* THÉRÈSE *turns round she runs away, stammering in her confusion.*

MAID: Oh, I'm sorry, mademoiselle. I was just going through—

She vanishes.

HARTMANN: Have you never noticed what she does? Every night she braves that forbidden stretch of garden – for you. She runs the risk of a scolding or dismissal, but she's shut up all day in the kitchen, and if only for a few seconds every night, she wants to see you, to draw her sustenance from you. You are her idol, Thérèse.

THÉRÈSE: Me? But that's absurd!

HARTMANN: She must think you so beautiful, and clean and scented. She doesn't have you one single minute to herself, yet she doesn't rebel against her lot.

THÉRÈSE: But, Hartmann. . . .

HARTMANN: And who knows, maybe she has a dog tied up in the yard, which waits for her each night, and thrives on a brief glimpse of her, and which she doesn't even notice.

A pause. FLORENT *is heard playing.*

THÉRÈSE (*quietly*): It's good of you to help me, Hartmann. But how one has to scrape away the remnants of one's pride to love like this.

HARTMANN: Take life as it comes. You'll see, little by little, a strange thing will work a change inside you. You'll grow to think in the way they do, quite naturally. I was a human being pitted against the world myself once. But the serene days glided over me, one after the other. You'll see, soon you won't feel any pain at all. Soon, you'll ask nothing more from them but a warm corner in their joy.

A pause.

THÉRÈSE: But that's a little bit like being dead.

HARTMANN: A little.

THÉRÈSE: I love him, I don't mind being a dead thing beside him. But what about you, Hartmann? He told me you had money of your own, that you don't need to be his manager.

HARTMANN (*quietly*): I love the god that dwells in his hands.

A pause. FLORENT *is still playing.* THÉRÈSE *is curled up in a deep arm-chair. Suddenly she says in a small voice:*

THÉRÈSE: The important thing is never to think that there are others who live and fight and die . . . I shall stay here all my life and when I go out it will always be with them, in their handsome trains and aeroplanes and their fine hotels with their silky-smooth head waiters – won't I, Hartmann?

HARTMANN: Yes, Thérèse.

THÉRÈSE: My eyes will only rest where theirs do, on flowers, and precious stones and kindly faces. And I'll become translucent and serene too, just like them – and not know anything any more. (*She repeats it, like a wonderstruck child.*) To know nothing . . . That must be good, Hartmann, to know nothing any more.

HARTMANN: Yes, Thérèse.

THÉRÈSE: Happiness is a knack the clever ones have; the ones who know the ropes. But don't worry, I'll learn it too.

HARTMANN (*with a hint of nostalgia*): Yes, Thérèse, you'll learn it too.

The HEAD HOUSEMAID *comes rushing in.*

HOUSEMAID: Mademoiselle! Mademoiselle! Your father has just arrived!

THÉRÈSE (*turning pale*): My father?

HOUSEMAID: Yes, mademoiselle. He looks most upset. He says he must see you at once.

HARTMANN: I'll leave you, Thérèse. If you should need me, I'll be in the garden.

He goes out. TARDE *comes in greatly agitated. He makes a sweeping gesture which* THÉRÈSE'S *attitude cuts short. The* HOUSEMAID *goes.* TARDE *repeats the same gesture with rather less abandon.*

THÉRÈSE: Well, what is it?

TARDE: It's horrible!

THÉRÈSE: What is? I told you you weren't to come here.

TARDE: It's horrible – horrible I tell you! Your poor mother . . .

THÉRÈSE: What about her?

TARDE: Oh, my God!

THÉRÈSE: Speak, can't you? Is she hurt? Dead?

TARDE: All but! She fell on the corner of the piano.

THÉRÈSE: And you've come all this way to tell me that?

TARDE: Oh, you are a heartless girl! She fell on her head, half dead – and why? I'll tell you why! Oh, the shame, the disgrace! She had a lover.

THÉRÈSE: What?

TARDE: Gosta.

THÉRÈSE: But you've known that for the last thirteen years!

TARDE: Nobody else did. Now every Tom, Dick and Harry knows it. A public scandal – a ghastly shindy right on the bandstand – a shouting and a yelling such as you never heard! I feel hot with shame now as I think of it. Gosta gave her a punch on the nose. It was on account of you, needless to say. I wasn't there, Lord be praised. (*A pause.*) When I came out of the toilet—

THÉRÈSE: You mean you were hiding in the toilet?

TARDE: I happened to be in the toilet, that's all. When I came out, he'd left – in the middle of the performance, as usual – and your mother was coming to. It seems he said he was going to kill your young man. He took his revolver. You know me. Quick as a flash, I leapt into a cab! A train! Another cab! There's two hundred francs for the first cab, five hundred and fifty for the train fare – had to take a first class. It was an express – no seconds and thirds. Taxi number two from the station, three hundred and twenty, plus tip . . . it's waiting outside . . . In the excitement I came away without a cent . . .

He pats his pockets for the look of the thing. THÉRÈSE *does not move. He pats his pockets again.*

The clock's ticking up . . . If you could let me have . . .
I'll just go and settle up with him. . . .

THÉRÈSE: Oh, be quiet. You'll get your money.

TARDE (*frantic at the thought*): But . . . the meter's running—

THÉRÈSE: Let it run.

TARDE: You don't seem very pleased to see me. You might
thank me for missing a show to come and warn you. You
know how the management feels about replacements. Gosta
flinging out – now me – your mother with her head done up
in gauze and sticking plaster . . . We'll get the push from
there too, I shouldn't wonder.

THÉRÈSE (*almost imploringly*): Be quiet. Please be quiet. I'll
give you all the money you want, only be quiet!

TARDE: Right.

THÉRÈSE (*after a pause*): Has Gosta been very unhappy since I left?

TARDE: A wreck. He hasn't stopped drinking. He'd even given
up knocking your Ma about, that shows you! This'll make
you laugh! – One night, I found him crying like a baby over
the little quilted cover you used to put over your fiddle – you
remember, that red satin thing he gave you years ago.

THÉRÈSE: Is that true?

TARDE: What a character! That makes two fights he's had
over you. The first time was with old Lebonze, over some
remark he made about you. Between you and me, I wasn't
at all sorry at his giving that old blood-sucker his ticket.
Do you know the old bastard didn't pay us our full money?
We had to drag him to court over it. Anyhow, that's another
story. The second time was with the waiter over at the Royal.
You know, the lanky dark fellow – big chin, flat nose.
Sniggered and asked Gosta how you were keeping. That time
it wasn't funny. Gosta seized a soda syphon, the other one
pulled out a knife. They ended up in the police station.
Imagine the name the band is getting with all this. And here
am I, working my fingers to the bone . . . However, after
that little flare-up, I thought we'd have a bit of peace. What
a hope! This afternoon, your Ma, the great fool, goes and
tells him you were very happy down here.

THÉRÈSE: And he hit her because of that?

TARDE: Just because of that, girlie, without a word of a lie.

THÉRÈSE: But what business is it of his whether I'm happy or not!

TARDE: You took the words out of my mouth, girlie. (*Suddenly remembering the taxi.*) But look, there's no point in keeping the taxi waiting – the meter's ticking up . . . If you could give me—

THÉRÈSE (*in sudden anguish*): Why did you have to come and tell me all this, Father?

TARDE: Are you serious? You're my daughter. He's my son-in-law, at least, my future son-in-law. I wasn't going to stand by and see you murdered! We must call the police! Personally, I don't mind telling you I'd as soon Gosta didn't know I came. So if you could give me. . . . There's a train back in half an hour . . . (*A pause. He adds, in spite of himself*) and the taxi is outside. I shan't have to pay the starting charge because, as I said, he didn't stop his . . . (*He mimes the action.*)

THÉRÈSE (*looking up, vacantly*): What?

TARDE (*repeating it with an effort*): I said if I took the taxi on to the station now, I shouldn't have to pay a second starting charge, because he didn't stop his meter.

THÉRÈSE (*incoherently*): Why did you come, Father?

TARDE: You are a funny girl. I came here, regardless of danger and at considerable expense, because I thought it was my duty. If you could give me two hundred and fifty plus six hundred and fifty plus three hundred and twenty plus, say four hundred – that comes to—

THÉRÈSE: Here's two thousand. Now be quiet.

TARDE (*the shrewd businessman*): But you're forgetting the return journey, my lass.

THÉRÈSE: Here, here . . .

TARDE: Now you've given me too much! (*He pats his pockets.*) I haven't any change. I'll send you a postal order, or would you rather have cash?

THÉRÈSE: He was weeping on my little red cover?

TARDE (*wheezing with mirth*): Like a baby! (*Seeing that* THÉRÈSE *is not laughing.*) Well, like a desperate man . . . (*anxious again*) a desperate man who'll be here in five minutes! With those automatics they use nowadays, they're none too fussy about the number of corpses. If you don't want a bloodbath, you'd better do something! (*He pulls out his watch.*) As for me, if I don't want to miss that train . . .

THÉRÈSE (*murmuring*): Gosta is on the march now too. All the figures of my past will have come here, one by one, to take me back.

TARDE: I hope, when he does come, you'll see to it he'll find a couple of coppers ready to slip the bracelets on! Blubbing is one thing, but larking about with loaded firearms is another. Who does he think he is?

THÉRÈSE: Yes, who does he think he is, who do you think you are, all of you?

TARDE: He's your mother's fancy man – all right. Let him act his love drama with her – God help us! – if he's that short of fun. But you, my little pretty! To come badgering *you,* under your fiancé's roof, the night you're trying on your chaste white dress! It's gorgeous, by the way. But I'm beginning to have doubts about everything now. You're sure you never slept with Gosta?

THÉRÈSE (*smiling despite herself*): Quite sure, Father.

TARDE: Then what does he hope to achieve? When he's fired his shots here, whether he hits your young man or not – I ask you, where will it get him? What will he gain by it?

THÉRÈSE: The certainty of having lost me, irrevocably, at last. Of having reached the farthest limits of his pain. You may not know it, but at the far end of despair, there is a white clearing where one is almost happy.

TARDE: Queer sort of happiness.

THÉRÈSE: Yes, Father, a frightful happiness. A foul, a shameful happiness. (*She clings to him, suddenly, seized with panic.*) But I don't want it any more! I want to be happy! I want to be happy like everybody else! I don't want to know anything more about you all!

The HOUSEMAID *comes in.*

HOUSEMAID: Mademoiselle, there's another gentleman asking
   to see you.
TARDE (*yelling*): Gentleman? – what sort of gentleman? Who
   is it, for God's sake?

GOSTA *appears.*

GOSTA: It's me, Thérèse.
THÉRÈSE (*to the maid*): Leave us.

The HOUSEMAID *goes out.*

GOSTA (*dully*): Where's your fiancé?

He steps forward. TARDE *backs away and puts up his hands.*

TARDE (*yelling*): Not me, Gosta! Not me! I haven't done any-
   thing! I just dropped in – by chance – by chance – quite by
   chance! (*He tries to scream, but his voice breaks.*) Help! Police!
GOSTA: Shut your trap, you!
TARDE (*cringing behind* THÉRÈSE): Yes, I will, I will! This is
   none of my business! I'll just keep my trap shut!
GOSTA: Where is your fiancé?
THÉRÈSE: Take your hand out of your pocket, Gosta.
GOSTA: Where is your fiancé? I want to talk to him.
THÉRÈSE: Gosta, do as I say.
TARDE (*safe in his corner*): Go on, do as she says!
GOSTA: Where's your fiancé, Thérèse?
THÉRÈSE (*struggling with him*): Take your hand out of your
   pocket, I tell you! Take your hand out and give me that!
TARDE (*from the other end of the room*): Careful, girlie – careful,
   now!
GOSTA (*trying to shake her off*): Thérèse, let me alone.
THÉRÈSE (*panting*): Give me that gun! Don't fight with me,
   Gosta, or I'll send a bullet through my heart! That's what
   you want, isn't it? Isn't it? (*She snatches the gun away.*)
TARDE: Phew!
THÉRÈSE: Now look at me.

GOSTA *hangs his head.*

Look at me, Gosta.

GOSTA *looks up.*

You wanted to kill him.
GOSTA: Yes.
THÉRÈSE: Why?

A pause. GOSTA *looks away.*

Why? Answer me.
GOSTA: I don't know.
TARDE (*exploding, now quite reassured*): Oh, that's rich, that is! He doesn't know! Give me that gun, girlie, give it to me.

He takes the weapon and puts it in his pocket. A pause.

GOSTA (*in a murmur*): I'm a brute to have come, Thérèse. Call your young man and tell him to kick me out. It's all I deserve.
THÉRÈSE (*in a hard voice*): No, I won't have him think that someone had sufficient claims on me to come here and make a scene. Go of your own accord.
GOSTA: You're right. I'm not even worth a scene.
THÉRÈSE (*quietly*): I've never loved you, Gosta. Even if I'd never met him, I could never have loved you. Did you think of that when you came here?
GOSTA: Yes, I thought of that.
THÉRÈSE: And you came just the same?
GOSTA: I've been hanging about outside the drive gates for half an hour.
THÉRÈSE: Then why did you come in? I don't want to see you. I'm happy, do you hear? I don't want anything more to do with you and your bundle of woes! I love him, do you hear? I love him. What are you doing here, with your wretchedness exposed for all to see? And how dare you smile when I say I love him? You're ugly, Gosta, you're useless, you're lazy. You're always saying you could have done better than anybody else, but you've never done a thing.

GOSTA (*looking intensely at her*): No, Thérèse.

THÉRÈSE: You spend all your money on liquor because when you're drunk you imagine you could do something in life. You've only one suit left to wear and you're proud of that, too, because you think a coat that's out at elbows and covered in stains is the hall-mark of a genius. Well, that courage, that strength you feel so full of, might perhaps consist in giving up drink and buying yourself some shoes.

TARDE: Girlie, girlie, don't exasperate him!

THÉRÈSE: Your hands shake on the keyboard, you strike wrong notes more and more often, don't you? Well, your love, your great love of music, might perhaps be to stop drinking and to practise every day.

GOSTA: Yes, Thérèse.

THÉRÈSE: Your love for me might have prompted you not to come here, too. You seized that revolver and you set out, like an avenging hero bent on justice. Well, I'll tell you what that justice of yours was, if you don't already know it. It was your hatred. The hatred of a failure for all that's finer and cleverer than you!

GOSTA: That's not true, Thérèse!

THÉRÈSE: It is true! (*Crying out.*) Do you think I don't know everything that goes on in your mind? I know it all, better than you do yourself!

A pause. GOSTA *hangs his head. She goes on in a strange, hoarse voice.*

The vanity – the odious conceit of it! I'll sympathize, I'll willingly feel sorry for you, but if you thought our squalor, our misery, our grime were tokens of nobility, you made a big mistake.

GOSTA (*dully*): And you can say that, Thérèse?

THÉRÈSE: Yes. I can and I do. What else have you to say to me?

GOSTA: Nothing. You're right, Thérèse.

THÉRÈSE: Then go away! Get out, both of you ! I want to be happy and never think of you again! You're unhappy, but

I don't care! I found my own way out of it! You're ugly
and unwashed and you're full of dirty thoughts and the rich
are quite right to hurry past you in the street! Get out! Get
out quickly! Get out of my sight! (*Suddenly she collapses on the
sofa, sobbing, and moans.*) Oh, go away for pity's sake! Can't
you see I'm weak with the ache of carrying you in my heart!

*She slips on to the floor, sobbing like a child. The two men look at
her, speechless, not daring to move. The music starts again next
door.* GOSTA *stands listening. Gradually,* THÉRÈSE'S *sobs die
down.*

GOSTA: Who's that playing?
THÉRÈSE (*softly*): It's he.

A pause.

GOSTA: Is it his own stuff he's playing?
THÉRÈSE: Yes, it's his.
GOSTA (*after another pause*): How does he do it?
THÉRÈSE: That's the way he does everything, Gosta – without
taking pains, without spoiling it or starting again. Without
heartache . . .

Another pause. The music sweeps over them.

GOSTA: How does he do it, Thérèse? I sweat and strain and
score out and start afresh and everything slips through my
fingers.

Another silence, filled with music. GOSTA *moves at last. He goes
to* THÉRÈSE *and says soberly:*

You must forget us. We ought never to have shown our
ugly faces here. But it won't be long now. We'll go out into
the garden, you'll see us walk through that patch of light
and then the dark will close around us. We'll be dead and
you'll have peace at last.

They stand listening a while longer, as the music swells. Then GOSTA
breaks out of the spell and goes to the door.

Thérèse, one day, later on, tell him I came to kill him and that I went away again.

TARDE *follows him, an old, decrepit figure suddenly.*

TARDE: And you can tell him, girlie, that I've been thinking it over about the money and I'll try and give him back a part of it . . .

The FITTER *and her girls come in again.* TARDE *sees them and takes* GOSTA *by the arm.*

Come on, let's go. No need for anyone to see us here.

He pulls GOSTA *away and they both disappear.*

FITTER (*very bright and talkative*): There we are! I kept you waiting, mademoiselle. I do apologize. We'll just slip the little jacket on, then you can see the whole ensemble. It simply makes the dress! (*To the little workgirl.*) Come along, wake up! (*They set to work.*) Oh, this will be the wedding of the year!

THÉRÈSE (*like a sleepwalker throughout this scene*): Yes.

FITTER: What colour are the bridesmaids wearing?

THÉRÈSE: Rose pink.

FITTER: Monsieur Lapérouse was so sorry not to be doing their dresses. I must tell you he had an utterly entrancing idea for them! But he quite understands, Mademoiselle France has her own loyalties. There are six of them, I believe?

THÉRÈSE: Yes.

FITTER: Too enchanting! They manage to achieve quite deliciously elegant ceremonies in those little country churches. There will be little children to carry the train, no doubt?

THÉRÈSE: Four little boys.

FITTER: Oh, how adorable! And the flowers, and the music and the colour! You'll have planned a divine honeymoon trip, I'm sure? Oh, I'm being very indiscreet – do forgive me!

THÉRÈSE: Switzerland and Italy.

FITTER: Switzerland and Italy. The classic honeymoon, but

there's still nothing to touch it. May I wish you both joy?
I'm sure you'll be quite blissfully happy!

THÉRÈSE (*murmuring*): Blissfully happy, yes . . .

She shudders and slips away from them.

Please – leave me for a second, could you? I'd like to be
alone . . .

FITTER: But, mademoiselle—

THÉRÈSE: Please . . . leave me alone. . . . The dress is fine.
Please . . .

FITTER: But our train goes in half an hour and this is the final
fitting!

THÉRÈSE: I tell you it fits very well . . . Go up to the linen
room, I'll join you. I'll come straight up, I promise. Only
leave me now – leave me . . .

FITTER (*tight lipped*): As mademoiselle wishes. (*Venting her
irritation on the little girl.*) Well, don't sit there dreaming!
Pick up your pins! You'll make us miss that train!

They go out. THÉRÈSE *takes off her bridal wreath and goes out,
quickly. Next door, the music stops.*
A pause. FLORENT *comes in.*

FLORENT: Who are you talking to, Thérèse?

*He glances round the empty room, then goes on to the veranda and
looks out. When he comes back,* THÉRÈSE *has come in again,
wearing her outdoor clothes, and carrying the wedding dress over her
arm. She lays it on the sofa.*

I was looking for you. Where are you going, darling?

THÉRÈSE: Only into the garden for a minute.

FLORENT: You've put your coat on. But it's so warm . . .

THÉRÈSE (*softly*): I felt a little chilly.

FLORENT (*drawing her to him*): I went through the details of
our trip with Hartmann this afternoon. I want to take you
to all the places that I've loved. There's a rock I know on
Lake Lucerne where we'll go and sit, early in the morning,
before the sun comes up. And there's a painting of a little

Renaissance princess, who looks like you, that we'll go and look at in the Uffizi together.

THÉRÈSE: Yes, my darling . . .

FLORENT: Oh, I feel so happy tonight . . . It's a beautiful evening. And you?

THÉRÈSE (*smiling with difficulty*): Yes, my darling, I'm happy too. Were you working?

FLORENT: Did you hear me? The andante is shaping well.

THÉRÈSE: Go back and play, darling.

FLORENT: Will you listen to me out in the garden?

THÉRÈSE: Yes, my darling. Go quickly, go and play. You're dying to – I can tell from your eyes.

FLORENT (*giving her a light kiss*). It's going beautifully. I'm very happy . . .

THÉRÈSE: Yes, my dearest.

He goes. THÉRÈSE *stands a moment without moving. Then she says gently:*

You see, Florent, it wouldn't be any use cheating. However tight I shut my eyes, there will always be a stray dog somewhere in the world who'll stop me being happy.

The music starts again next door. She touches the beautiful white dress in a brief, unfinished caress and murmurs, turning towards the room where FLORENT *is playing, as if she still had many things to say.*

You see . . .

But she stops, turns abruptly and goes out into the night. The wedding dress lies on the couch, a dazzling patch of whiteness in the gloom.

HARTMANN *has appeared, unobtrusively, at the top of the stairs. He has watched* THÉRÈSE *go, without a word. He stands quite still a moment, looking through the windows and following her with his eyes as she disappears through the dark grounds.*

HARTMANN (*in a murmur*): There she goes, small, and strong and lucid, to pit herself against all the sharp corners in the world.

The music swells next door.

Curtain

Traveller without Luggage

Characters

GASTON

THE DUCHESS

MONSIEUR HUSPAR

MADAME RENAUD

GEORGES RENAUD

VALENTINE RENAUD

THE BUTLER

THE VALET

THE CHAUFFEUR

THE COOK

JULIETTE

A SMALL BOY

MR TRUGGLE

Original Title: Le Voyageur sans Bagage
Translator: Lucienne Hill
First produced in 1936

Act One

The drawing-room of a well-appointed house in a provincial town in France, with an extensive view over gardens.

When the curtain rises the stage is empty. Then the BUTLER *ushers in the* DUCHESS DUPONT-DUFORT, M. HUSPAR *and* GASTON.

BUTLER: What name shall I say?

DUCHESS: Duchess Dupont-Dufort, my lawyer, M. Huspar, and Monsieur – (*She hesitates.*) – Gaston. (*To* HUSPAR.) We'll have to call him that, for the time being.

BUTLER (*who seems aware of the situation*): I hope your ladyship will excuse M. and Mme Renaud, but M. and Mme Renaud were not expecting your ladyship until the eleven-fifty train. I will tell M. and Mme Renaud that your ladyship is here.

He goes.

DUCHESS (*watching him go*): Perfect butler, that. Oh, Gaston, my dear, I'm so wildly happy. I was positive you'd be the son of an excellent family.

HUSPAR: Don't get too carried away. We have five other possible families besides these Renauds, remember.

DUCHESS: No, no, Huspar. Gaston will recognize these Renauds as his own people, I know it! He will rediscover the flavour of his past here, in this house. Something tells me this is where he'll get his memory back. That something is my feminine intuition and it has seldom let me down.

HUSPAR (*bowing before such irrefutable logic*): In that case . . .

GASTON *has been moving round the room, oblivious of them, and looking at the pictures, like a child out visiting.*

DUCHESS (*calling to him*): Well, Gaston? You're excited, I hope?

GASTON: Not much.

DUCHESS (*sighing*): Not much. Ah, my dear boy, I wonder sometimes if you realize quite how poignant your case is.

GASTON: But, Duchess—

DUCHESS: No, no, no. Nothing you can say will make me alter my opinion. You don't realize, you just don't realize. Now you don't, do you? Admit it.

GASTON: Perhaps I don't, not very well.

DUCHESS (*satisfied*): That's better. You're a charming person and you'll always admit you're wrong, I will say that for you. But that doesn't alter the fact that this casual attitude, this total lack of interest on your part, is extremely reprehensible. Isn't it, Huspar?

HUSPAR: Why, I—

DUCHESS: It is, it is, it is! You really must back me up and make him see that he's got to be excited.

GASTON *has turned back to the pictures on the wall.*

Gaston?

GASTON: Duchess?

DUCHESS: Are you made of stone?

GASTON: Stone?

DUCHESS: Yes. Is your heart harder than granite?

GASTON: I – I don't think so, Duchess.

DUCHESS: A very good answer! I don't think so either. And yet, to a less well-informed observer than either of us, your behaviour would lead one to believe that your heart is made of granite.

GASTON (*flatly*): Oh.

DUCHESS: Gaston, perhaps you don't grasp the gravity of what I'm saying. I forget sometimes that I'm speaking to an amnesia case and that there are some words you may not have re-learnt in the last eighteen years. Do you know what granite is?

GASTON: It's a kind of stone.

DUCHESS: Quite right. But do you know what kind of stone? The hardest stone there is, Gaston. Do you understand?

GASTON: Yes.

DUCHESS: And don't you care that I'm comparing your heart to the hardest stone there is?

GASTON (*embarrassed*): Well . . . no . . .

A pause.

It's a bit of a giggle really.

DUCHESS: Did you hear that, Huspar?

HUSPAR (*pouring oil*): He's a child.

DUCHESS (*peremptorily*): Child, rubbish! He's an ingrate. (*To* GASTON.) I see. Here you are, one of the most disquieting cases in psychiatric history, one of the most heart-rending enigmas of the war – and if I translate your vulgar phraseology correctly, it makes you laugh? You are – as one clever journalist so aptly put it – the living unknown warrior, and it makes you laugh. Are you quite incapable of respect, Gaston?

GASTON: But it's me, isn't it, so—

DUCHESS: Never mind! In the name of what you represent, you ought to forbid yourself to laugh at yourself. This may sound like a witty sally, but it fully expresses what I mean. When you see yourself in the glass, Gaston, you ought to take your hat off to yourself.

GASTON: Me – to myself?

DUCHESS: Yes, you, to yourself. *We* all do, when we think of what you stand for. Who do you think you are, that you should be exempt?

GASTON: Nobody, Duchess.

DUCHESS: Wrong answer! You think you're someone very important. The fuss the papers have made over your case has turned your head, that's all.

He tries to say something.

Don't answer me back, you'll only put me in a rage!

He drops his head and goes back to the pictures.

How does he strike you, Huspar?

HUSPAR: Him? Indifferent.

DUCHESS: Indifferent. That's the word. It's been on the tip of my tongue for a week. Indifferent. That's it exactly. Yet, good God, it's *his* future that's at stake, not ours! *We* haven't lost our memory, *we* aren't searching for our family! Are we, Huspar?

HUSPAR: Definitely not.

DUCHESS: Well then!

HUSPAR (*with a worldly wise shrug*): You're new to it all, your illusions are still fresh. He's been meeting all our efforts with this apathy for years now.

DUCHESS: It's unpardonable of him not to realize the trouble my nephew is taking on his behalf. If you knew how beautifully he's taking care of him, what devotion he's put into this whole enterprise! I hope he told you about the great event before you left?

HUSPAR: Dr Jibelin wasn't at the hospital when I went to collect Gaston's case history. Unfortunately I wasn't able to wait for him.

DUCHESS: What's this, Huspar? You mean you didn't see my little Albert before you left? Then you don't know the good news.

HUSPAR: What news?

DUCHESS: At the last pentothal injection he gave him, he succeeded in getting Gaston to talk in his delirium. Oh, he didn't say much. He said 'piddleprick'.

HUSPAR: Piddleprick?

DUCHESS: Yes, piddleprick. You may say that's not much, but the interesting thing is that it's a word nobody has ever heard him utter when he's awake, a word nobody remembers ever using in his hearing, a word which therefore has every likelihood of belonging to his past.

HUSPAR: Piddleprick.

DUCHESS: Piddleprick. It's a very tiny clue, but it *is* something. His past isn't just a black hole any more. Who knows if that 'piddleprick' won't set us on the right track? (*Dreamily.*) Piddleprick. A friend's surname perhaps. A common swear word, who knows? We have a small basis to build on now.

HUSPAR (*ruminatively*): Piddleprick.

DUCHESS (*repeating it delightedly*): Piddleprick. When Albert came to announce this unhoped-for result, he flung open the door and he cried 'Aunt! My patient has said a word from out of his past. It was a term of abuse.' I shook from head to foot, my dear. I was expecting some piece of filth. Such a charming lad, I should have been desolated if he turned out to be of low extraction. A pretty waste of effort it would be for my little Albert to spend nights on end – he's lost pounds over it – asking him questions and sticking needles in his rump, if the fellow recovers his memory only to tell us that before the war he was a plumber's mate! But something tells me different. I'm a romantic, my dear Huspar. Something tells me that my nephew's patient was an extremely famous man. A playwright, for preference. An eminent playwright.

HUSPAR: Eminent – it's unlikely. He would have been recognized by now.

DUCHESS: The photographs of him were all terrible. Besides, war takes such a toll of a man, doesn't it?

HUSPAR: I don't recall a well-known playwright ever reported missing during the hostilities. People of that sort always announce their slightest movements to the Press. Let alone their disappearance.

DUCHESS: Ah, Huspar, you're very cruel! You're destroying such a lovely dream. But he *is* a man of breeding, I'm quite sure of that. See how distinguished he looks in that suit. I sent him to Albert's tailor.

HUSPAR (*putting on his pince-nez*): Why, yes, I was going to say. That doesn't look like a hospital suit.

DUCHESS: You surely don't expect me to put my nephew's patient up in my own house, and parade him round myself to all the families who are claiming him, dressed in putty-coloured flannelette!

HUSPAR: An excellent idea, I think, these house-to-house visits.

DUCHESS: Aren't they? My little Albert said to me, the moment he took up his case, 'What he needs to do, in order to find his past,' he said, 'is to saturate himself in the atmosphere of that past.' The next step was obvious: take him along to the four or five families who had produced the most telling evidence. But Gaston isn't his only patient. Albert couldn't take time off from the hospital to conduct these visits himself, that was out of the question. So what was to be done? Ask the Bureau of Missing Persons for funds to carry out an official investigation? You know how stingy those folk are. What would you have done? I shouldered arms and jumped into the breach. Like in 1914!

HUSPAR: Very laudable.

DUCHESS: When I think that in Dr Bonfant's day families came in hordes to the asylum every Monday, saw him for a few minutes each and then went home by the next train! How could you find your nearest and dearest under those conditions, I ask you? Dr Bonfant is dead, I know, and we must hold our peace. But the least one could say about him, if silence over a grave weren't a sacred duty, is that the man was an idiot and a criminal.

HUSPAR: A criminal – oh come . . .

DUCHESS: Don't exasperate me, Huspar. I just wish he weren't dead, so I could fling the word in his face. A criminal! It's all his fault if this poor unfortunate boy has been languishing in mental homes ever since 1918! When I think that he kept him at Pont-au-Bronc for nearly fifteen years without getting him to say one word about his past, and my little Albert has had him for three months and he's already made him say 'piddleprick' – well, I'm speechless! He's a great psychiatrist, Huspar, is my little Albert.

HUSPAR: And a charming young man, too.

DUCHESS: The dear lad. Things are changing fast now he's in

charge, thank heaven. Identification parades, graphological evidence, chemical analyses, police investigations – nothing that's humanly possible will be spared to help Gaston find his rightful family. On the clinical side, too, Albert insists on the most up-to-date methods. Just think – he's already given him seventeen pentothal injections!

HUSPAR: Seventeen! But that's an enormous lot!

DUCHESS (*delightedly*): Enormous! And it's extremely brave of my little Albert, too. Because – we have to face the fact – it's risky.

HUSPAR: What about Gaston?

DUCHESS: What could he have to complain about, pray? It's all for his own good. He'll have a bottom like a pincushion, but he'll get his past back. And our past is the best part of all of us! What right-thinking man would hestitate between his past and the skin of his behind?

HUSPAR: It's not a question that arises much.

DUCHESS (*to* GASTON *as he passes by her*): Isn't that so, Gaston? Aren't you grateful to Dr Jibelin, after all those wasted years with Dr Bonfant, for taking such trouble to give you back your past?

GASTON: Very grateful indeed, Duchess.

DUCHESS (*to* HUSPAR): There, you see! He says it himself! Oh, Gaston my dear, isn't it moving – don't you find? – to think that on the other side of that door there may be a mother's heart beating, an old father waiting to open his arms to you!

GASTON: Well, you know, I've been through it so many times; so many deluded old women kissing me with their damp noses, so many fond old men rubbing their beards on me . . . Imagine having four hundred families, Duchess. Four hundred families all avid to clasp you to their bosom. That's a lot of families.

DUCHESS: But children, Gaston, dear little children! Little babies waiting for their father! Will you dare to say you don't long to kiss the little darlings – to bounce them on your knee?

GASTON: That would be a bit awkward, Duchess. The youngest couldn't be much under twenty.

DUCHESS (*sighing*): Oh, Huspar . . . He feels a need to defile all that's most sacred in life!

GASTON (*lost in thought suddenly*): Children . . . I should have some of my own now, real ones, if they'd let me live.

DUCHESS: You know that was impossible.

GASTON: Why? Because I couldn't remember anything before that spring evening in 1918, when they found me in a railway siding?

HUSPAR: Quite so, alas . . .

GASTON: Yes, I dare say it frightened people to think of a man living without a past. Foundlings aren't too well thought of, as it is . . . But at least there's time to instil a few little notions into them. But a man, a grown man, who scarcely had a country, no place of birth, no background, no name . . . Good God, the fellow's a bleeding outcast.

DUCHESS: In any case, Gaston my dear, everything points to the fact that your education wasn't all it might have been. I've already forbidden you to use that word.

GASTON: What – outcast?

DUCHESS: No . . . (*She hesitates.*) The other one.

GASTON (*continuing his reverie*): And a police record, too, maybe . . . Have you thought of that, Duchess? You trust me with your silver at table; my room is a step away from yours . . . Supposing I'd already killed three men?

DUCHESS: Your eyes tell me you haven't.

GASTON: You're lucky they honour you with their secrets, then. I stare into them until I'm dizzy sometimes, trying to find out a little of all the things they've seen. They give me nothing.

DUCHESS (*smiling*): You haven't killed three men, though, don't you worry. One needn't know your past life to know that.

GASTON: They found me in a trainload of returning prisoners from Germany. So I'd been to the front. Like the others, I must have hurled lumps of lead and iron at other men. Oh,

I'm a bad shot; I know that much about myself. But during the war the High Command reckoned more on the number of bullets than on the skill of those who fired them. Let's hope, anyway, that I didn't manage to hit three men.

DUCHESS: Gracious me, the very idea! On the contrary, I fondly hope you were a hero. I meant killing people in peacetime!

GASTON: A hero is fairly vague in wartime, too. The back-biter, the miser, the thief, the coward even, they were all condemned alike by regulations to be heroes – cheek by jowl, and in the same way almost.

DUCHESS: Don't worry. A little voice inside me tells me – and it's never wrong – that you were a very well brought up young man.

GASTON: That's a slender basis for asserting that I never did an evil thing. I must have hunted. Well brought up young men always hunt. So let's hope I was a hunter everybody laughed at; let's hope I didn't hit three animals.

DUCHESS: My dear boy, it takes all my fondness for you not to laugh, to listen to you talk. Your scruples are exaggerated.

GASTON: I was so content in the asylum. I'd grown used to myself. I knew that self well and now I have to leave it and find another me and put that on like an old coat. Will I recognize myself tomorrow, I who drink nothing but water, in the lamplighter's son who had to have his four full jugs of red wine every day? Or – me with my tiny store of patience – in the haberdasher's son who collected, and graded according to size, twelve hundred different sorts of buttons?

DUCHESS: Exactly! That's why I was set on visiting these Renauds first. They're a better class of people altogether.

GASTON: That means they have a grand house and a grand butler, but what kind of son did they have?

The BUTLER *appears in the doorway.*

DUCHESS (*seeing him*): We'll know in a second. (*Raising her hand to stop the* BUTLER.) Wait a second, my good man, before

you show in your master and mistress. Gaston, would you
go out into the garden for a little while? We'll send for you.

GASTON: Very well, Duchess.

DUCHESS (*drawing him aside*): Oh, and do stop calling me
Duchess. It was different when you were only my nephew's
patient.

GASTON: Right.

DUCHESS: Go along. And don't peep through the keyhole!

GASTON (*as he goes*): I can wait. I've already seen three hundred
and eighty-seven of them.

He goes out.

DUCHESS: Delightful boy! Ah, Huspar, when I think that Dr
Bonfant used to put him to planting cabbages, I shudder
from top to toe. (*To the* BUTLER.) You may show in your
master and mistress, my good fellow. (*She takes* HUSPAR'S
arm.) Oh, my dear Huspar, I'm so terribly wrought up! I feel
as if I'm embarking on a pitiless struggle against fate, against
death, against all the dark forces in the world. I came in
black, I thought the occasion called for it.

The three RENAUDS *come in. They are upper middle class, and
clearly rich.*

MME RENAUD (*in the doorway*): You see! I told you! He isn't
here.

HUSPAR: We just asked him to leave the room for a moment.

GEORGES: Let me introduce myself. I'm Georges Renaud.
(*Introducing the two ladies who came in with him.*) My mother.
And my wife.

HUSPAR (*bowing*): Lucien Huspar. I am the patient's solicitor.
(*Indicating the* DUCHESS.) Duchess Dupont-Dufort, presi-
dent of various charitable bodies connected with the mental
home at Pont-au-Bronc. The Duchess very kindly consented
to accompany the patient here, in the absence of her nephew,
Dr Jibelin, who is detained at the hospital.

They exchange bows.

DUCHESS: Yes, I have allied myself, as far as my feeble strength allows, to my nephew's good work. He has put such enthusiasm, such burning faith into the task in hand!

MME RENAUD: We will always be deeply grateful for the way he's taken care of our darling Jacques. It would have given me great joy to tell him so personally.

DUCHESS: Thank you.

MME RENAUD: Oh, but do sit down, won't you? Please forgive me – this is such a moving moment . . .

DUCHESS: I do feel for you, believe me.

MME RENAUD: You can imagine how impatient we are to see him. It's two whole years since we first saw him at the asylum.

GEORGES: And despite repeated applications, we haven't set eyes on him since.

HUSPAR: There were so many similar cases. You must bear in mind that there are four hundred thousand men listed as missing in France alone. Four hundred thousand families, and very few of them have given up hope, believe me.

MME RENAUD: Yes, but two years! And if you knew in what conditions they showed him to us! I'm sure you aren't to blame, nor your nephew either, as he wasn't in charge of the asylum then. But the patient swept past us in a great crush of people – we couldn't even get near him! There were over forty people there.

DUCHESS: Those identification parties of Dr Bonfant's were a downright scandal.

MME RENAUD: They certainly were! Of course, we didn't give up. My son had to get back to his business. But we took rooms in a near-by hotel, my daughter-in-law and I, in the hope that we might get in to see him again. After repeated bribes, an attendant let us see him alone for a few minutes – without any results, I'm afraid. Another time, my daughter-in-law contrived to take the place of a sewing-woman who was ill. She saw him on and off for a whole afternoon, but they weren't alone, so she couldn't say anything to him.

DUCHESS (*to* VALENTINE): How very romantic! But suppose they'd unmasked you? I hope you can sew!

VALENTINE: Yes.

DUCHESS: And you didn't manage to be alone with him at all?

VALENTINE: No, not for a second.

DUCHESS: Ah, that Dr Bonfant has a lot to answer for!

GEORGES: But why, seeing the amount of proof we've given you, were any other families even considered? That's what I can't understand.

HUSPAR: Yes, it seems extraordinary, I know. But do you realize that after our last cross-check, which was extremely thorough, there still remain five families – apart from yourselves – with more or less equal chances?

MME RENAUD: Five! But there can't be!

HUSPAR: I'm afraid there are.

DUCHESS (*consulting her list*): The families Bougran, Brigaud, Grigou, Legropatre and Madensale. But I want you to know that I insisted we should see you first, because I like you so very much.

MME RENAUD: Thank you, that's very kind.

DUCHESS: No, no, don't thank me! I mean it. From the very first your letter gave me the impression that you were charming people, and meeting you confirms that in every way. After you, Lord knows what kind of people we're going to stumble on! There's a milkman, a lamplighter—

MME RENAUD: A lamplighter?

DUCHESS: A lamplighter, yes, madame, a lamplighter! We live in impossible times! These people all have ideas far beyond their station. But they won't give Gaston to a lamplighter, not while I'm alive they won't!

HUSPAR (*to* GEORGES): Yes, you see, we had announced that claimants would be visited in alphabetical order – which was logical enough – but as that would have made you the last, her ladyship insisted, a little unwisely perhaps, that we should waive the rules and come and see you first.

MME RENAUD: Why unwisely? Those in charge of the patient are entitled to please themselves, I should have thought!

HUSPAR: Possibly. But you have no idea what a hornet's nest of feeling – often mercenary, alas – Gaston has stirred up. His pension as a wounded serviceman, which he has never been able to draw, comes to quite a tidy sum, you know. Arrears and compound interest amount today to more than two hundred and fifty thousand francs.

MME RENAUD: How can money enter into a situation as tragic as this?

HUSPAR: It does, unfortunately. And while we're on the subject, I'd like to say a word or two on the patient's legal position.

MME RENAUD: Later, M. Huspar, later, if you wouldn't mind.

DUCHESS: M. Huspar has a law book where his heart should be. But he's a dear fellow – (*She pinches him.*) – so he's going to fetch Gaston for us right away, aren't you, Huspar?

HUSPAR (*bowing to superior force*): Very well, ladies. But I must ask you not to get too emotional. Don't rush at him the moment he appears. He's been through that sort of thing so many times, it puts him in a most distressing nervous state.

He goes out.

DUCHESS: You must be terribly anxious to see him again.

MME RENAUD: A mother could hardly feel otherwise, surely.

DUCHESS: I'm quite overcome myself, in sympathy! (*To* VALENTINE.) You knew our patient, too, madame – at least, the man you believe our patient to be?

VALENTINE: Yes, of course. I told you, I went to the asylum.

DUCHESS: So you did! What a featherbrain I am!

MME RENAUD: Georges, my elder son, married Valentine when she was very young. She and Jacques were great friends. They were devoted to each other, weren't they, Georges?

GEORGES (*shortly*): Very.

DUCHESS: Yes, a brother's wife is almost a sister, isn't she?

VALENTINE (*oddly*): Quite.

DUCHESS: You must be insanely happy at the thought of seeing him again.

JACP–R

VALENTINE, *ill at ease, looks at* GEORGES.

GEORGES: Very happy indeed. As a sister.

DUCHESS: I'm such a romantic soul! Do you know, I always
   dreamed that a woman he'd been passionately in love with
   would be there to recognize him and give him a lover's kiss
   – his first kiss on emerging from that sepulchre! I see it isn't
   to be.

GEORGES (*shortly*): No, I'm afraid not.

DUCHESS: So much for my dream!

She goes to the window.

M. Huspar is taking a long time. Your grounds are very big,
   and he's rather near-sighted. I expect he's got lost.

VALENTINE (*aside to* GEORGES): Why are you looking at me
   like that? You aren't going to rake all that up again?

GEORGES (*gravely*): I put it out of my mind when I forgave
   you.

VALENTINE: Then don't look daggers at me each time that old
   lunatic opens her mouth.

MME RENAUD (*who has heard none of this and apparently knows
   nothing*): Darling Valentine. Look, Georges, she's quite
   upset. It's nice to think she remembers our little Jacques so
   kindly, isn't it, Georges?

GEORGES: Yes, Mother.

DUCHESS: Here he comes!

Enter HUSPAR *alone.*

I knew it! You couldn't find him?

HUSPAR: Yes, I did, but I didn't like to disturb him.

DUCHESS: What do you mean? What was he doing?

HUSPAR: Standing in front of a statue.

VALENTINE (*with a cry*): A hunting goddess, with a circular
   stone seat, at the far end of the garden?

HUSPAR: Yes. Look, you can see it from here.

They all look.

GEORGES (*abruptly*): Well, what does that prove?

DUCHESS (*to* HUSPAR): My dear, isn't this exciting!

VALENTINE (*softly*): I don't know. I seem to remember he was very fond of that statue, that seat.

DUCHESS (*to* HUSPAR): We're getting warmer and warmer!

MME RENAUD: You surprise me, Valentine dear. That corner of the garden used to be part of the Dubanton's property. True, we'd already bought it in Jacques' day, but we didn't knock the wall down until after the war.

VALENTINE (*flushing*): I don't know, yes, I expect you're right . . .

HUSPAR: He looked so odd standing there, by that statue, I didn't dare interrupt him before I'd inquired whether this might have some special significance. Apparently it doesn't, so I'll go and fetch him.

He goes out.

GEORGES (*quietly, to* VALENTINE): Is that where you used to meet? On that seat?

VALENTINE: I don't know what you mean.

DUCHESS (*to* MME RENAUD): I'm sure you're feeling very wrought up – and who can blame you? – but I must ask you to keep absolutely calm.

MME RENAUD: You can rely on me.

HUSPAR *comes in with* GASTON.

(*Murmuring.*) Yes, it's he, it's Jacques . . .

The DUCHESS *goes to* GASTON *with a sweeping dramatic gesture and screens the others from him.*

DUCHESS: Gaston, try not to think, let yourself go, don't make any effort at all. Now look carefully at all these faces . . .

Silence. They all stand there motionless. GASTON *comes to* GEORGES, *looks at him, then passes on to* MME RENAUD. *Before* VALENTINE, *he stops for a second. She murmurs, barely audibly:*

VALENTINE: My darling . . .

He looks at her, surprised, then he passes her, goes back to the
DUCHESS, *and spreads his arms in a helpless gesture of regret.*

GASTON (*kindly*): I'm very sorry . . .

Curtain

SCENE 2

A big ornate double door, closed.

The RENAUDS' *servants are grouped round it, whispering. The*
COOK *is bent double at the keyhole. The others crowd round her.*

COOK: Wait – wait! They're all staring at him like a monkey
in the zoo. The poor boy doesn't know where to put himself.

CHAUFFEUR: Let's have a look.

COOK: Wait a minute! He just jumped up off his chair.
Knocked his cup over, too. Had enough of their questions
by the look of it. Master Georges is taking him over to the
window. He's holding his arm, very kindly, just as if nothing
had happened . . .

CHAUFFEUR: Well, I'll be—

JULIETTE: My word, you should have heard him when he
found their letters after the war! He looks mild as a lamb,
does Master Georges, but the sparks flew then, I can tell
you!

VALET: And I'll tell *you* something. He was right.

JULIETTE (*furiously*): What? Right, was he? Saying nasty
things about the dead – is that right? Do you think it's a
decent thing to do – picking quarrels with the dead?

VALET: The dead had no call stealing other men's wives in the
first place.

JULIETTE: Oh, you and your wife-stealing! You haven't
stopped bleating about it ever since we got married! It's not

the dead who do you wrong, much good they'd be at it, poor things. It's the living. And the dead have nothing to do with the carryings on of the living.

VALET: Very convenient, that is! You mess about with someone's wife and flip-flip, out of sight out of mind and everything's lovely. All you have to be is dead.

JULIETTE: It's no fun being dead, you know!

VALET: Being a cuckold's no fun either!

JULIETTE: On and on and on! It'll happen to you one of these days the way you keep harping on it.

The CHAUFFEUR *tries to push the* COOK *aside.*

COOK: Wait, wait! They're all going over to the bookcase. They're showing him some photographs.

She gives him her place.

With the old-style keyholes you could see something. But these newfangled things . . . Eyestrain, that's all they're good for.

CHAUFFEUR (*peering through the keyhole*): It's him! It's him! The bastard. I'd know his ugly little snout anywhere!

JULIETTE: Here! What do you want to say that for? You shut your own ugly snout.

VALET: Why are you sticking up for him?

JULIETTE: I liked him; he was nice, was Master Jacques. And what do you know about him, anyway? You never knew him. I liked him a lot.

VALET: Well, what of it? He was your master. You cleaned his boots for him.

JULIETTE: What's that got to do with it? I liked him.

VALET: Huh! Like his brother, I'll bet. A first-class swine.

The CHAUFFEUR *gives up his place to* JULIETTE.

CHAUFFEUR: Worse, man, worse! God, the times he's kept me hanging about till four in the morning, outside night clubs. And then, at dawn, when you were frozen stiff, out he'd

come, red in the face and stinking of drink from five yards
off, and he'd throw up all over the back seat – the pig!

COOK: You can say that again. The times I've stuck my hands
into it, as true as I stand here! And all of eighteen years old!

CHAUFFEUR: And the abuse you'd get! Language as made *me*
blush, even!

COOK: And a brute with it! Do you remember, there was a
little potboy in the kitchens then. Gave him a kick or a clout
whenever he saw him, poor little devil.

CHAUFFEUR: And for no reason, too. A regular little thug,
that's what he was. And when we heard he'd caught it, back
in 1918 – we're no worse natured than most – but we all
drank to it, remember? – and said serve him right.

BUTLER: Come along now, that's enough. Back to work.

CHAUFFEUR: What? Don't tell me you don't think the same
as us, Monsieur Jules?

BUTLER: I could tell you a thing or two, don't you worry! I've
heard their scenes at table. I was there when he raised his
hand to his mother! What about that?

COOK: His own mother! A boy of eighteen!

BUTLER: And as for his bits of nonsense with Madame
Valentine, they're known to me, I may say, in every particular.

CHAUFFEUR: Well! Very good of you to have shut your eyes
to it, Monsieur Jules, if I may say so.

BUTLER: Above stairs is above stairs, my lad. That's their
affair.

CHAUFFEUR: Here, let's have another look at him.

JULIETTE (*moving away for him*): It is him, I'm sure it is! Master
Jacques . . . He was a lovely-looking boy, you know, in
those days. Really handsome. And so genteel.

VALET: Oh, shut up about him, girl. There's a heap of handsome
fellows besides him, and younger, too.

JULIETTE: That's true. Twenty years nearly. It's a long time.
Do you think he'll think I've changed a lot?

VALET: What's it to you if he does?

JULIETTE: Oh, nothing . . .

The VALET *thinks a minute, while the others make faces behind his back.*

VALET: Here . . . why have you been mooning about the place ever since you heard he might come back?
JULIETTE: Me?

The others giggle.

VALET: Why do you keep looking at yourself in the mirror and asking if you've changed?
JULIETTE: What – me?
VALET: How old were you when he went to the front?
JULIETTE: Fifteen.
VALET: The postman, was he your first?
JULIETTE: You know he was! He gagged me and gave me a sleeping pill – I told you!
VALET: You're sure he *was* your first?
JULIETTE: What a thing to ask! It's not something a girl forgets! He flung his sack down in the kitchen, the brute, and all his letters fell out on to the floor!
CHAUFFEUR (*still at the keyhole*): Look at that Valentine; she can't take her eyes off him. If he stays here old Georges will sprout another pair of horns, I'll bet you anything!

The BUTLER *takes his place at the keyhole.*

BUTLER: Disgusting, that's what it is.
CHAUFFEUR: Perhaps he likes it that way, Monsieur Jules!

They all snigger.

VALET: They make me laugh, with their 'amnesia'. If they were his real family, he'd have recognized them by now, it stands to reason. He's been here all day. Amnesia nothing. Eyewash, the lot of it.
COOK: I don't know so much. As God is my judge, there are times when I can't even remember if I've put salt in my sauces.
VALET: Yes, but – a family!

COOK (*shrugging*): For all the interest he took in them. Little gallivanter!

BUTLER (*at the keyhole*): It's him all right, though. I'll bet my head on it.

COOK: Yes, but they say there are five other families besides! And all with the same amount of things to prove it.

CHAUFFEUR: I'll tell you my opinion, if you want to know. There's no sense even hoping that little swine isn't dead, not for our sakes, not for anybody's, and that's a fact.

COOK: You're right!

JULIETTE (*witheringly*): Oh, it's lovely being dead – you should try it!

BUTLER: Nor for his sake either, if you ask me. He's better off dead. Start off life the way he did and you come to no good anyway.

CHAUFFEUR: Besides, what if he's got attached to his quiet life in the asylum? Look at the pile of things he'll have to know about. That Grandchamps boy, the Valentine business, that row over the hundred thousand francs – and a whole lot more that we don't know about.

BUTLER: You're right. I'd rather be in my shoes than his.

VALET (*looking through the keyhole*): Look out, they're getting up. They'll be coming out in a minute.

The servants scatter.

JULIETTE (*dreamily, as she goes*): That Master Jacques, though . . .

VALET (*suspiciously, as he follows her out*): Master Jacques what? What about him?

JULIETTE: Oh, nothing.

They have gone out.

Curtain

Act Two

JACQUES RENAUD'S *room and the long ill-lit corridors of the old mansion which lead into it. On the opposite side a paved hallway and a big stone staircase, with a wrought-iron handrail leading down from it.*

MME RENAUD, GEORGES *and* GASTON *appear at the top of the stairs and cross the hall.*

MME RENAUD: Excuse me, I'll lead the way. Now this, you see, is the passage you used to walk through to your room.

She opens the door.

And this is your room.

They all three go inside.

Oh really, how careless! I particularly said to open the shutters!

She opens them. Light floods into the room. It is furnished in the elaborate style of 1910.

GASTON (*looking round him*): My room.

MME RENAUD: You wanted it decorated to your own plan. You had such advanced ideas!

GEORGES: Yes, very bold you were in your tastes!

GASTON: So I see.

He notices an absurd-looking piece of furniture.

What's that? A tree in a thunderstorm?

GEORGES: It's a music stand.

GASTON: Was I a musician?

MME RENAUD: We wanted you to learn the violin, but you
   just wouldn't. You flew into insane rages if we tried to make
   you practise. You kicked all your instruments to pieces.
   Only that music stand survived.

GASTON (*smiling*): Very silly of it.

He goes to look at a portrait.

Is that him?

MME RENAUD: Yes, that's you, when you were twelve.

GASTON: I always pictured myself as shy and fair.

GEORGES: You had dark hair, almost black. You used to kick
   a ball around all day; you smashed everything to bits.

MME RENAUD (*showing him a big trunk*): Look what I had
   brought down from the attic.

GASTON: What's that – my old trunk? You're beginning to
   make me think I lived in the Second Empire!

MME RENAUD: No, silly! It's your Uncle Gustave's trunk and
   it's full of your toys.

GASTON (*opening the trunk*): My toys! Did *I* have toys, too? Yes,
   of course, I must have . . . I'd forgotten about the toys.

MME RENAUD: Look. Your catapult.

GASTON: A catapult. And it's no toy either!

MME RENAUD: My God, the birds you killed with that thing!
   A real fiend, you were. And you weren't content with the
   birds in the garden either. I had an aviary full of prize song-
   birds. One day you went into it and you slaughtered the lot.

GASTON: Birds? Little birds?

MME RENAUD: Yes.

GASTON: How old was I?

MME RENAUD: Seven – nine perhaps.

GASTON (*shaking his head*): That wasn't me.

MME RENAUD: Yes, it was, it was!

GASTON: No. At seven I'd go into the garden with bread-
   crumbs and coax the sparrows to peck out of my hand.

GEORGES: What? You'd have wrung their necks, poor things!

MME RENAUD: Yes, look at that dog whose paw he broke
   with a stone!

GEORGES: And the mouse he led about on the end of a string.

MME RENAUD: And the squirrels, later on, and the ferrets and the weasels. The amount of little creatures you killed! You'd stuff the best specimens. There's a whole collection of them upstairs. I must have them brought down.

She rummages in the trunk.

Here are your knives, your first shotguns . . .

GASTON (*searching, too*): Are there no teddy bears, no Noah's arks?

MME RENAUD: Even as a tiny boy, all you ever wanted were scientific toys. Look, your gyroscopes, your test tubes, your magnets, your mechanical crane.

GEORGES: We wanted to turn you into a brilliant engineer.

GASTON (*spluttering with laughter*): Me?

MME RENAUD: But the things you liked best of all were your geography books. You were always top of your class in geography.

GEORGES: At ten years old, you could place any city in the world on the map blindfold.

GASTON: Blindfold . . . True, I've lost any memory I had . . . But I tried to learn the capitals of Europe again in the asylum. Well, even with my eyes open . . . Let's shut this treasure chest. I doubt if it will teach us anything. I don't see myself like that as a child at all.

He shuts the trunk, wanders about the room, touches various objects, sits in the chairs. Then he asks suddenly:

Did he have a friend, that little boy? Another boy who went everywhere with him, who shared his secrets and his stamp collection?

MME RENAUD (*volubly*): Of course, of course! You had dozens of playmates. All the boys at school, and then at college, why—

GASTON: Yes, but . . . not playmates. A friend . . . You see, before I ask you who my women were—

MME RENAUD (*shocked*): Oh but, Jacques, you were so young
  when you went away!

GASTON (*smiling*): I'll ask about them just the same . . . But
  before I do, it seems to me far more urgent to ask who was
  my friend.

MME RENAUD: Why, you can see them all in the school
  photographs. I'll show them to you. Then, later, there were
  the boys you went out with, in the evenings.

GASTON: But the boy I liked going out with most, the one I
  told everything to?

MME RENAUD (*hastily, with a quick glance at* GEORGES): There
  wasn't any one boy you preferred, not really.

GASTON (*looking at her*): Your son didn't have a best friend,
  then? Pity. I mean it's a pity if we find out that I was he.
  I don't think there's anything more comforting for a grown
  man than seeing the reflection of one's childhood in the eyes
  of another grown-up little boy. It's a pity. I'd even hoped,
  you see, that this imaginary friend would give me back my
  memory – as a good turn, the way friends do.

GEORGES (*after a slight hesitation*): Well, you did have a friend,
  yes. One you were very fond of. You even stayed friends
  until you were seventeen . . . We didn't want to mention
  it; it was such a painful business . . .

GASTON: Did he die?

GEORGES: No, no. He didn't die, but you stopped seeing each
  other, you fell out – for good.

GASTON: For good? At seventeen?

A pause.

Did you ever know why?

GEORGES: Vaguely . . .

GASTON: And neither your brother nor that other boy ever
  tried to make it up?

MME RENAUD: There was the war, remember. Besides . . .
  Well, I'll tell you. You quarrelled over some futile thing or
  other. You had a fight, as boys do at that age. And – without
  meaning to, I'm sure, you . . . did something violent,

something – unfortunate, let's say. You pushed him down some stairs. His spine was injured. He was in plaster for a long time, and he's been a cripple ever since. Now you can see how awkward, how painful it would have been if you'd attempted to see him again.

A pause.

GASTON: I see. And where did we have this fight – at school – at his house?

MME RENAUD (*quickly*): No, here. But let's not talk about it; it's too dreadful. That's one of the things you'd do best not to remember, Jacques.

GASTON: If I remember one thing, I'll have to remember them all; you know that. A past comes wholesale, not by the piece. Where are those stairs? I'd like to see them.

MME RENAUD: There. Just outside your room. But what's the point, Jacques?

GASTON (*to* GEORGES): Will you show me?

GEORGES: If you like, but I really don't see why you should want to see that spot again . . .

They go out into the hall.

MME RENAUD: There.

GASTON *looks round, then leans over the handrail.*

GASTON: Whereabouts were we fighting?

GEORGES: Oh, we never knew exactly. One of the maids told us about it afterwards. She saw the whole thing.

GASTON: It's not an everyday occurrence. I imagine she described it in considerable detail. Where were we fighting? This landing is so wide . . .

MME RENAUD: Right on the edge, I should imagine. He must have lost his footing. Who knows, you may not have pushed him even!

GASTON (*going back to her*): If that's the case, if it was just an accident, then why didn't I sit with him every evening in his room? Give up my Saturdays to keep him company, instead of going out into the sunshine, so he shouldn't feel the unfairness of it all too much? Why?

GEORGES: Everybody gave a different version of it, you know . . . And then, local gossip made things worse, as you can imagine . . .

GASTON: Which maid was it who saw us?

MME RENAUD: What's the use of your knowing that? Anyway, she isn't with us any more.

GASTON: There must be other servants in the house who were here at the time. I'll ask them.

MME RENAUD: I trust you won't listen to backstairs gossip. They'll tell you some tales, you may be sure, if you start questioning the servants! You know what that class is like!

GASTON (*turning to* GEORGES): *You* must know how I feel. So far I haven't recognized one single thing in your house. What you've told me about your brother's boyhood seems about as remote from my own temperament as it could possibly be. But – perhaps because I'm tired, or perhaps it's something else – I feel, for the first time, a strange stirring inside me as I listen to people telling me about their child.

MME RENAUD: There! Oh, Jacques darling, I knew it! I knew—

GASTON: No! Don't be affectionate. Don't call me darling Jacques too soon. We're investigating a case, like the police, as toughly – as callously, if possible – as the police. This contact with a total stranger, whom I may have to accept in a minute as part of me: this uncanny betrothal with a ghost – all that's painful enough without having you to struggle with on top of it. I'll bow to all the evidence, I'll listen to all the anecdotes, but something tells me that before anything else I must know the truth about that fight. The truth, however cruel.

MME RENAUD (*hesitantly*): Well now . . . you came to blows over some stupid little thing – you know how quick-tempered one is at that age—

GASTON (*interrupting*): No, not you. That servant *is* still here, isn't she? You were lying just now?

A pause.

GEORGES (*shortly*): Yes. She's still here.

GASTON: Send for her, please. Why temporize? You know I'll find her anyway.

GEORGES: It's too stupid – stupid and horrible.

GASTON: I'm not here to learn something pleasant. And anyway, suppose that's the one episode that brings my memory back? You've no right to keep it from me.

GEORGES: All right, if you insist, I'll call her.

He rings the bell.

MME RENAUD: Why, Jacques, you're trembling! I hope you aren't sickening for something?

GASTON: Am I trembling?

MME RENAUD: Perhaps there's a glimmer of light inside you now – is there?

GASTON: No. Darkness. The darkest night.

MME RENAUD: Then why are you trembling?

GASTON: It's silly. But of all the thousands of memories there could have been, it was the memory of a friend I yearned for most. I've built a whole edifice on that imaginary friend. Our long walks, the books we read together, the girl we both loved and I gave up for his sake, and even – you'll laugh at this – the time I saved his life on a sailing trip. So, you see, if I really am your son, I shall have to get used to a reality so very different from that dream . . .

JULIETTE *comes in.*

JULIETTE: You rang, madame?

MME RENAUD: Master Jacques would like to speak to you, Juliette.

JULIETTE: To me?

GEORGES: Yes. He wants to ask you about that unfortunate accident of Marcel Grandchamps's.

MME RENAUD: You know the truth, my dear. Master Jacques may have been a violent boy, but you know he could never have done anything deliberately evil.

GASTON (*interrupting again*): Don't say anything to her, please. Where were you, mademoiselle, when the accident happened?

JULIETTE: On the landing, with the two young gentlemen, Master Jacques.

GASTON: Don't call me Master Jacques yet. How did the quarrel begin?

JULIETTE (*with a glance at the* RENAUDS): Well . . .

GASTON (*going over to them*): Would you mind letting me speak to her alone? I feel you're embarrassing her.

MME RENAUD: I'll do anything you want if only you'll come back to us, Jacques.

GASTON (*seeing them out*): I'll call you.

They both go. GASTON *turns to* JULIETTE.

Sit down, won't you?

JULIETTE (*flustered*): May I?

GASTON: How old are you?

JULIETTE: Thirty-three. You know I am, Master Jacques; I was fifteen when you went to the front. So why ask?

GASTON: In the first place, because I didn't know. In the second place, I tell you I may not be Master Jacques at all.

JULIETTE: Oh yes, you are. I'd recognize you anywhere, Master Jacques.

GASTON: Did you know him well?

JULIETTE (*bursting into tears*): You can't have forgotten *everything*! Don't you remember anything at all, Master Jacques?

GASTON: Absolutely nothing.

JULIETTE (*wailing*): Asking me a thing like that after what happened! Torture it is, torture for a woman!

GASTON (*dazed for a second, then suddenly realizing*): Oh . . . Oh, I see. I'm sorry. So then Master Jacques was . . .

JULIETTE (*sniffing*): Yes.

GASTON: I'm very sorry . . . And you were how old?

JULIETTE: Fifteen. He was my first.

GASTON (*smiling suddenly, all tension gone*): Fifteen and he was seventeen . . . Why, that's a very sweet story. It's the first thing I've heard about him that strikes me as a little endearing. And how long did it last?

JULIETTE: Until he went away.

GASTON: And I tried so hard to guess what his sweetheart looked like. Why, she was charming.

JULIETTE: Charming she may have been, but she wasn't the only one, don't think it!

GASTON (*still smiling*): Oh, really?

JULIETTE: I should say not!

GASTON: Well, that isn't so dislikeable either.

JULIETTE: I suppose you think it's funny! But you must admit, for a woman, it's—

GASTON: Yes, of course, for a woman . . .

JULIETTE: It's agony for a woman, I can tell you, bearing the cruel pangs of thwarted love!

GASTON (*blinking*): The cruel pangs of . . . Yes, I suppose it is . . .

JULIETTE: I was only a tuppeny ha'penny little kitchen maid, but that didn't stop me draining the bitter cup of sorrow to the dregs.

GASTON: Bitter cup of . . . er – yes . . .

JULIETTE: Haven't you ever read *Ravished on her Wedding Night*?

GASTON: No.

JULIETTE: Oh, you should. There's a situation almost exactly like ours in it. Bertrande's dastardly seducer goes away, too – to America actually, to his millionaire uncle. And that's when she tells him – Bertrande does – that she's drained the bitter cup of sorrow to the dregs.

GASTON: Oh, I see! It's something out of the book!

JULIETTE: Yes, but it applied so terribly well to me!

GASTON: Yes, of course . . .

He rises abruptly and asks:

And he loved you very much did he – Master Jacques?

JULIETTE: Passionately. Well, I'll tell you, he used to say he'd kill himself for my sake.

GASTON: How did you come to be his mistress?

JULIETTE: Oh, it was my second day in this place. I was doing his room, and he pushed me on to the bed. I was laughing like a mad thing. Well, can you wonder, at that age! It all happened in spite of myself, as you might say. But afterwards, he swore he'd love me all his life.

GASTON (*looking at her with a smile*): Funny Master Jacques.

JULIETTE: Why funny?

GASTON: No reason. Anyway, if I become Master Jacques, I promise I'll talk this whole situation over with you very seriously.

JULIETTE: Oh, I'm not asking for any sort of amends, you know. I'm married now.

GASTON: Even so, even so . . .

A pause.

But I'm playing truant, I'll never pass my exams this way. Let's get back to that fight – that whole horrible story I'd give anything in the world not to have to know.

JULIETTE: Oh, yes, the fight with Master Marcel.

GASTON: Yes. You were there?

JULIETTE (*proudly*): Of course I was there!

GASTON: You saw the quarrel right from the start?

JULIETTE: I certainly did!

GASTON: Then perhaps you can tell me what unlikely nonsense they were fighting about so savagely?

JULIETTE (*calmly*): What do you mean – unlikely nonsense? They were fighting over me.

GASTON: Over you?

JULIETTE: Of course it was over me. What's so surprising about that?

GASTON (*reiterating, stunned*): Over you!

JULIETTE: Yes, I tell you! You see, I was Master Jacques's girl – I'm telling you this, because you've got to know, but don't go blurting it out, will you? I don't fancy losing my place over something that happened twenty years ago. Yes,

I was Master Jacques's mistress and – I may as well admit it – Master Marcel used to run round me a bit too.

GASTON: And?

JULIETTE: Well, one day he tried to kiss me in the passage. Of course, I didn't let him, but you know what a man's like when he's got that sort of thing in mind. Just at that moment Master Jacques came out of his room and saw us. He made a grab at Master Marcel, and Master Marcel hit back. They started fighting, then they both went down and rolled about on the floor.

GASTON: Where were they?

JULIETTE: On the first-floor landing. Just outside this room.

GASTON (*with a sudden mad cry*): Where? Where? Where? Show me! Come and show me! I want to see the exact spot!

He drags her out by the wrist into the hall.

JULIETTE: You're hurting me!

GASTON: Where? Where?

JULIETTE (*snatching her wrist away and rubbing it*): Here, I tell you! They fell just here, half in the hallway and half on the landing. Master Marcel was underneath.

GASTON (*shouting*): But they weren't anywhere near the edge! How could he possibly fall down the stairs? Did they both roll over as they were fighting?

JULIETTE: No. Master Jacques managed to get to his feet and he took hold of Master Marcel's leg and dragged him over to the stairs.

GASTON: And then?

JULIETTE: Then he pushed him over! And he shouted 'There, you little swine, that'll teach you to mess about with someone else's girl!'

A pause.

Oh, he was quite a lad, was Master Jacques.

GASTON (*dully*): And he was his best friend.

JULIETTE: I should say so! They'd been going to school together ever since they were six years old.

GASTON: Since they were six years old . . .

JULIETTE: Yes, it was a frightful thing, I know. But there! Love conquers all!

GASTON (*looking at her and murmuring*): Love, yes, of course, love . . . Thank you, mademoiselle.

GEORGES *knocks on* JACQUES'S *far door, opens it and, seeing the room empty, goes out into the hall.*

GEORGES: Excuse my coming back. You didn't call us. Mother was getting anxious. Well, did you find out what you wanted to know?

GASTON: Yes. Thank you. I found out what I wanted to know.

JULIETTE *has gone out.*

GEORGES: I know, it isn't a pretty story, is it? But no matter what anybody said, I'm still convinced it was an accident, basically . . . and you were only seventeen, one mustn't forget that . . . A prank, that's all it was – a sinister prank.

A pause. He looks uneasy.

How did she describe it?

GASTON: Just as she saw it, I imagine.

GEORGES: She told you it was over your rowing-club championships, did she? You were in rival crews – and keen sportsmen, both of you – well, it's understandable, you . . .

GASTON *says nothing.*

Anyway, that's the version I chose to accept. Of course, the Grandchamps family spread a different tale, but I for one have always refused to believe it. Don't try to find out; it was stupid and foul.

GASTON (*looking at him*): Were you fond of him?

GEORGES: He was my brother. In spite of everything. Because there was a great deal more besides that. Oh, you were terrible.

GASTON: So long as I still can, I shall ask you to say '*he* was terrible'.

GEORGES (*with a wan smile as he thinks back*): Terrible . . . You caused us a lot of worry, I can tell you. If you do come back to us, I'm afraid there's a lot more you'll have to know about, things worse even than that wretched fight. At least you can keep the benefit of the doubt about that.

GASTON: So there's still more I have to know.

GEORGES: Well, what can you expect? – you were a child. A boy left to his own devices in a disrupted world. Mother with her rigid principles pitched herself against you in her clumsy way without achieving anything – except to drive you further back into yourself. I didn't have enough authority . . . You did one very silly thing, among others – something that cost us a great deal . . . Well, we older ones were all away at the front. Youngsters of your age did as they liked . . . You tried to float a company. Now, whether you ever believed in the scheme, or whether you used it as a pretext for reasons of your own, I don't know. Only you can tell us that, if you ever get your memory back. The fact remains that you bewitched an old woman, a friend of the family – and bewitched is the word – into giving you a large sum of money. Nearly five hundred thousand francs. You were the so-called go-between. You had some letterheads printed, of some fictitious place of business – you signed fake receipts, and so on . . . One day the whole thing came out. But it was too late. There were only a few thousand francs left. You'd spent the rest in bars and night spots, with women and odd drinking friends . . . We paid her back, naturally.

GASTON: Your delight at the prospect of your brother's homecoming is positively saintlike.

GEORGES (*avoiding his eyes*): More so than you think, Jacques.

GASTON: What? Is there more to come?

GEORGES: We'll talk about it some other time.

GASTON: Why not now?

GEORGES: Better not, I think. I'll call Mother. She must be getting anxious.

GASTON (*stopping him*): You can tell me. I'm almost sure I'm not your brother.

GEORGES *looks at him for a moment in silence. Then he says dully:*

GEORGES: You look very like him . . . It's the same face, only as if a kind of storm had swept across it.

GASTON (*smiling*): Eighteen years . . . Yours, too, no doubt, although I was never privileged to see it without lines.

GEORGES: It isn't only the lines. It's a worn look you have. A wearing away. But one that instead of furrowing your face and hardening it had as it were softened it and rubbed it smooth. It's as if a turmoil of kindness and goodwill had swept across your face.

GASTON: Yes, I can see there's every chance that your esteemed brother's face wasn't particularly stamped with kindness.

GEORGES: No, no, you're wrong about him. He was hard, yes – and frivolous and irresponsible. But . . . I cared for him a lot, with all his faults. He was better looking than I was. Not cleverer perhaps – the cleverness you need at school or in business – but more sensitive, more brilliant definitely . . . (*He adds heavily*): More . . . attractive. He was fond of me, too, you know, in his own way. He even had – as he grew out of childhood anyway – a sort of grateful tenderness that touched me very much. That's why it was so hard when I found out.

He hangs his head as if he were in the wrong.

I hated him then, yes, I hated him. And then, very quickly, I just couldn't go on holding it against him.

GASTON: But for what?

GEORGES *lifts his head and looks at him.*

GEORGES: Are you Jacques?

GASTON *moves his hand in a gesture of helplessness.*

I keep telling myself he was young, and weak underneath like all violent people . . . I keep telling myself it's all too easy for a handsome pair of lips on a summer's night when you're about to leave for the front. I keep telling myself that I was miles away, that she was only a little girl herself . . . But . . .

GASTON: I don't follow, quite. He stole a girl from you?

A pause.

Your wife?

GEORGES *nods dumbly.* GASTON *says tonelessly:*

The bastard.

GEORGES (*with a rueful little smile*): It may be you.

A pause.

GASTON (*hoarsely*): Georges – that is your name, isn't it?
GEORGES: Yes.

GASTON *looks at him a moment, then makes an awkward gesture of affection.*

GASTON: Georges . . .

MME RENAUD *comes into the hall.*

MME RENAUD: Are you there, Georges?
GEORGES (*gruffly, ashamed of his emotion*): Excuse me, will you?

He goes out quickly. MME RENAUD *comes into the room.*

MME RENAUD: Jacques?
GASTON (*motionless*): Yes.
MME RENAUD: Guess who's just arrived? The effrontery of it!
GASTON (*wearily*): I can't remember anything as it is. So as for guessing games . . .
MME RENAUD: Aunt Louise, my dear! Aunt Louise!
GASTON: Aunt Louise? And that's effrontery, is it?
MME RENAUD: I should think so indeed! After what happened! I hope you'll do me the favour of refusing to speak to her if she ever tries to see you behind our backs. She behaved in a way that . . .! Not that you ever liked her anyway. My

word, if there's someone in the family you really loathed, my dear, and with good reason, it was your cousin Jules.

GASTON (*still motionless*): So I have a genuine loathing for someone and I didn't know it?

MME RENAUD: What – for Jules? Why, don't you know what he did to you, the little wretch? He gave you away to the Board of Examiners for having some logarithm tables. It's true! I have to tell you these things or you might be nice to all those people, as you don't remember anything. There's Gerard Duboc, who's sure to come fawning over you in that sugary way of his. He did you out of a very good job in the Fillière Company – and you had a much better chance of getting it than he did, with your uncle in the firm. He told lies about you to the managing director. We found out later that he was behind it. I hope you'll slam the door in his face, and the same with certain others I'll tell you about, too, who stabbed you in the back.

GASTON: It's full of pretty things, a past, isn't it?

MME RENAUD: On the other hand, you'll have to be very nice to old Madame Bougron, although she's rather repulsive since she had her stroke, poor thing. She helped to bring you into the world.

GASTON: That doesn't seem a good enough reason.

MME RENAUD: And she nursed you through pneumonia, too – I was ill myself at the time. She saved your life, my dear.

GASTON: Yes, that's true, there's gratitude too. I'd forgotten gratitude.

A pause.

Obligations, hatreds, injuries . . . What did I expect memories to be?

He stops and then adds thoughtfully:

And I was forgetting remorse. I have a complete past now.

He smiles a funny little smile and goes to her.

But you see how demanding I am. I should have preferred

a different model, one with a few joys in it. A spark of feeling, too, if possible. Have you nothing to offer me?

MME RENAUD: I don't understand you, my child.

GASTON: It's simple enough. I would like you to tell me about one of my old delights. My hatreds and my remorse have taught me nothing. Give me something that delighted your son, so I can test the ring of it inside me.

MME RENAUD: That's easy enough. You had a lot of enjoyment, you know. You were so pampered.

GASTON: Tell me one thing, just one.

MME RENAUD: All right . . . It's annoying having to remember on the spur of the moment . . . I don't know which to choose from.

GASTON: Say any one thing you think of.

MME RENAUD: Well, let's see . . . Yes, when you were twelve—

GASTON (*interrupting*): A man's joy. The others are too remote.

MME RENAUD (*suddenly ill at ease*): The thing is . . . You didn't tell me much about those. Well, goodness, a grown-up son! You went out such a lot. Like all boys. You were gods in those days. You went to the races, you went out to parties. You had fun with your friends, but with me . . .

GASTON: Did you never see me happy?

MME RENAUD: Well, of course I did, good heavens! Why, on your last prizegiving day, I remember—

GASTON (*interrupting*): No! Not prize day. Later on. Between the time I put away my school books and the day they put a gun into my hands; during those few months which were to be, without my knowing it, my entire life as a man.

MME RENAUD: I'm trying to think. You were out such a lot . . . You acted the man so much.

GASTON: Yes, but however much he plays the man, a boy of eighteen is still a child! There must have been a burst pipe in the yard that nobody could stop, or a day when the cook uttered some frightful barbarism, or we met a comic bus conductor . . . and you saw me laugh. A day when I was gladdened by a gift, a ray of sunshine. I'm not asking for an

overwhelming joy. Just a tiny moment of delight. I wasn't
neurotic, was I?

MME RENAUD (*suddenly ill at ease*): Well, you see, Jacques
dear . . . I was going to tell you all that later, when we
had more time . . . But the fact is, you and I weren't on
very good terms just then. Oh, it was nothing, childish sulks
that's all. I'm sure it will seem much more serious now, after
all these years, than it was at the time. Yes, as I was saying,
at the particular time you mentioned, between your leaving
school and the army, we weren't speaking to each other.

GASTON: Oh?

MME RENAUD: Yes. Oh, for quite futile reasons really.

GASTON: And did this . . . feud last for very long?

MME RENAUD: Almost a year.

GASTON: A year! We had some staying power, both of us.
Who stopped speaking first?

MME RENAUD (*hesitating slightly*): Oh, I did, I suppose. But
you were to blame for it. You were so stupidly pigheaded
over something.

GASTON: What youthful pigheadedness could possibly have
induced you not to speak to your son for a whole year?

MME RENAUD: You did nothing whatever to end this state of
affairs. Nothing!

GASTON: But when I left for the war, we did make it up then,
didn't we? You didn't let me go without kissing me good-
bye?

A pause.

MME RENAUD (*abruptly*): Yes.

A pause.

It was your fault. I waited for you in my room. You waited
in yours. You expected me to make the first move – me, your
mother! After the way you'd behaved towards me. The
others pleaded with you. It was no good. Nothing would
make you give in. Nothing! And you were going to the
front!

GASTON: How old was I?

MME RENAUD: Eighteen.

GASTON: Perhaps I didn't know where I was going. At eighteen war is a gay adventure. But it wasn't 1914 any more, when mothers hung garlands on the rifles. *You* must have known where I was going.

MME RENAUD: I was sure the war would be over before you'd left the training camp. I thought I'd see you again on your first leave. Besides, you were always so curt, so hard with me.

GASTON: But couldn't you have come in to me and said, 'Don't be so silly, kiss me.'

MME RENAUD: I was afraid of your eyes. Of how you'd stiffen in that proud way you had . . . Suppose you'd told me to get out? – you easily might, you know.

GASTON: Then you'd have come back again, wept at my door, gone down on your knees and begged me to kiss you before I went away. You did wrong, you did wrong not to go down on your knees.

MME RENAUD: But, Jacques, your own mother!

GASTON: I was eighteen and they were sending me away to die. I may have behaved like a boor, shut myself up like a fool in my own ridiculous pride, but even so – I'm a little ashamed at saying this, but you should have gone down on your knees, all of you and begged my pardon.

MME RENAUD: Pardon for what? *I* hadn't done anything.

GASTON: And what had I done, for that great gulf to open up between us?

MME RENAUD (*speaking suddenly as she did all those years ago*): Oh, you'd taken it into your head to marry some little shopgirl you'd picked up, and who refused to sleep with you no doubt . . . Marriage isn't a fairy tale. Were we supposed to let you ruin your life – bring this girl into the family? Don't tell me you loved her. How can you be in love at eighteen – I mean, deeply, lastingly enough to marry on and raise a family – with a little shopgirl you'd met at a dance three weeks before?

GASTON (*after a pause*): Yes, of course, it was folly . . . But my year were due for call up in a few months, you knew that. Suppose that was the one piece of folly I was ever to commit? It was calf love and couldn't last – but suppose the boy who clamoured for it had only a few months to live, not even time enough for it to fade?

MME RENAUD: But we didn't think you were going to be killed! And I haven't told you everything. Do you know what you shouted, right into my face, with your mouth all twisted and your hand raised to strike me – me, your own mother? 'I hate you! I hate you!' That's what you screamed at me.

A pause.

Now do you understand why I stayed in my room hoping you would come up, right until the street door banged behind you?

GASTON (*quietly, after a pause*): And I died at eighteen, without my moment of joy, because it was a piece of foolishness, and without your speaking to me again. I lay on the ground for a whole night with a wound in my shoulder and I was twice as lonely as the others who cried out for their mothers.

A pause. He says suddenly, as if to himself:

Yes, it's true. I do hate you.

MME RENAUD (*terrified*): Jacques, what is it?

GASTON (*coming back to himself*): What? I'm sorry . . . Please forgive me.

He moves away, hard and impenetrable.

I'm not Jacques Renaud. I recognize nothing here of what was his. Just for a second yes, as I stood listening to you, I merged with him. I'm sorry. But you see, for a man without a memory an entire past is too heavy to take on to one's back at one go. If you want to please me, if you want what's best for me, you'll let me go back to the asylum. I grew lettuces, I polished floors, the days went by . . . But even after eighteen years – the second half, exactly, of my life – those days, added one to the other, never managed to make up that devouring thing you call a past.

MME RENAUD: But, Jacques—

GASTON: Don't call me Jacques any more. He's done too many things, that Jacques. Gaston is all right. He's no one in particular, but I do know *what* he is. But this Jacques, with his name already swamped with the bodies of so many dead birds, this Jacques who betrayed, and murdered and went away all alone to the war with nobody to see him off, that Jacques who never even loved, he frightens me.

MME RENAUD: But, my dear child—

GASTON: Go away. I'm not your child.

MME RENAUD: You're talking to me just as you used to in the past!

GASTON: I have no past. I'm talking as I talk today. Go away.

MME RENAUD (*stiffening as she did long ago*): Very well, Jacques! But when all the others have proved to you that I really am your mother, you'll have to come to me and beg my pardon.

She goes out without seeing VALENTINE, *who has overheard the last few remarks, out in the passage.*

VALENTINE (*coming into the room*): You say he never loved. How do you know, when you know nothing?

GASTON (*looking her up and down*): Go away. You, too. Go away.

VALENTINE: Why are you talking to me like that? What's the matter?

GASTON (*shouting*): Go away! I'm not Jacques Renaud.

VALENTINE: You're shouting it as if you were afraid you were.

GASTON: It's partly that.

VALENTINE: Fear I can understand. The shadow of Jacques at eighteen is a frightening burden to take on. But why should you hate me?

GASTON: I don't like the little smiles you've been giving me ever since I arrived here. You were his mistress.

VALENTINE: Who dared to say so?

GASTON: Your husband.

A pause.

VALENTINE: Well, if you're my lover, and I want you back –
  are you absurd enough to think that's wrong?

GASTON: You're talking to a sort of aborigine. I'm a man of
  mature years, yet I'm landing wide-eyed and fresh into this
  world. Perhaps it isn't so wrong after all to take my brother's
  wife, a brother who was fond of me and wished me well.

VALENTINE (*quietly*): When we met on holiday at Dinard, I
  swam and played tennis with you much more than with your
  brother. I went for more walks along the seashore with you.
  It was you, only you, who shared my kisses. I came to your
  mother's house, later, to parties and your brother fell in love
  with me, but it was you I came to see.

GASTON: It was him you married, though, wasn't it?

VALENTINE: You were a child. I was an orphan, a minor,
  without a penny to my name. And with a charitable aunt
  who'd already made me pay dearly for the first few offers of
  marriage I'd refused. Should I have sold myself to some
  other man rather than to him, who brought me nearer you?

GASTON: There's a column in women's magazines that deals
  with problems of that sort.

VALENTINE: We became lovers – when I returned from my
  honeymoon.

GASTON: Oh, so we did wait a little while.

VALENTINE: A little while? Two months, two horrible
  months! Then we had three years all to ourselves, because
  the war came and Georges went on the fourth of August.
  And now, after these seventeen years, Jacques—

She touches his arm. He recoils.

GASTON: I am not Jacques Renaud.

VALENTINE: Even if you aren't . . . Let me look at the ghost
  of the only man I ever loved.

She gives a little smile.

Oh, you're curling your lip!

She looks into his face. He turns away, ill at ease.

Does nothing in me strike a chord in you – a look, a tone in my voice?

GASTON: Nothing.

VALENTINE: Don't be harsh with me. It means a great deal, you see, for a woman who was once in love to find one day, after an interminable absence, if not her lover, at least, in the faintest curl of his upper lip, the scrupulously exact copy of his ghost.

GASTON: I may be a highly exact ghost, but I am not Jacques Renaud.

VALENTINE: Look at me.

GASTON: I am looking at you. You're a charming woman, but I am not Jacques Renaud.

VALENTINE: Do I mean nothing at all to you – are you sure?

GASTON: Nothing.

VALENTINE: Then you'll never get your memory back, ever.

GASTON: I'm beginning to hope I shan't.

A pause. He adds, a little anxiously:

Why will I never get my memory back?

VALENTINE: Because you don't even remember someone you saw two years ago.

GASTON: Two years ago?

VALENTINE: A sewing-maid, a temporary sewing-maid.

GASTON: A sewing-maid?

A pause. He asks abruptly:

Who told you about that?

VALENTINE: Nobody. I put on that disguise – with my mother-in-law's full approval, by the way – so I could get really near you. Look at me, man without memories.

GASTON (*disturbed, in spite of himself*): That girl in the laundry who only stayed for a day – was that you?

VALENTINE: Yes, that was me.

GASTON: But you didn't say anything that day?

VALENTINE: I didn't want to say anything before we . . . I
hoped – you see what faith I have in love, in your love – I
hoped that in taking me you'd get your memory back.

GASTON: But afterwards?

VALENTINE: Afterwards, just as I was going to tell you, we
were interrupted, don't you remember?

GASTON (*smiling at the memory*): Oh, the housekeeper.

VALENTINE (*smiling too*): Yes, the housekeeper.

GASTON: But you didn't tell anybody that you'd recognized
me.

VALENTINE: Yes, I did, but there were fifty other families all
doing the same thing.

GASTON (*with a quick, nervous laugh*): Why, yes, that's right, how
stupid of me; everybody recognizes me! That doesn't prove
I'm Jacques Renaud at all!

VALENTINE: But you did remember your sewing-maid with
her big pile of sheets to mend?

GASTON: Yes, of course I remembered her. Apart from my
amnesia, my memory's very good.

VALENTINE: Do you want to hold her in your arms again?

GASTON (*pushing her away*): Let's wait until we find out if I'm
Jacques Renaud.

VALENTINE: And if you are?

GASTON: If I am, I won't hold her in my arms again for anything in the world. I don't want to be lover to my brother's
wife.

VALENTINE: But you already have been!

GASTON: It was so long ago and I've been so miserable since,
I've washed my youth away.

VALENTINE (*with a little triumphant laugh*): You're forgetting
your sewing-maid. If you're Jacques Renaud, you were your
brother's wife's lover as little as two years ago. You yourself
as you are now, not some remote boy of eighteen.

GASTON: I'm not Jacques Renaud.

VALENTINE: Listen, Jacques, you really will have to give up
this wonderfully simple life of yours. It's too easy to live
without a memory. You'll have to accept yourself, Jacques.

Our entire life, with our fine moral code and our precious freedom, consists ultimately in accepting ourselves as we are. Those seventeen years in hospital, during which you kept yourself so pure, that's the exact length of adolescence, your second adolescence, and today you've come of age. You're about to become a man again, with everything that entails in the way of failures and blemishes – and moments of happiness, too. Accept yourself and accept me, Jacques.

GASTON: If some conclusive proof forces me into it, I shall have to accept myself. But I'll never accept you!

VALENTINE: But you've already done it, whether you like it or not, two years ago!

GASTON: I won't take my brother's wife.

VALENTINE: When will you drop your fine phrases? You'll see, now that you're going to be a man – none of your new problems will be simple enough to sum up in a formula. You took me from him, yes. But he took me from you before that, merely because he was a man and master of his actions, before you were.

GASTON: Besides, there isn't only you. I don't care to have swindled old ladies and violated maids.

VALENTINE: What maids?

GASTON: And another little thing . . . I don't much care to have raised my hand against my mother, nor any of the other eccentricities of my appalling little double.

VALENTINE: Listen to you shouting! Why, not ten minutes ago you very nearly did exactly that yourself.

GASTON: I told an inhuman old woman that I hated her. But that old woman wasn't my mother.

VALENTINE: She was, Jacques. And that's why you said that to her so vehemently. And, you see, it was enough for you to rub shoulders for an hour with the characters out of your past for you to drop unconsciously into your old attitudes with them. Listen, Jacques, I'm going up to my room, because you're about to get very angry. In ten minutes you'll call me down again, because your rages are terrible, but they never last longer than ten minutes.

JACP—T

GASTON: How do you know? You're beginning to get on my nerves. You talk as though you knew me better than I know myself.

VALENTINE: But I do! Listen, Jacques, listen. There is one definite piece of proof which I've never been able to tell the others . . .

GASTON (*shrinking*): I don't believe you!

VALENTINE (*smiling*): Wait. I haven't told you yet.

GASTON (*shouting*): I won't believe you! I won't believe anybody! I won't listen to any more about my past!

The DUCHESS *bursts in, followed by* HUSPAR. VALENTINE *hides in the bathroom.*

DUCHESS: Gaston, Gaston, something terrible has happened. Some people have just arrived, fighting mad and yelling their heads off. It's one of your families. I had to receive them. They screamed abuse at me. It was dreadfully rash of me not to keep to the schedule we announced in the Press, I see that now. They think they've been tricked. They're going to make a scandal, accuse us of all sorts of terrible things!

HUSPAR: I'm sure nobody would dare question your ladyship's good faith.

DUCHESS: They're blinded by those two hundred and fifty thousand francs, can't you see that? They're talking of favouritism, of wire-pulling and the Lord knows what. Give them a bit longer and they'll be saying my little Albert is conspiring to give Gaston to the Renauds so they can all share out his money!

Enter the BUTLER.

BUTLER: Begging your ladyship's pardon, but some more persons have arrived and are asking for your ladyship and M. Huspar.

DUCHESS: Their names?

BUTLER: They gave me this card, which I did not presume to present to your ladyship straight away, as it pertains to trade.

He reads it with great dignity.

'Butter, eggs, cheeses. Bougran and Son.'

DUCHESS (*consulting her list*): Bougran? Bougran you say? It's the milkman!

The VALET *knocks and comes in.*

VALET: I beg your pardon, madame, but there's a gentleman, or rather a man, asking to see your ladyship. Judging by his attire, I'm afraid I didn't dare to ask him in.

DUCHESS (*looking at her list*): What name? Legropatre or Madensale?

VALET: Legropatre, your ladyship.

DUCHESS: Legropatre, that's the lamplighter. Show him in with all due ceremony. They've all come on the same train. The Madensales will be arriving at any minute. I've just telephoned Pont-au-Bronc. I'll try to keep them quiet.

She goes quickly out, followed by HUSPAR.

GASTON (*in a harassed murmur*): You all of you have proof, photographs that look like me, memories as cut and dried as crimes. I listen to you all and I can feel looming up behind me a monstrous hybrid creature, with a little bit of all your sons in it and nothing of me. Because your sons have nothing of me.

VALENTINE *has come in again.*

Me! Me! I exist, in spite of all your stories. You talk of the blissful simplicity of life without a memory. That's very funny . . . You try taking all the virtues, all the vices and loading them on to your back!

VALENTINE: Life will be much simpler for you if you'll only listen to me for a minute, Jacques. I'm offering you a past – a rather heavy one perhaps, but it will seem quite light because it frees you from all the others. Will you listen?

GASTON: Well?

VALENTINE: I've never seen you naked, have I? Well, you

have a scar, a very small scar which none of the doctors who examined you ever discovered, I'm sure – just under your left shoulder blade. It was made by a hatpin – the things we wore in 1917! – and I gave it to you one day when I thought you'd been unfaithful to me.

She goes out. He stands there stunned for a moment, then slowly takes off his jacket.

Curtain

SCENE 2

The CHAUFFEUR *and the* VALET *are standing on a chair in the passage, looking through a small inner window.*

VALET: Hey, look! He's taking his clothes off!

CHAUFFEUR (*elbowing him out of the way*): Go on! He's mad as a hatter, that one! What's he doing? Looking for fleas? Wait, wait! He's climbing on to a chair to look in the mantelpiece mirror.

VALET: Don't be daft, man! Climbing on to a chair?

CHAUFFEUR: I'm telling you!

VALET (*taking his place*): Let's have a look! Well, would you believe it! And just so he can look at his back! I tell you he's cracked. He's getting down now. He's seen what he wanted to see. He's putting his shirt on. Now he's sitting down. . . . Hullo? Well, I'll be done!

CHAUFFEUR: Why, what's he doing?

VALET (*turning round and goggling*): He's crying!

Curtain

Act Three

JACQUES'S *room. The shutters are closed, the russet gloom is streaked with light. It is morning.*

GASTON *is lying on the bed, asleep. The* BUTLER *and the* VALET *are bringing in the stuffed animals which they set around the bed. The* DUCHESS *and* MME RENAUD *are directing operations from the passage outside. All this is performed on tiptoe and in whispers.*

BUTLER: Shall we put these round the bed too, your ladyship?

DUCHESS: Yes, yes, all round his bed, so he'll see them the moment he wakes up.

MME RENAUD: Oh, if only the sight of these little creatures could bring him back to us!

DUCHESS: It may affect him very deeply.

MME RENAUD: He did so love trapping them! He'd climb trees up to giddy heights to put glue on the branches.

DUCHESS (*to the* BUTLER): Put one on his pillow. Yes, go on! Right on his pillow.

BUTLER: Don't you think it might frighten him, your ladyship, seeing this creature right by his face?

DUCHESS: An excellent thing, fright, in his case, my good man. An excellent thing. (*She goes to* MME RENAUD.) I'm sick with worry, you know, quite sick! I managed to quieten those people down last night by telling them that Huspar and my little Albert would be here first thing this morning. But God knows if we'll ever get rid of them without a riot.

The VALET *comes in again.*

VALET: M. Gaston's presumptive families have arrived, your ladyship.

DUCHESS: There, you see! I told them nine o'clock, and they're here at five minutes to. That class never gives an inch.

MME RENAUD: Where have you put them, Victor?

VALET: In the drawing-room, madame.

DUCHESS: Are there as many as yesterday? Safety in numbers – that's the peasant mentality all over.

VALET: There are more of them, your ladyship.

DUCHESS: More? How is that?

VALET: Yes, your ladyship, three more. They came together. A gentleman of good appearance, with a little boy and his nurse.

DUCHESS: Nurse? What sort of nurse?

VALET: An English one, your ladyship.

DUCHESS: Ah, those are the Madensales. Charming people, I believe. It's the English branch of the family who are claiming Gaston. Very touching to come all this way to find a loved one, don't you find? Please ask them to wait for a few minutes, will you?

MME RENAUD: But these people aren't going to take him away before he's decided about us, are they?

DUCHESS: No, no, don't distress yourself. The experiment began with you; we'll have to conclude it properly whether they like it or not. My little Albert promised he would be adamant on that point. However, we'll have to be extremely diplomatic if we're to avoid the faintest sniff of scandal.

MME RENAUD: I do feel you're exaggerating the danger of that, really!

DUCHESS: Not a bit of it! The Left Wing Press has its eye on my young Albert, I know it has. I have my spies. That lot will pounce on this like vultures on a carcass. And I cannot allow that to happen – much as I should like to see Gaston joining an enchanting family like yours. You're a mother – well, I'm an aunt. My flesh and blood come first.

She squeezes her hand.

But believe me, I'm just as lacerated as you are by the strain, the torment of it all!

The VALET *comes in with some stuffed squirrels. She watches him as he goes by.*

Why, it's ravishingly pretty, that squirrel fur. Why on earth has nobody thought of making coats out of it?

MME RENAUD (*dazed*): I don't know . . .

VALET: Too small, I expect.

BUTLER (*by the door, watching*): Hush! He's just moved.

DUCHESS: He musn't see us, whatever happens! (*To the* BUTLER.) Open the shutters.

Light floods into the room. GASTON *opens his eyes. He sees something close to his face. He recoils, and sits up.*

GASTON: What's that?

He looks around at all the stuffed squirrels, ferrets and weasels, his eyes starting out of his head, and shouts:

What are all these animals? What do they want with me?

BUTLER (*stepping forward*): They're stuffed, sir. They're the little creatures you used to kill, sir. Great fun you had. Don't you recognize them, sir?

GASTON (*hoarsely*): I've never killed any animals!

He has got up. The VALET *rushes over with his dressing-gown. They both go out to the bathroom.* GASTON *comes back a second later and goes over to the animals.*

How did he catch them?

BUTLER: Don't you remember, sir, the steel traps you used to pore over in the catalogues? For some of them, though, sir, you preferred to use glue.

GASTON: So they weren't dead when he found them?

BUTLER: Mostly not, sir, no. You used to finish them off with your knife. Very handy with it you were, sir.

A pause.

GASTON: What can one do for dead animals?

He goes to them with a timid gesture, too shy for a caress, and looks at them, murmuring:

How can one stroke these tight, leathery skins? I'll throw bread and nuts to other squirrels every day. I'll forbid anyone, on any land I own, to do the slightest harm to ferrets. But how can I comfort these for the long night when they were afraid and in pain and didn't know why, with their paws held in those cold steel jaws?

BUTLER: Oh, you mustn't fret yourself like that, sir. They don't matter much, not these little things. Besides, it's all over now.

GASTON: It's all over now . . . And even if I were powerful enough to make all little woodland creatures happy ever after, as you say – it's all over now.

Going into the bathroom:

Why am I wearing a different dressing-gown this morning?

BUTLER: This one belongs to you, too, sir. Madame told me to see you tried them all on, sir, in case you recognized one.

GASTON: What's this in the pockets? More souvenirs, like yesterday?

BUTLER: No, sir. This time it's mothballs.

The bathroom door shuts. The DUCHESS *and* MME RENAUD *come out of their hiding-place.*

(*As he goes.*) You heard what he said, madame. I don't think he recognized anything at all.

He goes out.

MME RENAUD (*tight-lipped*): If you ask me, he's doing it on purpose! He isn't even trying!

DUCHESS: If that were so, I should speak to him very severely, I promise you. But I'm afraid it goes deeper than that.

GEORGES *comes in.*

GEORGES: Is he awake?

DUCHESS: Yes. But our little plan didn't work, I'm sorry to say.

MME RENAUD: He was surprised and pained at seeing those dead animals, but that's all.

GEORGES: Would you mind leaving me alone with him? I'd like to talk to him if he'll let me.

MME RENAUD: Pray God you succeed, Georges! I'm beginning to lose hope.

GEORGES: No, no, Mother, you mustn't do that. We must keep hoping, whatever happens. However hopeless it looks.

MME RENAUD (*rather crossly*): Well, I'm getting rather tired of his attitude. Do you know what? I think he's sulking with me as he did in the old days.

GEORGES: But he hasn't even recognized you.

MME RENAUD: He was such a bad-tempered boy. Lost memory or no lost memory, why should he be any different now?

DUCHESS (*as they both move to go out*): I think you're exaggerating his hostility towards you. Of course, it's not for me to give you any advice, but you do act rather coldly towards him, if you don't mind my saying so. Gracious me, you're a mother, aren't you? Be pathetic, weep at his feet, grovel a little!

MME RENAUD: It is my dearest wish to see Jacques take up his rightful place here, Madame. But I really cannot go as far as that! Especially after what happened.

DUCHESS: That's a pity. I'm sure it would have a great effect on him. Why, if anyone was threatening to take my little Albert away from me, I'd be as savage as a tigress, I know I should. Did I ever tell you? – when he failed his matriculation, years ago, I marched in to the Professor of the Faculty and nearly tore his beard off.

They go out. Meanwhile, GEORGES *knocks on the bedroom door and goes in timidly.*

GEORGES: May I speak to you, Jacques?

GASTON (*from the bathroom*): Who is it now? I said I wanted to be left alone! Can't I even have a wash without somebody firing questions at me and shoving their reminiscences down my throat?

The VALET *pops his head through the bathroom door.*

VALET: Monsieur Jacques is in his bath, sir. (*To the invisible* GASTON.) It's Monsieur Georges, sir.

GASTON (*off, a little more affably*): Oh, it's you.

GEORGES (*to the* VALET): Leave us for a moment, will you, Victor?

The VALET *goes out.* GEORGES *moves nearer to the door.*

I want to say I'm sorry, Jacques . . . I quite realize we're annoying you with all our dramas. But what I want to tell you is important. If it doesn't bother you too much, I'd just like to say that—

GASTON (*interrupting*): What new filth in your brother's past are you going to rub my nose in this time?

GEORGES: It's not filth, Jacques, on the contrary. It's something I've been thinking. I'd like to tell you about it if you'll let me. (*He pauses for a second and then goes on.*) You see, just because one's honest, and always has been, just because one never did anything bad – which is easy, after all, for some – one tends to think one can say what one likes to people . . . One talks down to them, blames them for things, feels sorry for oneself . . . Are you angry with me about yesterday?

The answer comes after a slight pause, gruffly, almost reluctantly.

GASTON (*off*): Angry about what?

GEORGES: All the things I said. Acting the injured party, making it out to be worse than it was . . . The sort of moral blackmail I treated you to, with my pathetic little tale.

A sound from the bathroom. GEORGES *jumps up hastily.*

Wait! Don't come out yet! Let me finish, it's easier. If I see you I'll put on my elder-brother voice again and I'll never be able to drop it. You see, Jacques, I thought it all over very carefully last night. What happened wasn't very pretty, I know, but you were just a child – and so was she. And then again, at Dinard, before we got married, it was you she always wanted to be with, not me. Perhaps you were already in love by then and couldn't help yourselves, poor things . . . I came along and stepped between you with my clumsy great feet, my position, my age . . . I played the serious-minded suitor . . . Her aunt must have pressed her into accepting me. Anyway, the conclusion I came to last night was that I had no right to reproach you as I did, and I take it all back. That's all.

He drops into a chair, exhausted with the effort.
GASTON *comes out of the bathroom, goes to him and lays his hand gently on his shoulder.*

GASTON: How could you love that worthless little brute so much?

GEORGES (*almost apologetically*): He was my brother . . .

GASTON: He never once acted like a brother. He robbed you, he betrayed you . . . You would have hated your best friend if he'd done the half of what he did.

GEORGES: A friend is different; he was my brother . . .

GASTON: And anyway how can you want him back, even altered as he is, and older, and see him come between you and your wife again?

GEORGES (*simply*): Even if he were a murderer, he's one of the family. He belongs here.

GASTON (*repeating, after a pause*): He's one of the family, he belongs in the family. It's so simple, isn't it? (*He goes on, as if to himself:*) He thought he was a kind man; he isn't. He thought himself honest, and he's hardly that. I'm alone in the world, he thought, and free – in spite of the asylum walls – and instead the world is full of people to whom he is committed, and who are waiting for him. And his humblest acts and gestures can only be extensions of acts and gestures in the past. So simple! So very simple!

He seizes GEORGES *roughly by the arm.*

Why did *you* have to come along with your tale of woe into

the bargain? Why did you have to throw your affection in my
face? To make it simpler still, I suppose?

He drops on to the bed, strangely weary.

You've won.

GEORGES (*bewildered*): But, Jacques, I don't understand. What
have I done wrong? I came to tell you all this – and it
wasn't easy, believe me – so that you'd feel a little warmer in
the loneliness you must have known, ever since yesterday
morning.

GASTON: That loneliness wasn't the worst of my enemies.

GEORGES: You may have caught looks from the servants,
sensed a kind of embarrassment around you. But you mustn't
think nobody loved you . . . Mother—

GASTON *looks at him. He cannot finish. Instead, he says:*

And anyway, there was me; I was very fond of you.

GASTON: And apart from you? Who?

GEORGES: Well – er . . . (*Embarrassed.*) Well, Valentine, I
expect.

GASTON: She was in love with me, that's different. No, there
was only you.

GEORGES (*his head bent*): Perhaps, yes.

GASTON: Why, though? I simply can't understand why.

GEORGES (*gently*): Did you never dream of a friend, a friend
who was first a little boy who'd hold your hand and go for
walks with you? You care about friendship – just think what
a boon it can be to have a friend so new that he owes the
secret of his first carefully spelled out letters to you, his first
shaky rides on a bicycle, his first floundering strokes in the
water. A friend so defenceless that he needs you there all the
time to protect him.

A pause.

GASTON: Was I very young when our father died?

GEORGES: You were two.

GASTON: And you?

GEORGES: Fourteen. So I had to look after you, didn't I? You were so little.

A pause. He tells him his real reason.

You've always been so little – for everything. For the money we gave you far too soon, fools that we were. For mother's harshness and for my own weakness too, for my incompetence. That pride, that violence in you, which you wrestled with even at two years old, they were devils you couldn't be blamed for and it was up to us to save you from them. Not only were we incapable of doing so, but we condemned you for them and we let you go off all alone to the front. With your rifle and your kitbag and your gas mask, you must have made such a little soldier, standing there on the station platform.

GASTON (*shrugging*): The ones that looked so fierce with their big moustaches were just little soldiers, too, I imagine.

GEORGES (*with a cry of pain almost*): Yes, but you were eighteen! And apart from Latin verbs and the multiplication tables, the very first thing grown men were going to require of you in life was mopping up a slit trench with a kitchen knife.

GASTON (*with a hollow laugh*): What of it? Dealing out death strikes me as an excellent initiation into life, for a young man.

The BUTLER *comes in.*

BUTLER: Her ladyship requests you to be so kind as to join her in the drawing-room as soon as you are ready, sir.

GEORGES (*getting up*): I'll leave you. But please, despite all they may have told you, don't hate that Jacques too much. I think he was, more than anything else, a poor little lad . . .

He goes. The BUTLER *helps* GASTON *to dress.*

GASTON (*abruptly*): Butler?
BUTLER: Sir?
GASTON: Have you ever killed a man?
BUTLER: You're joking, I trust, sir. If I had ever killed anybody I certainly shouldn't be in madame's service, sir.

GASTON: Not even during the war? A sudden tussle in a shell hole, man to man?

BUTLER: I fought the war as a corporal in the quartermaster's stores, sir, and I must say, sir, we had very few openings of that sort in the supply depot.

GASTON, *motionless and very pale, says very quietly:*

GASTON: You're a lucky man. Because it's an appalling sensation to kill somebody so that one can live.

BUTLER (*not knowing whether to laugh*): Appalling is right, sir. Especially for the victim.

GASTON: You're wrong, butler. It's all a question of imagination. And the victim often has much less imagination than the murderer.

A pause.

Sometimes, even, he's no more than a shadow in the murderer's dream.

BUTLER: In that case, I can see he wouldn't suffer much, sir.

GASTON: But the murderer has the privilege of two lots of suffering. Do you like living, butler?

BUTLER: As much as the next man, sir.

GASTON: Imagine that in order to live you had to hurl a young man into oblivion, for ever. A young man of eighteen. A young thug, a young swaggerer, but even so, a poor little lad. You will be free, the freest man on earth, but in order to be free you have to leave that innocent little corpse behind you. What are you going to do?

BUTLER: I must confess I've never asked myself the question, sir. But if detective stories are anything to go by, the last thing you want to do is leave a corpse behind.

GASTON (*bursts out laughing*): But what if nobody except the murderer can see the corpse, anyway? (*He goes to him and says kindly:*) There. The deed's done. He's there, at your feet. Do you see him?

The BUTLER *looks down at his feet, jumps aside, looks around and then scuttles out in terror, as fast as his dignity will allow.* VALENTINE *comes quickly into the passage. She runs into the room.*

VALENTINE: What's this Georges tells me? Haven't you told them yet? I didn't like to come into your room before the others this morning, but I was expecting they'd call me any minute with the good news. Why didn't you tell them?

GASTON *looks at her and says nothing.*

Are you trying to send me out of my mind? That scar – you saw it in the mirror yesterday, you must have!

GASTON (*quietly, without taking his eyes off her*): I saw no scar.

VALENTINE: What did you say?

GASTON: I said I looked at my back very carefully and I saw no scar on it at all. You must have made a mistake.

VALENTINE *looks at him for a second, dazed, then she understands and cries:*

VALENTINE: Oh, I hate you! I hate you!

GASTON (*very calmly*): I think it's better that way.

VALENTINE: But do you realize what you're doing?

GASTON: Yes. I am refusing my past and all the characters in it – myself included. You may all be my family, my loves, the true story of my life. But you see . . . I don't like you. I'm rejecting you, all of you.

VALENTINE: But you're mad! You're a monster! One can't reject one's past! One can't reject oneself!

GASTON: Yes, I expect I'm the only man who's ever had the God-given chance to do what must be everybody's secret dream. I'm a grown man, and if I choose to I can be as new and unmarked as a child. It would be criminal not to use that privilege. I refuse you. I have too many things to forget about myself as it is, since yesterday morning.

VALENTINE: And my love, my love for you, what are you going to do with that? You aren't interested enough to want to find out about that either, I suppose?

GASTON: All I can see of it just now is the hatred in your eyes. It must be one of the aspects of love that only a man without a memory could wonder at. In any case, it's a very useful one. I don't want to see another. I am a lover who doesn't know his mistress's love, a lover who doesn't remember the first kiss, the first tear, a lover who's shackled by no memories, who'll have forgotten everything tomorrow. That's a rare enough gift, too. I mean to make full use of it.

VALENTINE: And what if I shout it to the world that I recognized that scar?

GASTON: I've envisaged that possibility. From the point of view of love: I think the old Valentine would have done it long ago and it's a fairly cheering sign that you've become so cautious. From the legal point of view: you are my sister-in-law, you claim to be my mistress. What court of law would make a decision as serious as this one on an unsavoury bedroom intrigue which only you can vouch for?

VALENTINE (*with clenched teeth*): I see. Congratulations, you must be feeling very pleased with yourself. But don't imagine, apart from all that claptrap about your lost memory, that your behaviour is particularly unusual for a man. Why, I'm sure you're secretly quite proud of your grand gesture. It's so flattering, isn't it, to repulse a woman who's waited for you for so long? Well, I'm sorry if this hurts you, but I *have* had other lovers, you know, since the war!

GASTON (*smiling*): Thank you. It didn't hurt.

The VALET *and the* BUTLER *appear in the passage. From their dumbshow, it is clear they consider it safer to approach* GASTON *together.*

VALET (*in the doorway*): Her Grace the Duchess Dupont-Dufort requests me to request you to hurry and join her in the drawing-room as soon as possible, sir, as your families are getting restive.

GASTON *has not moved. The servants go out again.* VALENTINE *bursts out laughing.*

VALENTINE: Your families, Jacques! Oh, I have to laugh, it's too silly! Because, you see, you're forgetting one thing. If you refuse to come to us, you'll have to go to them, won't you? Whether you like it or not. You'll have to sleep in their dead son's sheets, wear their dead son's flannel waist-coats, put on his reverently kept old slippers. Your families are getting restless. Come. You're so afraid of your past – come and see their screwed-up little tradesmen's faces, come and ask yourself what a past of avarice and penny-pinching they have to offer you.

GASTON: They'll find it difficult to outdo you, at any rate.

VALENTINE: You think so? Those ill-gotten five hundred thousand francs spent on laughter and gay living may seem very light beside certain tales of stolen widows' savings and greasy banknotes hoarded in old stockings. Come along. Since you don't want us, you owe yourself to your other families now.

She tries to pull him out.

GASTON: No. I won't go.

VALENTINE: Oh. What are you going to do, then?

GASTON: I'll go away.

VALENTINE: Where?

GASTON: Where? Anywhere.

VALENTINE: That's an amnesia word. The rest of us, who have a memory, know that one always has to pick a destination at the railway station and that one never goes any farther than the price of one's ticket. If you had money, the world would be open to you, but you haven't a penny in your pocket. So what are you going to do?

GASTON: Upset your plans, leave on foot, across country, and make for Chateaudun.

VALENTINE: Do you feel so free since you got rid of us? To the police you're only an escaped lunatic from an asylum. They'll arrest you.

GASTON: I'll be miles away. I walk very fast.

VALENTINE (*shouting in his face*): Do you think I won't give the alarm if you take one step out of this room?

He goes abruptly to the window.

Don't be absurd. The window's too high up and that isn't a solution.

He turns back to her like a trapped animal. She looks at him and says softly:

You may get rid of us, but you won't rid yourself of your habit of letting your thoughts flit across your eyes as you think them. No, Jacques, even if you killed me to gain one hour's start, they'd catch you. You can't escape.

He drops his head and stands at bay in the corner of the room.

Besides, you know perfectly well that I'm not the only one who's on your trail and wants to keep you. All women do, and all men. Even the right-minded dead, who can sense in some vague way that you're trying to let them down. One can't escape so many people, Jacques. And whether you want to or not, you'll have to belong to somebody or go back to your asylum.

GASTON (*dully*): Then I'll go back to my asylum.

VALENTINE: You forget I worked for a whole day in your asylum. I saw you hoeing lettuces very happily, but I saw you emptying slops and washing dishes too; hustled by the attendants; begging the kitchen staff for a pinch of tobacco for your pipe . . . You're acting proud with us; you snarl at us, you mock us, but without us you're nothing but a helpless little boy who isn't allowed to go out by himself and who has to hide in the lavatories if he wants to have a smoke.

GASTON (*when she has finished*): You can go. I haven't the smallest rag of hope left now. You've done your work.

She goes out without a word. GASTON *remains alone. He casts a weary glance around the room. He stops in front of the mirror and gazes at himself for a long while. Suddenly, he picks up an object from the table, without taking his eyes off his reflection, throws it at the mirror and shatters it. Then he slumps down on the bed and buries his head in his hands. Then, very quietly, the music starts, rather sad at first, then gradually, despite* GASTON, *despite us, it grows gayer. After a while a* SMALL BOY *in an Eton suit opens the door of the little hall, casts a furtive glance around, then carefully closes the door and ventures into the passage on tiptoe. He opens all the doors as he passes and casts an inquiring look inside the rooms. He gets to the bedroom door and does likewise. He finds himself face to face with* GASTON, *who looks up in surprise at the apparition.*

SMALL BOY: Excuse me, sir. I'm sorry to disturb you, but could you tell me where the little place is?

GASTON (*coming out of a dream*): Little place? What little place?

SMALL BOY: The little place where you can be by yourself.

GASTON *looks at him and then bursts into a sudden, good-natured laugh.*

GASTON: Well, isn't that funny? Do you know, that's just what I'm looking for, a little place where I can be by myself.

SMALL BOY: I wonder who we could ask, then?

GASTON (*still laughing*): I wonder too.

SMALL BOY: Anyway, you haven't got much chance of finding it if you stay there. (*He sees the broken glass.*) Oh dear, was it you broke the glass?

GASTON: Yes.

SMALL BOY: I can see why you look so worried, then. But if I were you, I'd own up straight away. You're a grown-up; they can't do much to you. They say it means seven years bad luck, though . . .

GASTON: They do say that, yes.

SMALL BOY (*going out*): I think I'll walk along the passage. I might meet one of the servants. I'll ask him and then I'll come back and tell you where it is.

GASTON *looks at him.*

The little place we're both looking for, I mean.

GASTON (*smiling and calling him back*): Wait a second. Your
little place, where you can be by yourself, is much easier to
find than mine is. You have one right here, in the bathroom.
SMALL BOY: Thank you very much, sir.

*He goes into the bathroom. The music takes up its mocking little
theme again. The* SMALL BOY *comes back after a second or two.*
GASTON *has not moved.*

I'd better get back to the drawing-room now. Is it this way?
GASTON: Yes. Are you with the families?
SMALL BOY: Yes. It's full of all sorts of strange people who've
come to identify a man who lost his memory in the war.
That's what I've come for, as a matter of fact. We rushed over
by plane, because it seems there's some funny business going
on. Of course, I don't really know what it's all about. You'll
have to talk to Uncle Job. Have you ever been up in an
aeroplane?
GASTON: Which family do you belong to?
SMALL BOY: The Madensales.
GASTON: Madensales. Ah yes, the English people. I remember
the file very well. Next of kin: uncle. Why, I even copied the
name down on the list. There *is* an uncle among the
Madensales, am I right?
SMALL BOY: Yes, sir . . .
GASTON: Yes, of course, Uncle Job. Well, you can tell Uncle
Job that if he takes my advice he won't hold out too much
hope over his nephew.
SMALL BOY: Why do you say that?
GASTON: Because there's every chance that the said nephew
may never recognize Uncle Job.
SMALL BOY: But there's no reason why he should. It isn't
Uncle Job who's looking for his nephew.
GASTON: Oh. Is there another uncle, then?
SMALL BOY: Yes, of course there is. And it's rather funny,
actually. You see, it's me.
GASTON (*blinking*): You? You mean your father, don't you?

SMALL BOY: No. Me. And it's very awkward for a small boy to be a grown-up person's uncle, I can tell you. It took me ages just to grasp it. But my father had children very late in life, you see, so that's how it happened. I was born twenty-six years after my nephew.

GASTON *bursts out laughing and draws the* SMALL BOY *on to his knee.*

GASTON: So you're Uncle Madensale?
SMALL BOY: Yes. But don't make fun of me, it's not my fault.
GASTON: But then, that Uncle Job you were talking about – who's he?
SMALL BOY: Oh, he's an old friend of my father's; he's the lawyer who deals with all the business about my heirs. I just call him uncle; he isn't really.
GASTON: But how do you come to be the sole representative of the Madensale family?
SMALL BOY: It's because of a dreadful disaster at sea. Have you ever heard of the sinking of the *Neptunia*?
GASTON: Yes. Years ago.
SMALL BOY: Well, my entire family went for a cruise in her.

GASTON *looks at him in wonder.*

GASTON: So all your relations are dead?
SMALL BOY (*kindly*): Yes. But you needn't look at me like that, you know. It's not so sad really. I was only a baby when it happened. To tell the truth, I didn't even notice it.

GASTON *sets him on the ground, looks at him, then pats him on the back.*

GASTON: Little Uncle Madensale, you're a great character, did you but know it.
SMALL BOY: I'm not bad at cricket, actually. Do you play cricket?
GASTON: What I don't understand is why Uncle Job should come all the way from England to find a nephew for his

young client. A nephew who'll complicate his finances more than somewhat, I should think.

SMALL BOY: Oh, you can't know much about the rights of succession then. It's very involved, but I think it goes like this. If I don't find my nephew, then most of my money gets whisked away from under our nose. I'm very worried about it because among the property that's supposed to come to me there's a lovely house in Sussex with some marvellous stables with ponies. Do you like riding?

GASTON (*suddenly thoughtful*): So Uncle Job must be very keen indeed to find your nephew?

SMALL BOY: I should just say he is! For his sake as well as mine. He won't admit it, but my nurse told me that he gets a percentage on all my income.

GASTON: Ah, I see. And what sort of a man is this Uncle Job?

SMALL BOY: He's rather round, with white hair.

GASTON: No, I didn't mean that. But I don't suppose you can really tell me what I want to know. Where is he at the moment?

SMALL BOY: Smoking his pipe in the garden. He didn't want to wait in the drawing-room with the others.

GASTON: Good. Will you take me to him?

SMALL BOY: If you like.

GASTON *rings the bell. The* VALET *appears.*

GASTON: Tell her ladyship that I have an announcement of vital importance to make to her. Do you get that? Of vital importance. Will you ask her to be so good as to come up here, please?

VALET: Of vital importance. Very good, sir. You can rely on me.

He goes out, highly excited, muttering:

Of vital importance . . .

GASTON *leads the* SMALL BOY *towards the other door.*

GASTON: Let's go this way.

He gets to the door, stops and asks:

Tell me, you're quite sure everybody's dead in your family?
SMALL BOY: Yes, everybody. Even their best friends. They all
went on that cruise together.
GASTON: That's perfect.

*He ushers him ahead and follows him out. The music starts again,
mocking. The stage is empty for a while, then the DUCHESS comes
in, followed by the VALET.*

DUCHESS: What do you mean, he wants to see me? But he
knows I've been waiting for him downstairs for the last
twenty minutes! An announcement, you said?
VALET: Of vital importance.
DUCHESS: Well, where is he?

GASTON, *followed by* UNCLE JOB *and the* SMALL BOY, *comes
solemnly into the room. The orchestra performs a tremolo or something like it.*

GASTON: Duchess, may I introduce Mr Truggle, solicitor to
the Madensale family. And this is their sole surviving
member. Mr Truggle has just told me something very
disturbing. He maintains that his client's nephew had a slight
scar, an inch or so below the left shoulder blade, which
nobody knows about. An old letter he came across in a book
recently informed him of this fact.
TRUGGLE: The letter in question will, of course, be at the
disposal of the hospital authorities as soon as I get back to
England.
DUCHESS: But this scar, Gaston – have you ever seen it? Has
anybody?
GASTON: Nobody.
TRUGGLE: It's so small, madame, that I guessed it might have
gone unnoticed until now.
GASTON (*taking his coat off*): We'll soon find out. Would you
care to look?

He pulls up his shirt. The DUCHESS *takes her lorgnette.* MR
TRUGGLE *puts on his thick glasses.* GASTON *leans forward to talk
to the* SMALL BOY *while the others examine his back.*

SMALL BOY: That scar really is there, isn't it? I'd be terribly
disappointed if it wasn't you.

GASTON: Don't you worry. It's me all right. Tell me, don't
you really remember anything about your family? Not a
single face? Not even a little story?

SMALL BOY: No stories at all. But if that bothers you, I might
try to find out.

GASTON: No. Don't.

DUCHESS (*peering at his back, cries out suddenly*): There! There!
There it is! Oh my God, it's there!

TRUGGLE: So it is! So it is!

DUCHESS: Kiss me, Gaston! I insist you kiss me! Oh, it's such
a marvellous adventure!

TRUGGLE (*quite straight-faced*): And so unexpected.

DUCHESS (*sinking into a chair*): Oh, the shock! I think I may be
going to faint.

GASTON (*helping her to her feet with a smile*): I don't think you
will.

DUCHESS: Nor do I. I'll telephone Pont-au-Bronc instead.
But tell me, Monsieur Madensale, there's something I should
so like to know. At the last pentothal injection he gave you,
my little Albert managed to make you say 'Piddleprick' in
your delirium. Is that a word which connects you to your
past life now?

GASTON: Shush. Don't tell a soul. That was my pet name for
him.

DUCHESS (*horrified*): My little Albert! (*She hesitates, then changes
her mind.*) Never mind, we forgive you. (*She turns to
TRUGGLE, simpering.*) It's his English sense of humour, I
realize that now.

TRUGGLE: Precisely.

DUCHESS (*as the thought strikes her*): But what a terrible blow for
the Renaud family! However am I going to break it to them?

GASTON (*cheerfully*): I'll leave it to you. I shall be out of this house in five minutes and I shan't be seeing them again.

DUCHESS: Haven't you even a message for them?

GASTON: No. No message. Oh, yes, on second thoughts . . . (*He hesitates.*) Tell Georges Renaud that his brother's light ghost lies sleeping in a common grave somewhere in Germany. He was never anything but a child deserving all forgiveness, a child he can love now without fear of reading anything vile on his man's face. There. And now . . .

He opens the door wide, and ushers them out with a kind little wave of the hand. He holds the SMALL BOY *close.*

Leave me alone with my family. We have to compare our memories . . .

Triumphant music. The DUCHESS *goes out with* MR TRUGGLE.

Curtain

Dinner with the Family

Characters

PROPRIETRESS

GEORGES

EMILE

DELMONTE
(*an Actor*)

MME DE MONTRACHET
(*an Actress*)

BARBARA

JACQUES

M. DELACHAUME

ESMÉ

MME DELACHAUME

ISABELLE

DOCTOR

Original Title: Le Rendez-vous de Senlis
Translator: Edward Owen Marsh
First produced in 1937

Act One

A rococo drawing-room of a large house in Senlis, some twenty-five miles from Paris. The time is the present. The owner of the house – the PROPRIETRESS *– and* GEORGES *are in the dining-room. The door at the back, leading out of it, is wide open, and the* PROPRIETRESS *is reading from a large-size document.*

PROPRIETRESS: '. . . And four copper flower-pots chased and ornamented.'

GEORGES (*in tired repetition*): 'Four ornamented flower-pots.' Yes . . . they're there . . . they would be!

PROPRIETRESS: I beg your pardon?

GEORGES: I was saying how lovely they are.

PROPRIETRESS: I should think so! They were a wedding present!

GEORGES (*defeated by this argument*): Oh! Of course . . .

They have now moved into the drawing-room.

PROPRIETRESS: That's finished the dining-room. Now we come to the large drawing-room. We'll begin with the walls again. Let me see . . . (*She reads.*) 'Walls covered in figured silk with a delicate pattern of flowers, trees and birds.'

GEORGES: I'm sorry. Do you mind if I stop you there? . . . I can't see any birds.

PROPRIETRESS: Can't you? Really?

GEORGES: No. I'm not trying to be awkward. There just aren't any birds. Let me see your inventory. (*Reads.*) 'Walls covered in figured silk, with a delicate pattern of flowers, trees *and birds.*' We are in the drawing-room, I suppose?

PROPRIETRESS: Of course! I know my own house, I hope!

GEORGES: Trees, yes . . . at a pinch you could even guess at

the flowers, but, with the best will in the world, I can't see a
bird. Look for yourself.

PROPRIETRESS (*putting some effort into searching for the birds, her
eyes glued to the wall*): I'm not wearing my spectacles, you see.

GEORGES: The day I leave this house I don't want to find I'm
legally bound to pay for a flock of imaginary birds!

PROPRIETRESS (*bewildered*): I've had these inventories a
terribly long time, just as they are. No one's ever questioned
them before. It was a very competent man indeed who did
them for me. . . .

GEORGES: Perhaps the birds were taken away by the previous
tenant.

PROPRIETRESS (*attempts a wan smile*): From a wall pattern? . . .

GEORGES: There's no limit nowadays to what people steal.
Anyway, there's no disputing it, there isn't a trace of a bird
on that wall! Not a feather!

PROPRIETRESS (*who hasn't yet lost all hope*): This little design
here? Don't you think . . .? Here, the head . . . there, the
tail?

GEORGES: A bird with a beak growing out of its stomach?

PROPRIETRESS: What shall we do, then?

GEORGES (*laughs*): I can only see one thing to do: scrap the
inventory.

PROPRIETRESS: You think that's funny! Anyone can see
you're young. If you were my age you'd have something else
to think about, a worry or two to spoil some of the fun you
seem to get out of life. . . .

GEORGES (*with a sudden sad crease in his lips*): Oh, worry's got a
taste for young flesh, too, sometimes.

PROPRIETRESS: Listen! I'll leave just the 'trees and flowers'.
Let's forget about the birds, shall we?

GEORGES: Thank you. Now, have we many more rooms to
see?

PROPRIETRESS: How impatient you are! We've only done the
dining-room and the hall, so far; there are still the two
drawing-rooms and seven rooms upstairs.

GEORGES (*looks at the time*): It's taken us thirty-five minutes to

do those two rooms. There are nine more. That makes about
– three hours if we work steadily through the lot.

PROPRIETRESS (*very proudly*): Yes! This inventory runs to
ninety-two pages!

GEORGES: Does it really? I'm afraid I'm expecting some
people by the seven-ten train and it's now two minutes to
seven. So I have a total of twelve minutes at your disposal
. . . Which room shall we do?

PROPRIETRESS (*hopping with emotion*): Twelve minutes! Why,
it's ridiculous!

GEORGES: Quite!

PROPRIETRESS: But you can't blame me, can you, when you
come wanting the house all in five minutes? You took it as
from the first of the month, I know, but you didn't move in.
I couldn't check the inventory without you. And now you
drop on me without warning, just when I'm sitting down to
dinner, and everything's got to be done in a flash. I think
I'm being very accommodating in allowing you to move in
at all at this time of day . . . It's not usual, you know.

GEORGES: My plans changed unexpectedly . . . I must have
the house this evening.

PROPRIETRESS: Well, if you must, you must, but an inventory
is an inventory, remember. (*She tries a bold stroke.*) Come, we'll
go through it quickly. We won't look at the servants' rooms
today . . . You see, I'm doing my best to meet you. (*Picks
up her list.*) Let me see: '. . . with flowers and trees. At the
windows, two large red damask curtains and holders made
of the same metal.'

GEORGES: The same metal? . . . What metal?

PROPRIETRESS: How do you mean, what metal?

GEORGES: I think you'd better read that item again. Then
you'll see for yourself.

PROPRIETRESS: 'Two large red damask curtains and holders
made of the same metal.' (*She repeats.*) '. . . of the same
metal.' (*She thinks for a moment.*) . . . Yes, there must be a
mistake, or a line missed out. He was a very competent man,
you know, but, of course, he was rather old. . . .

JACP–X

GEORGES: Far too old. It's crawling with mistakes . . . And you want me to sign that? I'm ready to believe in your good faith, but there is a limit . . . 'Curtains and holders of the same metal!' There's no mention of any metal! What if, the day I leave, you come down on me for a set of gold holders for your damask curtains?

PROPRIETRESS: Gold holders? Oh, no, you're joking. . . .

GEORGES: You would be well within your rights. I know what a signature can involve. I'm not prepared to spend any more time on this fantastic inventory. You can tell the aged and competent gentleman responsible for it . . .

PROPRIETRESS: He's dead. . . .

GEORGES: Then you mustn't disturb him! Give me the inventory, I'll sign it. This is just to stop you worrying – people always exaggerate their worries at your age. It's such a mistake. You can always smooth out life's little difficulties, you know, somehow. At least for one evening. With a little imagination a man can live his whole life in the space of an evening. (*He signs.*) 'Read and approved. Georges Delachaume.' There! Now, it will all seem much simpler . . . (*He looks at his watch.*) . . . In eleven minutes' time everything in your house must be mine, including the invisible birds on the figured silk and the curtain holders made of the same metal.

PROPRIETRESS (*a little frightened by this flow of words*): Yours . . . yours? But we must understand one another, please, M. Delachaume . . . I mean . . . I know you've rented it for the month, but that gives you no right to . . .

GEORGES: No rights at all, Mme Guillaume. I know . . . but listen to me. (*He sits her down and seats himself opposite her.*) You seem to be quite a nice old lady. . . .

PROPRIETRESS (*wondering what's behind all this*): Oh, I'm not at all . . . really. . . .

GEORGES: What's more, you have a charming old house, but you never manage to let it, do you? Now I've paid you quite a high price to have this place, for a month. . . .

PROPRIETRESS (*plaintively*): I wanted to let it for the year. . . .

GEORGES (*amused*): And I wanted to take it for the year! We all want to do things by the year, Mme Guillaume, but we can never manage them for more than a week, sometimes only a day. That's what life's like.

PROPRIETRESS: A day! Oh, no! Never! It's humiliating enough already to let by the month. I'm not a boarding-house landlady!

GEORGES (*seriously*): You're too finicky, Mme Guillaume, believe me! I'd be the happiest man alive, if I could live in your house a whole month.

PROPRIETRESS: There's nothing to stop you! You've paid until the first of July!

GEORGES: Yes, I know. But I shall only stay here for one night. Tonight.

PROPRIETRESS: It's nothing to do with me, but what I don't understand is . . .

GEORGES: What?

PROPRIETRESS: . . . why a young man who lives alone should need a large house like this, miles away from Paris, buried in the country. . . .

GEORGES: I have to entertain relations. Incidentally – I am sure you'll understand – it would be rather embarrassing for me to have to explain to . . . er . . . these relations – that I only moved in this evening. Would you be very kind and stay upstairs in your room? And do please hide this inventory somewhere.

PROPRIETRESS: I'll leave you the copy. You can check it over tomorrow when you have more time.

GEORGES: I'll do my best with it.

PROPRIETRESS: May I say that I make a point of never disturbing my tenants. Ah, I forgot . . . you can't use this telephone. It hasn't any wires, you see. It's a souvenir . . . Oh, and be careful of this arm-chair; one leg is broken. If your relatives are heavy people, you'd do better to give them the sofa. Do be careful of the window, too, the glass is so fragile. There are sixty-three separate little panes; one of them's just been reglued. This one.

GEORGES (*resigned*): This one's reglued. I'll guard it with my life.

PROPRIETRESS (*goes off, but stops with a little cry – she points to the wall with a feverish finger*): Oh, look there, to the left of that candelabrum. Wouldn't you say that looks rather like a bird?

GEORGES (*pitiless*): No.

PROPRIETRESS (*sighs and goes out reading her inventory*): 'Flowers, trees *and birds.*'

A ring at the door.

GEORGES: That's for me. I'll open the door myself.

PROPRIETRESS (*going out*): But won't your relatives think it odd, your living in this big house without any servants?

GEORGES: Thank you, I've thought of that.

They have gone out. The stage is empty for a moment. GEORGES *comes back with the* BUTLER.

Dufort's do things promptly; it's scarcely an hour since I telephoned. . . .

BUTLER: We always have a few choice dinners in readiness, sir. It just means putting the dishes into a van and off we go. My assistants are in the kitchen already, sir. The champagne is on ice, the claret at the right temperature. In a quarter of an hour dinner can be served. (*He recites.*)

'Nothing warmed up, all quite hot.
Time and distance, trouble not:
   A miracle, just one more,
   From the firm of Jean *Dufort.*' (*Bows.*)

GEORGES: Do *you* believe in them?

BUTLER: In what, sir?

GEORGES: Miracles.

BUTLER (*changing his tone*): No, sir. Still, Dufort's is one of the best-organized and best . . .

GEORGES (*giving him money*): How old is the vol-au-vent which is 'never warmed up, always hot'?

BUTLER (*modest*): Oh, sir, beautifully mature. If you have any little pets, sir, they're usually fond of the crust . . . as for the sauce, well . . . (*A vague gesture.*)

GEORGES: I see we understand one another. Serve what you're sure is all right and that's all. And don't let it look too much like a banquet! Now there's one special thing, that may sound rather odd, I suppose, to you . . . Please don't serve anything that obviously comes from Dufort's!

BUTLER: I don't quite follow, sir.

GEORGES: Listen, I've had to improvise this meal. I turned to a caterer because I had so little time, but, so far as my guests are concerned, everything has been cooked here in the house. Do you follow me now?

BUTLER: Perfectly, sir.

GEORGES: What are your assistants like? Pretty rough-looking individuals?

BUTLER (*with scorn*): Just assistants, sir . . .

GEORGES: Don't have them too much in evidence.

BUTLER: I intended to keep them out in any case, sir. One because of his smell, sir, and the other has a glass eye.

GEORGES: In the kitchen, definitely! I want very simple service. Nothing *Dufort* about it. Is that clear?

BUTLER: Very well, sir, but . . .

GEORGES (*giving him another tip*): But what?

BUTLER (*tucking the note away quickly*): There is no 'but'.

GEORGES: Have you always been a hired butler?

BUTLER (*wounded*): One is not born so, sir, one becomes it in self-defence. I was seventeen years with the Duke of Maine, sir.

GEORGES: Seventeen years? What made you leave him?

BUTLER (*flattered*): You are very kind to suppose that it was I who left, sir. It was the Duke who had to leave me.

GEORGES: Ruined?

BUTLER: Yes, sir, er . . . physically, through abuse, sir. His heart was finished; kidneys refused to function; the arteries, sir, just a lot of old piping . . .

GEORGES: Spare me the full description. The main thing is that you have been in a well-to-do household. What is your name?

BUTLER: Graduzac.

GEORGES: I meant your Christian name.

BUTLER: Emile. But the custom, sir, with a hired butler is . . .

GEORGES: Emile, what I want is not customary; that is precisely the point. You are a man with imagination, I can see . . . Now . . . picture yourself dandling me on your knee.

BUTLER (*stepping back*): Me, sir?

GEORGES: You, Emile.

BUTLER (*embarrassed*): I don't know if you realize, sir, that I am getting on in years, and I hope nothing in my appearance could lead anyone to suppose. . . .

GEORGES: We are at cross-purposes! The thing I'm asking is very simple and quite respectable. I want you to say, not that you are hired but that you are the permanent butler in this house? Is that clear?

BUTLER: Yes, sir. In nine cases out of ten, sir . . . vanity rules people's lives.

GEORGES: Well, that's the first point. Next, Emile, I want you always to have been here . . . since my childhood. Would it be asking too much for you to have been here when I was born?

BUTLER: It would be an honour, sir. An honour and a pleasure. I adore babies.

GEORGES: It's too late for the pleasure, I'm afraid. But take the honour, by all means.

BUTLER: Delighted. From now on, I say that I was here when you were born, sir.

GEORGES: Right. And you dandled me on your knee when I was no bigger than that. . . .

BUTLER (*with relief*): No bigger than that . . . The size makes all the difference.

GEORGES (*cutting in*): How much did I give you just now?

BUTLER: I have forgotten, sir . . . It is a principle with me.

GEORGES: Good. If I give you twice that amount to play the old family butler just for dinner this evening, will that be all right?

BUTLER: Could you go, sir, to another five thousand?

GEORGES: Done!

BUTLER (*suddenly warming up*): In that case, I've been with the family for years, sir. And my father was butler here before me. I worked in the kitchen when I was young, went off to various parts of the world to learn the business; and, when my father had to retire, I came back to take his place.

GEORGES: Fine! But don't embroider too much. I shall be introducing you to my parents in a moment.

BUTLER: Won't your parents be rather surprised, sir?

GEORGES (*smiling*): Not in the least, don't worry!

A ring at the door.

Emile. Go and let my parents in, will you?

BUTLER (*starting to go out*): Certainly, Baron.

GEORGES (*with a start*): What?!

BUTLER (*ingenuously*): Don't you think I should give you a title while we are about it, sir?

GEORGES: Listen, Emile. I'm not trying to put the grand family across – not that at all. Old retainer, simple and honest, almost one of the family, that's your line . . . If I hadn't been pressed for time I would probably have preferred an old Breton nursemaid. . . .

BUTLER (*reproachfully*): Oh! sir! Breton nursemaids are overdone . . . ten a penny, sir . . . no one with real taste, sir, would ever . . .

GEORGES: Anyway, simplicity's the keynote . . . no title. Do you see?

BUTLER: As you wish, sir . . . There is one point, though . . . Are we in your house, sir, or in your . . . er . . . parents' house?

GEORGES: My parents' house.

BUTLER: In that case would you be so good as to tell me your first name, sir? Custom requires that I call your father simply 'Monsieur', and you yourself 'Monsieur Jean' or 'Monsieur Lucien', or 'Monsieur . . .'?

GEORGES (*cutting in*): Georges.

BUTLER: Monsieur Georges. (*He repeats it.*) Monsieur Georges. Good. I must get it well into my head. (*Repeating it again gravely.*) Monsieur Georges. That's right. Now I'd better answer the bell. What room should I show them to, Monsieur Georges?

GEORGES: Straight in here, Emile.

The BUTLER *goes out, comes back almost at once and announces:*

BUTLER: Mme de Montrachet and M. Delmonte.

GEORGES (*going to the two who have just entered*): Very glad to see you. You are very punctual . . . Did you come together?

DELMONTE: We met at the station! We used to be the best of friends, inseparable, only we've lost sight of one another for ten years or more. Imagine our surprise! I rushed up to her with arms outstretched almost speechless: (*They mime their meeting on the spot.*) 'Emilienne! Darling! . . .'

MME DE M.: 'Ferdinand, darling! Fancy running into you like this! All those years of touring together and we've never clapped eyes on one another since!'

DELMONTE: 'Emilienne! This brings back all those wonderful tours in Egypt and Africa? Do you remember? *Saint Joan* at Ben Said, and *Romeo* at Hafi Moufa?' 'Oh! Do I remember that *Romeo*! . . .' she said to me. 'You were magnificent, Ferdinand dear. The way they cheered! And most of them couldn't understand a word, could they?' And so forth and so on . . . 'But . . . where are you going, darling?' I said. 'Where are *you*, Ferdinand, dear?' she said.

MME DE M.: 'Thirty-two rue Victor Hugo?' he said. 'So am I! . . .' I said. 'Not to a young gentleman's house? What's his name? . . . Delachaume? . . . Some mystery about it?'

DELMONTE: 'Both of us? No! Oh, it's too fantastic! Well, let's go together!' And off we started arm in arm like in the old days. . . .

GEORGES: Good!

DELMONTE: Wait, wait, though. As we come into the Place Clémenceau, Emilienne suddenly stops, so I say: 'What's the matter, my dear? Have you forgotten something?' She squeezes my arm: 'Ferdinand, we've acted in this town together before! A very long time ago!'—

MME DE M.: It was uncanny! I felt certain I was wearing ankle-length bloomers! (*To* GEORGES.) I'm not, of course.

GEORGES: Of course not.

DELMONTE: Then I say sceptically: 'There's a Place Clémenceau in nearly every town in France, darling . . .' 'But something tells me!' And suddenly she cries out: 'Look at the statue!'

MME DE M. (*with a gesture*): Ah! That statue!

DELMONTE: I look at the statue; and stand rooted to the ground. . . .

GEORGES (*interrupting*): You had played here before?

DELMONTE (*very simply*): No, it was a mistake.

GEORGES: Forgive me. I'd love to hear the rest of the story, but I have so much to get ready this evening, and very little time ahead of me.

DELMONTE: When Guillotard first spoke of this engagement, he said Tuesday *or* Wednesday. . . .

GEORGES: My plans were changed at the last minute. I need your help tonight. Do sit down, and I'll explain what I want you to do.

All sit.

MME DE M.: Yes, of course . . . I'm most intrigued, myself. What is it all about?

DELMONTE: Guillotard is a very old friend of ours, isn't he, my dear? *He* gave us to understand it was something out of the ordinary.

GEORGES: Yes, I suppose it is.

DELMONTE (*with the indulgence of a man quite used to the caprices of amateurs*): Very well, we are listening, my dear sir.

MME DE M.: We are all ears. (*She laughs.*) Do you remember, darling, how he used to say that every time we had a reading? Old Gado, you know, the stage manager at the Ambigu Theatre?

DELMONTE (*laughs, too*): Oh yes, Good Lord! (*Laughs.*)
What's happened to old Gado?

MME DE M.: What! Haven't you heard? He's dead!

DELMONTE: No?! Old Gado?

MME DE M.: Yes. 'We are all ears.' Ha! Ha! Been dead some
time!

DELMONTE (*laughs till the tears roll down his cheeks*): 'We are
all ears, all ears.' My God, he was a comic chap! (*Turns
suddenly sad.*) Poor old Gado!

MME DE M. (*who was roaring with luaghter at the same time, also
stops suddenly*): Poor old Gado!

They turn round together to GEORGES *with quite expressionless
faces.*

GEORGES (*a little surprised*): Well, now . . . I haven't brought
you here to act a play in a theatre. . . .

DELMONTE (*cuts in quickly*): One moment. I'm sorry, but I
must butt in there. It's not for the films, I hope?

GEORGES: No, no, nothing to do with films.

DELMONTE (*turns to* MME DE M.): I've just finished a few days'
filming with Bourbenski . . . They'll never get me at that
again! Those fellows on the other side of the Atlantic are
born in it and have grown a sixth sense by now, but *I* am a
theatre animal. Human contact, real human contact, that's
the thing for me. . . .

MME DE M.: I'm just the same. I must feel them there, vibrating
in front of me, their tears, their laughter, ready to flow at
the artist's touch. My audience! Difficult, unpredictable,
human! It makes me think of taming a mule . . . a wild,
stubborn, rebellious mule! That reminds me, darling, is
your health any better since we were at Biarritz?

DELMONTE: Health? My dear, with all their films and things,
I can't steal a minute to think of my health. (*He suddenly
remembers* GEORGES.) . . . Oh, do forgive us! Let's get
back to the point. As our old stage-manager always used to
say: 'We are all ears.'

They both break into laughter again, then suddenly stop.

Poor old Gado!

MME DE M. (*with a sigh*): Poor old Gado!

GEORGES (*somewhat annoyed*): I'm afraid I must have your full attention now. In half an hour my guests will be here and you must know your parts by then.

DELMONTE: I beg your pardon! I hope you've no intention of asking us to play parts we've not yet read? . . .

GEORGES: Yes, I have.

DELMONTE: But the script? Where are our lines?

GEORGES: There are no words for you to learn.

MME DE M.: Oh! We're not expected to improvise?

GEORGES: Don't get alarmed before you know what I'm asking of you, please. To tell the truth, I turned to professional actors so that I'd have every possible guarantee of success. What you have to do is very simple, almost anybody could pull it off.

DELMONTE: Amateurs, eh? . . . Well, sir, I can't do more than wish some on you.

GEORGES: Well, isn't this simple? I want you to have dinner here this evening and keep up as interesting a conversation as possible with my guests.

DELMONTE (*stands up, delighted*): Ah, now I understand. . . . I think you might go a long way with that scheme, you know! As a matter of fact, I had the same idea myself, some time ago. Original, Emilienne, isn't it? Most original! . . . If I understand you, sir, you're having a dinner-party, and you're afraid of its being rather flat. So you mix with your guests a few persons whose profession and exceptional gifts make them more interesting, more brilliant, more . . .

GEORGES (*interrupts*): Not exactly . . . I have no doubts about your charm, or your wit, of course . . . But what I really want to appeal to is your professional skill . . . Your ability to imitate traits in other people's characters and make them appear absolutely natural to you . . .

DELMONTE: Ah! There you are! If we didn't have that talent

we'd be knocking nails into shoes or polishing ball-bearings, I suppose . . . like everybody else!

MME DE M.: It's the gift, you see. Either it's there . . . or it's not.

GEORGES: That's why I want you to help me. I spoke of my 'guests' just now. I really mean my 'guest'. I am expecting a young lady at almost any minute. Let me be quite frank with you – for reasons which it would take too long to explain, I found myself lying to this young lady. Oh, nothing serious, really . . . All my lies can be put in a sentence or two . . . My real parents are dead, and I told her they were still alive and I lived just outside Paris . . . Why? . . . Why did I tell her that? (*Throughout the following, he is obviously improvising.*) Well, for a very simple reason . . . just to explain away my absences during the week . . . I was involved with someone else – an old affaire I could not bring myself to tell her about . . . That's not all. Actually, I have no friends. But you must know how weak a man in love can be. . . .

DELMONTE: Oh, do I know!

MME DE M.: And women, too!

GEORGES: When this young lady, who is pure and innocent and still believes in friendship – when she said one day how amazed she was that a man of my age had no friends . . . I just invented one, whole, so as not to disappoint her. And of course, while I was at it, I made a good job of it . . . I made him the best friend in the world: brave, sincere, devoted. I only wanted to please her, you see . . . so there was no need to be niggardly about it. . . .

DELMONTE: Ah, love! . . . Love! . . . I've spun a few yarns in my time, too. Once in Marseilles I made a little waitress believe I was an international soccer player. Ha! (*Rocks with laughter.*) An outside left! . . .

GEORGES (*going on without taking any notice*): I had no idea what a mistake I was making when I invented these people. The girl got into the habit of asking after them. Then, of course, I was forced to invent more and more things about them; they interested her and she began to wonder why I didn't let her meet them as they meant so much to me. For a long time I put her off with excuses; they were ill, or out of town. But tomorrow she's leaving for her home in the country . . . for the summer. I can't hold back any longer. So I've asked her here to dinner this evening to meet my parents, *and* the friend I've talked so much about.

DELMONTE: I'm beginning to see daylight . . . You want us to be the parents?

GEORGES: Yes . . . And to talk as they would talk if they really existed.

DELMONTE: Wonderful!

MME DE M.: Oh, splendid! I think it's too marvellous for words!

DELMONTE: Isn't it? But, tell me, who's playing the friend?

GEORGES: I didn't want an actor for that . . . Parents are straightforward enough to play. They always tell their son's girl about the comic things he used to say at eighteen months and the alarming way he shot up in his teens. She doesn't get any more out of them than that . . . But not a friend . . . There are so many things a woman can ask him . . . We'll lay a place for him and wait dinner for him as long as common courtesy requires. But his seat will stay empty. He won't come. (*He adds softly, to himself.*) That way he stands a chance of remaining a perfect friend.

There is a short silence.

DELMONTE: I'm sorry about that. I know a very talented youngster who would have done fine for the part.

GEORGES (*smiling*): I don't think so.

MME DE M.: I'm just too thrilled with the idea of playing the mother. Mothers are always magnificent parts. Especially when one is still a young woman, don't you think? . . . There's something irresistible about a young mother.

GEORGES: Yes, but don't let your imagination run on until we've gone over things together. As you can guess, I've talked to her in detail about you, so you'll have to call on every bit of talent you have. You have to bring to life, in flesh and blood, the exact characters I've already planted in her mind.

DELMONTE: Oh, wait! Wait a minute, old chap! I've got an idea for a rattling good father. Just a minute. I've got all I need for it here. (*And before* GEORGES *can make a move, he darts behind a screen with his little suitcase.*)

MME DE M. (*coyly*): So here am I with a big boy of my own! A big boy I just adore . . . or don't I? I hope you haven't cast me for a bad mother! I should be quite unable to play it.

GEORGES: An excellent mother. You dote on your son.

MME DE M.: Guillotard told me to wear a black dress . . . This one has a *touch* of colour . . . But she's not in mourning, is she?

GEORGES: No.

MME DE M.: You know, the most essential thing in playing a young mother is to give the feeling that, in spite of everything, she is still very feminine.

GEORGES: No, please! It's just the opposite I want. We mustn't feel that at all.

MME DE M. (*cross*): Well, just as you like. But with my looks, you must see I can't play an old hag!

GEORGES: Be patient just a little longer, please, and I'll give you all the details of your character, so that . . .

At this moment, enter a wrinkled and bearded old man, doubled up with age. GEORGES *steps back.*

What the. . . .?!

DELMONTE (*for it is he*): It's me! Ha, ha, ha, ha! That's very funny! He was caught in the trap himself.

GEORGES (*in consternation*): You're not going to sit down to dinner like that, I hope?

DELMONTE: No, no, don't worry. I shall do it all again . . . better. This was only to give you an idea of the general effect.

GEORGES: It's impossible! You've quite misunderstood me, I can see.

DELMONTE (*suddenly flying into a temper*): What the devil! You

told me a father character! I produce a father for you! . . .
You're not going to stand there and pretend you can teach
me my job, damn it all!

GEORGES: No . . . but . . . That's out of the question!
I'm sorry, but it's miles away from what I . . .

DELMONTE: Let's get this straight. Do you want a romantic
young lead or do you want a father? I understood you wanted
a father and *this is* a father!

GEORGES: Tell me, how old are you, in reality, M. Delmonte?

DELMONTE: Fifty-two, and thirty-four years on the stage. So
you're not talking to a mere call-boy remember . . .

MME DE M. (*trying to calm him*): Ferdinand . . . Ferdinand
. . . Don't upset yourself, darling.

GEORGES: You are fifty-two and I'm twenty-eight. So in all
seriousness it's no violation of nature to pass you off as my
father without false whiskers.

DELMONTE (*tearing his beard off in a fury*): Oh! Well! I was a
fool to go to so much trouble! If you want somebody
with the looks of a leading man to play the part of the father
straight . . . don't let me stop you! Anyway, the success of
the whole business is no one's concern but your own. But I
insist on your knowing that I'm giving way simply because
this is a young man's whim. And no more! It's unimportant!
I have a respect for my profession, sir, deep respect. If there'd
been any artistic principle at stake, the boot would have been
on the other foot, I can tell you!

*He goes back behind the screen to remove his make-up. He will
return, rather bad-tempered, in the course of the following speech.*

GEORGES (*who has suddenly begun to speak sharply*): You must
realize that I didn't bring you here just to play-act. These
characters exist . . . They're already half alive. Someone
believes in them . . . and expects special words, special
gestures from them: a special atmosphere around me . . .
You, you cling to your professional conscience . . . Well, it
must make you obey me as unquestioningly as you would
the most finicky producer in the theatre. You must help me

with all the talent you have. We have to bring to life the father, mother and friend that this young girl is expecting to meet.

The ACTORS, *surprised by his tone, draw near to him, abashed.*

You probably think I'm crazy – you're used to the sort of theatre where the different kinds of play never get mixed up – and here you find a young man with a sad face and trembling hands pushing you into a farce instead of a tragedy! Some people seem to carry tragedy at their fingertips – given only half a situation, a leave-taking, a mere hint of pain, they can turn on the tears in a moment and draw them from the onlookers, too. It so happens that I'm not made that way . . . I always have to play my life as a farce. (*He rises anxiously.*) So help me, will you? Help me bring these imaginary people to life just for one evening. I'm more anxious to see them than any man has ever been to see his real father and mother, or his real best friend, even after years of separation.

The ACTORS *cough, moved by his words.*

MME DE M.: You know how sentimental we women are . . . we're always ready to help lovers. . . .

DELMONTE: We are at your disposal, sir . . . Aren't we, Emilienne? And . . . er . . . I'm sorry for my show of temper just now . . .

GEORGES (*with a gesture to stop them*): Thank you . . . But please, from now on don't speak another word as your real selves. We must begin at once. We have so little time and so much to learn. One thing in particular is going to be difficult, I feel – hitting the exact tone of restraint that comes of long-standing affection, the sort of intimate silence I've always envied in people who understand one another so well they have no need of words . . .

DELMONTE: My dear sir, silence is the easiest thing to do in the theatre . . . I think you should tell us a few of the other things that matter, first. . . .

GEORGES: All right. Why did you imagine yourself wearing a

beard like one of those old cranks out of a museum? You're really a very charming man, still in the prime of life, with a youth that time cannot touch. You're the ideal father, you have no paternal manner – and no beard, I hope. You're much more like an older brother. You are my friend, Father. What's more you dress like me, you even dress younger than me – but that's only natural at your age.

DELMONTE: Still, you know – for a father? (*He shrugs.*)

GEORGES (*with a smile*): Of course, Father . . . there are times when a normal elder brother would think of himself first; when it's a question of making a sacrifice, or of lending a bit of money . . . That's when you turn into a real father again, strong and comforting, the sort a fellow can still act the little boy with for a moment, and not feel too embarrassed.

DELMONTE: Yes, Son.

GEORGES (*happily*): There, you see, it's true! You've called me 'son'. It's a bit ridiculous and I didn't tell you to, of course, but I like it.

DELMONTE (*patting his shoulder*): Really?

GEORGES: Yes, Father.

DELMONTE (*changing his tone*): You don't think the expression rather too sentimental for a retired judge?

GEORGES: But you've never been a judge! Where did you get that idea?

DELMONTE: . . . Just came to me . . . I would have quite liked to be a judge.

GEORGES: No, no. You're not a judge, Father – couldn't be! You always needed at least three weeks when we caught the maid pilfering, to bring yourself to give her the sack. Even then you always wrote her a glowing testimonial . . . I can't see you packing dozens of poor devils off to jail every day and then calmly sitting down to afternoon tea.

DELMONTE: What am I, then, Son? A chain-store owner? Stock-broker? Powerful industrialist?

GEORGES: No. People who spend their lives piling up money pick up such dreadful habits on the way. No. You can be a Civil Servant. I can see you quite well in that sort of work.

DELMONTE (*troubled*): Not some silly little pen-pusher, I hope. You'll at least put me in one of the upper grades of the service?

GEORGES (*generously*): Of course, I'll even make you a . . . First Secretary.

DELMONTE (*overwhelmed*): Oh, thanks.

MME DE M. (*annoyed and sulky*): Nothing's been said about me.

GEORGES (*suddenly serious*): Ah, yours is the more difficult part. There's such a range in mothers. Right from the grey-wigged tyrant, dearly defending her heritage, down to the sweet and gentle lady who trembles like a young girl in love and loses the thread of the conversation whenever her son comes into the room.

MME DE M.: A good mother's part ought to range over them all!

GEORGES: No, I want this one to be quite straightforward. Clear. Like one of those mothers in children's books. The sort little boys *dream* about as they wait in the kitchen with the maid, while their *real* mother – drenched in perfume – is out on one of those interminable afternoon calls. A mother who doesn't make trips to the shops all the time, and has no friends to visit at all. A wonderful mother.

MME DE M.: All mothers are wonderful; instinct tells me so.

GEORGES: But the slightest sign of neglect can ruin all that in a moment. An unguarded smile to a strange man. A hard word at the end of a trying day. A simple kiss that's forgotten when it's due . . . And there you have a child watching you, making demands on you, as big a tyrant as a sergeant-major. I know it's not easy to play the mother. It's a part that can have no understudy and that should never be lightly taken on.

MME DE M.: I'm quite familiar with mother parts – all sorts. You should have seen my 'mother' in *Brittany First*.

DELMONTE: Ah, my dear, yes! You were delightful!

GEORGES: I don't trust stage-mothers. Their devotion is much too facile.

MME DE M.: Oh, but I've played wicked mothers, too. In *She*

was Guilty, for instance, I abandoned my baby on the steps of
the church.

GEORGES: Exactly. I don't trust wicked stage-mothers either.
They're laid on too thick. With them a real child wouldn't
have time to be unhappy. He'd be dead or turned into a
lunatic straight away. In the first place, would anybody think
of leaving a baby on the steps of a church when there are
so many easier ways of abandoning a child? Some women
can do it by just keeping him at home until he's of age.

MME DE M.: Well . . . If you think I shan't be able to play
the part . . .

DELMONTE: No need for me to say, young man, that if that
is the case, I shall be forced to leave with my colleague.

GEORGES: What makes you think that? I'm convinced you'll
play it very well. Just to give us confidence if you like we'll
have a little rehearsal. Let's play one scene, a typical scene.
Here we are: I am twenty. I'm a weak young man, easily led,
not very good at facing up to life. Let us suppose, to get a
situation, that you have arranged a rich marriage for me . . .
(*He repeats this, suddenly very far away.*) . . . A very rich
marriage, a pure business deal, something you, my mother,
ought never to have considered. I've just come into your
room. I've talked about one or two things, then suddenly
awkward and embarrassed, I come up to you and say:
'Mother . . .!' Come, have a try, let's play the scene
together . . .

DELMONTE (*leaping to his feet*): One moment, one moment.
Emilienne de Montrachet, you're one of the oldest members
of the Union; are you going to agree to an audition *after*
being engaged for the job?

MME DE M.: It's not quite the same, Ferdinand. I just want
to convince this gentleman that . . .

DELMONTE: As you please, darling . . . but . . . it's not
like you at all! That's all I can say!

GEORGES: Well, 'Mother' . . .

MME DE M.: Shall I answer you?

GEORGES: Yes.

MME DE M. (*playing her part*): What is it, dear?

GEORGES (*with his eyes closed and in a curious voice; one feels one no
   longer knows to whom he is speaking*): Mother . . . I don't want
   to marry the girl you've chosen for me, however rich she
   may be. Being rich doesn't mean anything to me, Mother.
   And I'm in love with someone else. She's poor and has to
   earn her own living, and I know you won't want me to marry
   her. But I must, Mother. I can't marry anyone else . . .
   Please help me. . . .

MME DE M. (*hesitating: she is surprised by his tone, perhaps. Then
   she says, rather nobly*): I thought I was doing the right thing,
   dear. But if your happiness is really somewhere else, you
   mustn't hesitate; go and be happy. At your age, love is *the
   one thing* that counts and that cannot be bought.

GEORGES *has listened in silence, with closed eyes.*

(*A bit anxious, she changes her tone.*) Is that all right?

GEORGES (*opening his eyes, as if surprised*): I'm sorry. It's very
   good. In fact, it's exactly what the mother I've imagined
   would have said. Congratulations. Is that a speech from one
   one of your other parts?

MME DE M.: No. I made it up.

GEORGES: It couldn't have been better! Just as if you had a
   son who'd already asked you the same question!

MME DE M. (*simpering*): Well, yes . . . I admit I have. You
   wouldn't think so, would you, looking as young as I do? A
   grown-up son . . . He came to me with exactly the same
   story a year ago . . . so of course I was rehearsed, in a
   way. . . .

GEORGES (*looking at her, full of admiration*): And that's the
   answer you gave him?

MME DE M. (*suddenly carried away at the recollection*): What do
   you think? A tuppenny violinist! A flibbertigibbet without
   a sou to her name . . . I soon knocked all that nonsense out
   of his head, I can tell you! . . .

GEORGES (*smiles*): Please . . . Be the same as you were a few
   moments ago! There, that's it. Now that you've put your

child out of your mind, you make quite a wonderful mother again. This girl may arrive at any moment . . . so get yourselves used to the room . . . You've been living here for thirty years, remember. Look round for the little things in it that specially belong to you, that reflect you personally. . . . Mother, have you a bit of knitting with you, for instance?

MME DE M. (*goes and takes it from her bag*): I always carry some knitting; there's such a lot of waiting in the agencies these days.

GEORGES: Father, get a newspaper out. You've got one with you, I imagine?

DELMONTE: Two. I found them on my way here; they were lying on the seat in the train. *Figaro* and *La Vie Parisienne*.

GEORGES: Grand! Both indispensable signs of a normal middle-class life. But remember – you must make a show of reading the *Figaro*; only take a peep at *La Vie Parisienne* now and then on the sly.

The tableau is now set. He steps back, narrowing his eyes like a painter.

There . . . you don't dislike each other, you know – you're a very devoted couple. It wouldn't be overdoing it to bring your chairs a little closer to one another.

They do so.

That's it . . . Fine.

DELMONTE (*suddenly feeling in his pocket*): Damn. I was forgetting. . . .

GEORGES: What's that?

DELMONTE: Nothing, a minor point, just a little touch . . . but I like to have the details right in any character part. . . . It's the Legion of Honour for my buttonhole. (*He puts on the rosette.*)

GEORGES (*looks at them for a moment in silence*): It's very strange, and somehow very comforting, bringing all these lies to life.

In the silence a clock strikes eight, with a musical chime.

Eight o'clock! She'll be here in a second! Ah, I was forgetting! Can you play the piano, Mother? I specially asked M. Guillotard for someone who played the piano.

MME DE M.: I won the Napoleon Bronze Medal at the Dieppe Academy in 1925.

GEORGES: Splendid. You'll manage this piece quite easily. It's a tune I heard one evening when I was only ten years old. I was wandering through the streets alone . . . suddenly I heard music coming from an open window. I stood up on a wall and peeped through. In an old-fashioned sitting-room, rather like this, a little girl with plaits was playing the piano . . . and the whole family sat round listening.

MME DE M. (*trying out the piece softly at the piano*): It's a waltz, by Olivier Métra.

GEORGES: As soon as I made the acquaintance of the young lady who's coming tonight, I went round all the music-shops singing that tune, until someone recognized it. I had to sing it for two months. I'm tone-deaf, you see, I can't sing a note . . . so I had to be very patient . . . so did the assistants in the music-shops, of course. Ah! something else I was forgetting . . . (*He rushes out.*)

DELMONTE (*admiringly*): He's a most unusual fellow. We were fools, you know. We should have asked for a bigger fee.

GEORGES *has come back with a large photograph which he unpacks from its newspaper wrappings.*

GEORGES: A portrait of my mother, taken at a garden fête at about the time when . . . (*He hesitates.*) Well, at the time I lost her . . . (*He looks round for a place to put it.*) I'll put it here. (*He takes a portrait down from the wall.*) This bearded old boy looks quite a gentleman. He'll be delighted, I'm sure, to give up his place to a lady. (*He hides the old man behind a chair, looks round and says comically.*) Then at least there'll be something in the house that's real.

Enter BUTLER.

BUTLER: Excuse me, Monsieur, I know your order was for four persons, but sometimes . . . since people know that we do things on a quite generous scale at Dufort's. . . . Well, to come to the point, how many should I lay for?

GEORGES: Five.

BUTLER: Just as I thought. (*He goes out muttering.*) They're all the same. Very well, sir . . .

GEORGES (*calling after him*): Emile! There'll only be four of us to dinner in spite of that. The fifth person won't be eating.

BUTLER (*astonished at first, thinks he understands. He is charmed and most impressed with this touch*): Ah! I ask your pardon, sir. It's the poor man's place, no doubt? (GEORGES *looks at him.*) At the Duke's, where all the traditions were respected, we always laid an extra place on special occasions, for the poor. A poor man was always welcome at the Duke's table.

GEORGES: And did the poor man come, now and then?

BUTLER: No, sir, never. His place was laid, but as no one ever took the trouble to inform him of it . . . poor man . . . (*He goes out, very dignified, with a cynical gesture. As soon as he has gone out the bell rings.*)

GEORGES: Two rings, that'll be Isabelle! I told her to give two rings. In your places, quickly! You, Mother, at the piano. And start playing. You, Father, there, behind. I am reading. Be very careful what you say, keep your imagination well under control, don't let it run away with you. And keep your eye on me. I shall cut in as soon as anything gets too dangerous. Anyway, you know enough now to play your parts. There's no need for any hitches if you are careful.

MME DE M.: And you? What about you?

GEORGES: How do you mean?

MME DE M.: She's sure to ask us about you. You've told us nothing about yourself. Your character, your history . . .

GEORGES: Good God, that's true. (*He calls upstage.*) Emile, Emile!

BUTLER (*entering*): I was just going to answer the bell, sir.

GEORGES: It's the young lady I'm expecting. Take your time going to the door . . . and bringing her up here. Take as

much time as you can. (*He comes back to the* ACTORS.) Listen,
carefully, both of you . . . Ah! I haven't got time to tell
you much.

BUTLER (*reappears, very upset*): Monsieur! Monsieur!

GEORGES: What is it?

BUTLER: I've forgotten your Christian name!

GEORGES (*shouts at him*): Georges!

BUTLER: Monsieur Georges, that's it! It'll stick this time! (*He
disappears.*)

GEORGES (*takes the other two*): My name is Georges, my friend's
is Jacques.

MME DE M. ⎫
            ⎬ Yes.
DELMONTE ⎭

GEORGES: I'm very shy. Start playing.

MME DE M. (*quietly plays the waltz*): Very well.

GEORGES: I'm practical . . . No imagination.

DELMONTE: Hm!

GEORGES: I'm good-humoured, rather unsophisticated, rash
now and then, generous, kind.

DELMONTE: Good.

GEORGES: I was a wild and cruel little boy, but when anybody
even spoke to me I used to blush and burst into tears.

DELMONTE: How sweet!

GEORGES: I'm honest and uncomplicated, I have deep faith in
love and friendship. I'd gladly give my life for my friend
Jacques and he would give his for me.

DELMONTE: Bravo! Bravo!

GEORGES: He's just opened the door to her. (*He goes on
feverishly.*) I did my military service in the infantry at Tarbes.
You used to send me parcels of gingerbread and chocolates
every week.

MME DE M.: Gingerbread and chocolates, right.

GEORGES: I studied engineering. I had chicken-pox when I
was a child.

MME DE M.: All children have it.

GEORGES (*listening*): They're coming in now. There's no time
to tell you any more. (*He adds quickly.*) I am very loyal, and

a devoted son. (*A pause, they wait, fixed. He adds softly in the silence.*) And I adore climbing trees.

BUTLER (*comes in hesitantly*): Please, sir . . .

GEORGES (*sees his embarrassment. He stops* MME DE M. *with a wave of the hand*): What is it?

BUTLER: It's a hunchback, sir.

GEORGES: A hunchback?

BUTLER: Yes, sir. He says he's brought a message from Miss Barbara in Paris.

GEORGES (*leaping up*): Throw him out!

BUTLER (*with a gesture*): Oh! I couldn't, sir, a man with an affliction like that . . . Anyway, he's gone already. He lives next door; he brought a telephone message for you, sir. (*He recites.*) Miss Barbara in Paris couldn't find us in the directory, so she rang up number thirty-four next door. Miss Barbara wants you to ring her as soon as possible, sir. It seems there has been some rumpus regarding you can guess what, so the lady said, sir . . . and if you do not show some sign of life immediately there will be – I use Miss Barbara's own words, sir – there will be an awful bloody shindy!

GEORGES *hasn't moved; his fists are clenched. The* BUTLER *impassively repeats.*

She said 'An awful bl—'

GEORGES *goes out brusquely and returns with his raincoat.*

GEORGES: Yes – I heard you the first time – I shall have to go. Listen – if the young lady arrives while I'm away, make her welcome. If I'm not back in half an hour, it means I've had to go to Paris. So start dinner, don't wait for me.

And before DELMONTE *and* MME DE M. *can make a move he is gone. They turn again to the* BUTLER, *who repeats oracularly.*

BUTLER: An awful bloody shindy!

He makes a gesture and goes out with impenetrable composure. The ACTORS *exchange a wan smile.*

DELMONTE: Well! I'm beginning to wonder, darling, if we

oughtn't to have asked for payment in advance. (*He paces the room, and whistles softly. He wants to appear indifferent.*) Funny business though, isn't it?

MME DE M.: Oh, on the stage you come up with all sorts.

DELMONTE: Why's he putting on all this show for the girl? To seduce her? . . . Kidnap her? . . . Who knows? To . . . (*Throat-cutting gesture.*)

MME DE M. (*with a little cry*): Oh, please! No! Don't talk such nonsense.

DELMONTE: Oh, you never know these days! When the butler announced that telephone call just now, he gave me a wink.

MME DE M.: A wink?

DELMONTE: Yes, a wink. Did Guillotard seem to know this young man well when he told you about him?

MME DE M.: I gathered it was the first time he'd ever seen him.

DELMONTE: Ah! ah . . . (*He looks out of the window.*) It's quite dark already. A nice thing if we have to go out and look for help in this maze of little streets.

MME DE M. (*suddenly*): Let's phone.

DELMONTE: Who to?

MME DE M.: I don't know. Let's phone anybody. (*She picks up the receiver and cries out.*) Hello! Oh!

DELMONTE (*furious because he's frightened*): What the devil's the matter.

MME DE M.: It's cut off.

DELMONTE (*seizes the receiver, listens, then puts it back trembling*): Hello, hello! Well, there's nothing extraordinary about that. Perhaps the line's out of order.

At this moment MME DE MONTRACHET, *speechless, shows* DELMONTE *the door, which is opening of its own accord as in a thriller. They draw together instinctively. It is the* BUTLER; *he has pushed it with his foot. He enters with some sherry and glasses.*

BUTLER: May I be allowed to serve some sherry to the lady and gentleman while they are waiting?

MME DE M. (*in a faint voice*): You may be allowed . . . Yes.

The sherry served, they do not take their eyes off the BUTLER, *and he obviously has no intention of going out. He comes and goes, putting chairs in place, closing the double curtains. She murmurs, with a sign.*

He is closing the curtains.

DELMONTE: You mustn't drink the sherry! I don't like the fellow's face.

MME DE M., *who hasn't heard him, empties her glass.*

MME DE M. (*when the* BUTLER *is farther off*): What did you say?

DELMONTE (*seeing that she has drunk it, annoyed*): It doesn't matter now, my poor sweet.

BUTLER (*coming up and speaking confidentially*): Sir . . .

DELMONTE (*startled, shouts*): What do you want?

BUTLER (*mysteriously*): Sh!

DELMONTE (*stepping back and shouting*): What do you mean, Sh?! Why, Sh?

BUTLER: I beg your pardon sir, but do you know the house well, sir?

DELMONTE: No . . . but . . . what about you?

BUTLER: I am hired, from Dufort's. I was sent after the young man telephoned for a meal and servants, at six o'clock . . . I only know this room, the dining-room, where I've just laid the table, and the kitchen. That's why I asked you, sir. The house *seems* deserted. The young man said it was, anyway. Yet I can hear something pattering about up there.

DELMONTE (*filled with horror at this detail*): Pattering about? . . .

BUTLER: Pattering about. Like a big mouse.

DELMONTE (*repeats*): A big mouse?

The PROPRIETRESS *appears at the door in nightgown, curling papers and a white shawl.*

PROPRIETRESS: Oh! I'm sorry . . . I couldn't hear any more noise . . . I was getting worried . . . So sorry . . . Do forgive me.

She disappears discreetly. The BUTLER *and the* ACTORS *look at each other questioningly.*

BUTLER: Did you see that old lady, sir, when you arrived?

DELMONTE: No, did you?

BUTLER: No.

A ring at the door.

MME DE M. (*lets out a cry*): Oh! Someone's ringing at the door.

There is silence. They listen. A second ring.

BUTLER (*sepulchral tones*): Another ring.

MME DE M.: Don't let's open it!

DELMONTE: Still, we can't spend the night shut in here. See if you can see who it is through the window, without showing yourself.

BUTLER (*goes to the balcony window and comes back*): It's a young girl in a flowered dress and a white straw hat.

DELMONTE (*a gesture of cold resolution, a moment's hesitation, then*): Show her up!

The BUTLER *hesitates, then goes out reluctantly, while* DELMONTE *prepares a bold front for the enemy.*

Curtain

Act Two

The linen room in the basement of CHRISTINE'S *house in Paris.*
Two doors. Huge cupboards. Piles of laundry on the table. A telephone
on the wall. A young woman, BARBARA, *in evening dress, is*
telephoning.

BARBARA: Yes . . . yes . . . Georges, a dreadful scene. She
says divorce – and she really means it this time, I'm sure.
So, if you're not doing anything really important, you might
do worse than come back home . . . I know it's not my
business. No, I'm speaking from the linen room; no one
ever comes in here. Of course not, I won't say a word. You
are silly, darling. Do just as you please. Good night, Georges.
Have a good time.

She hangs up, thinks a little. Suddenly she bites her handkerchief.
JACQUES *comes in quickly. He is in a dinner-jacket.*

JACQUES: Barbara! I thought you'd gone out! What have you
been doing here for the last hour?
BARBARA: Nothing, Jacques.
JACQUES (*looks first at her, then the telephone*): I know that little
dodge, telephoning from the linen room. I thought of it
before you did, my pet.
BARBARA: Did you, Jacques?
JACQUES: Who were you ringing?
BARBARA (*looking him full in the face*): Who did you want me
to ring?
JACQUES (*hesitates, blinks a little under her gaze*): Nobody heard
anything of him?
BARBARA (*shortly*): Nobody.

JACQUES: Not even you.

BARBARA: Not even me.

JACQUES: If he isn't back before midnight, we're sunk!

BARBARA (*archly*): A fine respectable family – not to mention their friends – all thrown out on the street.

JACQUES: Just what are you trying to insinuate, sweetie? We are guests here. The hosts are our closest friends. I should hate to see them quarrel. It would be a double disappointment to me – first as their friend, and second, as their guest.

BARBARA: Guest? . . . For two years?!

JACQUES: We came to Georges when we had to move out of our house. In the first place it was for a fortnight. We were invited!

BARBARA: Yes, twenty-two months ago.

JACQUES (*with crashing complacency*): We haven't been able to find a flat! After all, is Georges my best friend, or isn't he? If a man can't stay at his best friend's any more, where is he going to stay? With strangers?

BARBARA: That's what people are usually reduced to.

JACQUES: Well, that's just the sort of thing I can't stand! I've always believed in friendship, and I always shall!

BARBARA: Yes, Jacques.

JACQUES: He's only done what I'd have done, if I'd landed a rich wife like he has, instead of being daft enough to marry you. I'd have said the same as he said to me: 'You're hard up, Jacques, old chap, so make yourself at home here on me, be my . . . secretary, I'll give you sixty thousand francs a month pocket money.'

BARBARA: He said thirty thousand.

JACQUES: That's right, but *I'd* have said sixty. That's what comes of having a generous nature. (*He sits down.*) It's nice down here, it was a very good idea of yours . . . it's private, and it's quiet . . . In the rest of the house people are slamming doors and moaning in corners all over the place. They keep bombarding you with questions and waving revolvers in your face . . . Melodrama stuff! Huh!

The door opens. Enter M. DELACHAUME, *hearty, well groomed, in tails.*

DELACHAUME (*overcoat on arm, top hat in hand*): Oh! There you are . . . I've been looking everywhere for you two. These quarrels wear my nerves to shreds! I'm going to slip out by the side door and have a cigar in the garden. She's got her eyes glued to the front door all the time. Still no news of the blighter?

JACQUES: None.

DELACHAUME: Outlook's pretty black.

JACQUES: Very black.

DELACHAUME: Just as we finished dressing for the opera my wife shot off like a lunatic; said she'd just had an idea. Have you any faith in her ideas?

JACQUES: No.

DELACHAUME (*going out*): Neither have I.

JACQUES (*when he has gone – comes quietly over to* BARBARA): All the same, it's a bit thick of your friend Georges to play a trick like this on us.

BARBARA: *Your* friend Georges.

JACQUES: *Our* friend Georges if you like. You're sure he's *not* said anything to you?

BARBARA: Why should he tell me any more than you, my dear?

JACQUES: Men always confide more in a woman; it's common knowledge. Besides, Georges is very fond of you. You go out a lot together.

BARBARA: Is that a complaint?

JACQUES: No. Simply a statement. Listen, Barbara my love – we're man and wife, I know, but that needn't stop us being friends . . . I may be wrong, of course, but I rather suspect you know something.

BARBARA: You are wrong.

JACQUES: You don't think he's done a bunk like two years ago, when he tried to join the Foreign Legion?

BARBARA: He's told me nothing.

JACQUES: Christine's having one attack of hysterics after another upstairs in her bedroom! And it's *our* fate that's being decided by all this, remember! If Christine insists on a divorce and we're all flung into the street, it means back to the typing-pool for you, honey.

BARBARA: Well then, back to the typing-pool it'll have to be, honey.

JACQUES (*looks at her, and in all sincerity, says*): You sicken me. That's all I can say. You make me sick!

At that moment the telephone rings. They both rush to it. There is a short struggle.

Ah! So that's what you were waiting for, eh, old girl?

BARBARA: Jacques, let go! . . . Let go, do you hear? I forbid you to answer it . . . Beast! Filthy beast!

JACQUES (*who has got hold of her with one hand*): Hello? Who? Am I who? No, of course I am not Esmé. Who's speaking? . . . Eh? What message? The little fair chap from the hairdresser's won't be able to go to the cinema this evening? Right! I'll tell her.

He has let go of BARBARA. *He hangs up, sheepishly.* BARBARA *bursts out laughing and goes to sit farther away. He looks at her for a moment resentfully, then approaches her.*

Shut up, Barbara . . . Let's forget ourselves for the moment . . . If Christine gets a divorce do you think *Georges* is going to be happy? Can you see him going back to carselling at fifty thousand francs a month, including expenses, after four years of luxury? . . . It's all very well his getting on his high horse with Christine, but if he hadn't stumbled on her and her money four years ago, where would he be today? He's got brilliant qualifications as a scrounger, but nothing else. Where do you think a chronic loafer like Georges would be if he hadn't married well?

BARBARA: Where will you be tomorrow if he can't keep you any longer?

JACQUES: In queer street, like he is himself. You're not telling me anything, Barbie! I know! That's why I'm humble, that's why I don't say anything . . . even when you go out with him a bit too often in the afternoons. 'Cos there's one thing you'll both have to learn – you two really taught me this – in this life nobody can play fast and loose with the people who provide the cash! Filthy lucre's sacred when you haven't got any, and so are the people who supply it! If you happen to earn your living in my lady Christine's arms, it's no good trying to be clever – your place is there, in my lady's arms and nowhere else! And you mustn't complain. (*He adds more quietly.*) I don't.

BARBARA (*quietly*): You revolt me, Jacques.

JACQUES: Yes. It's not very nice. I grant you . . . Less for me than for you, in fact. After all, you can comfort yourself with the thought that you do all this because you love him . . . whereas I . . .

He has got up and moved over to the mirror, and now combs his hair.

Oh, what the hell! (*Speaking to himself in the mirror and preening himself.*) Remember, Jacques, you've got a very respectable old mother in the country with a comfortable income. You endured a Catholic education from the priests. You learnt Latin! 'Bellum, bellum, bellum, belli, bello, bello.' You're not just a lout. You want to remind yourself of that, now and again . . . (*Turning to* BARBARA.) Look at Poppa Edgar outside wallowing in his cigar: he'd be shocked to death if you told him he was living by sponging on his son . . .

DELACHAUME (*comes back with his cigar*): I'm getting bored out there. Ah! This is no sort of life for a man of my age . . . Tell me, what the devil are you two doing in the linen room?

JACQUES: Getting a change of air.

DELACHAUME: Oh! . . . Quite right! The atmosphere in this house is too thick to breathe. (*He is carried away.*) Damn it, I'm not to blame just because my son decides to spend the night away from home! (*He suddenly thinks of something else.*) Do you think we shall go to the opera?

JACQUES: The chances look mildly jeopardized to me.

DELACHAUME: I was so looking forward to it! I think Tosca's wonderful! (*He sings.*) Tra la la, tra la la, tra la la la. (*He stops with a sigh.*) Ah, well! Still no news, of course?

JACQUES: Still no news.

DELACHAUME: I can't fathom that boy, playing the idiot like this! I mean . . . Christine's charming . . . A bit highly strung perhaps, and a bit jealous, but absolutely charming in spite of that . . . What's your opinion?

JACQUES: Charming. Has anyone managed to relieve her of that little pearl-handled revolver?

DELACHAUME: Esmé has, I think . . . I hope . . . I don't know – in my time men used to deceive their wives, of course, but they went about it more skilfully. It was no worse a sin for that, I'm sure. What's your opinion?

BARBARA: I haven't an opinion.

DELACHAUME: Of course, I don't say this boy of mine is absolutely obliged to deceive his wife . . . Far be it from me to suggest such a thing! But what I can't understand about you young people is this taste for crudity you all have. You say you like clear-cut situations. So we old people think: 'Good. They're going to put themselves into clear-cut situations. They're going to behave as we old ones never knew how to behave.' Nothing of the kind, nothing of the kind! You're men just the same as we are, and yet get into exactly the same old situations, old as the world itself . . . Only you're different, oh yes! You turn your behind square to the rest of the world and you think that makes the situation clear cut! (*He is furious and has got up.*) I prefer the old hypocrites by far! In the long run they did much less harm . . . What's your opinion?

JACQUES (*to* BARBARA): Your opinion?

BARBARA (*shakes her head*): Haven't got one.

JACQUES: She has none. Neither have I.

DELACHAUME: When I was your age I was never short of opinions about anything! Ah! We were lively youngsters in my generation. We didn't need to go out on the hunt, not us! But we picked up plenty of game and fine game it was too! I can't understand this youngster of mine. He has a lovely wife, madly in love with him, and she's fabulously rich. What more does he want? Answer me that!

JACQUES: What more does he want? Answer him that.

BARBARA: I wouldn't know.

JACQUES: She wouldn't know.

DELACHAUME (*continuing*): A mistress? I've told you what I think about that. Simply a question of tact . . . Well what else does he want?

JACQUES (*to* BARBARA): What else?

BARBARA *shakes her head.*

DELACHAUME: Nothing. There *is* nothing else. Money, love, you can't want anything else. Life's very simple after all, damn it! I don't understand you people. He says he's unhappy. Why is he unhappy? Take me. I'm an unsuccessful old artist . . . a failure, and I've had a hard life. But am I unhappy? Are you unhappy?

JACQUES: Speaking for myself, I'm very happy.

DELACHAUME (*to* BARBARA): And you?

JACQUES: And you, dear?

BARBARA (*feelingly*): Divinely happy.

DELACHAUME: Well then? He says he doesn't love his wife. Neither did I love my wife. Did I make such a fuss, just because of that? He says we pushed him into it. The family reserves were in three per cent and I'd just realized them all in an attempt to make a bit of money, when the franc devalued overnight! Is it my fault we're not properly governed? Georges was earning fifty thousand francs a month as a car salesman and he had three million francs' worth of debts to settle for the family. He would never have finished paying them off. He meets a young girl in high society, ravishing to look at and madly in love with him – and she inherits a fortune. He flirts with her, everything's going fine. Then, suddenly, whoosh! The boy develops a conscience: begins to have doubts about whether he should marry her or not! His mother and I, thank God, soon settled that for him. Don't you think we did the right thing? (*To* BARBARA.) What's your opinion?

JACQUES: She's certain not to have one.

ESMÉ, CHRISTINE'S *maid, comes in, beside herself.*

ESMÉ: Ah, here you are. Oh, lor. Oh, lor. . . .

JACQUES (*ingratiatingly*): What's the news, Esmé?

ESMÉ: Oh, Monsieur Jacques, if only you could see my arm! It's been like that since first thing this morning. She can't speak to me without digging her nails into my flesh. Oh, she's in such a state! Still no news of the master?

JACQUES: Still no news.

DELACHAUME: He can't be long now, I'm quite sure. Quite sure.

ESMÉ (*rubbing her arm*): Well, it's not for me to say, I know, but I think the master should consider us a bit.

A bell suddenly rings in the linen room. She shouts.

Coming, madame! (*To the others.*) I can't leave her for a minute. Monsieur Edgar, sir, would you like to ask cook for some camomile tea for madame?

DELACHAUME (*adjusts his monocle*): Camomile tea . . .

ESMÉ (*just going out of the door, while the bell keeps ringing*): Yes, please. But don't let Jeannette bring it up. She can't bear the sight of her. She'd scratch her eyes out!

DELACHAUME: I'll bring it up myself.

ESMÉ (*before disappearing*): Don't forget the tray-cloth, please, Monsieur Edgar. If you do, I'll be the one who's told off.

DELACHAUME: With a tray-cloth. It shall be done!

He turns to go out, then stops. MME DELACHAUME, *elegant, youngly dressed, comes sweeping in. She is in evening dress and cloak.*

MME D.: Ah, here you are! I've been looking everywhere for you. My darlings, I've got wonderful news for you!

JACQUES: Have you been to the police?

MME D. (*falling into a chair*): No, to Madame Lerida, the clairvoyante. I took one of Georges's hats, and she swears he's not left the Paris area!

She still has the hat in her hand. JACQUES *takes it and looks at it.*

JACQUES: That's *my* hat now. He gave it to me a month ago.

MME D.: Oh, there! That muddles everything up. Then it must be you who hasn't left the Paris area. What a pity. (*She stands up.*) I'll have to go back to Madame Lerida. She can tell us everything, she's frighteningly clairvoyant. Right in the first second she told me exactly how old I was. (*She sits down again.*) What's Christine feeling like?

JACQUES: She wants to die.

MME D.: Good! That's better! That proves she still loves him. We're not going to the opera now, I suppose?

JACQUES: No need. We're in the middle of an opera here, prima donna and all—

MME D.: No opera, good! One less bore to go through, thank God. Oh! I've got another piece of news. Very nasty, this one. The cook told me that Christine had a visitor this afternoon: Dupont-Duprés.

DELACHAUME: Her solicitor!

MME D.: Yes, alas!

DELACHAUME (*sits down in despair*): That boy has done for us now! (*He stands up and then says.*) Oh, my God, that camomile tea. . . . (*He rushes out.*)

MME D.: We must do something! We've got to do something! It's ridiculous to let so much happiness crumble away like this, for no apparent reason. I mean . . . Oh, I could slap Georges. I'd slap him like a baby . . . if I had hold of him.

JACQUES: That's just it. You can hardly slap him if you haven't got hold of him! Where is he?

MME D.: I can't give up living in this house. I think I'd rather die. Some people just can't breathe outside an atmosphere of luxury. Take away their luxury and they die! (*She suddenly notices her reflection in the mirror.*) What do you think of my little hat?

JACQUES (*coldly polite*): Revolutionary.

MME D.: Christine gave it me. She'd only worn it once. It cost twenty thousand francs, this hat. (*Silence. She sighs.*) It's so easy for him. Christine's madly in love with him. She's generosity itself to him, and to us. We could all have been so cosy together, you know . . . with no troubles at all . . . But he never thinks of us. . . .

ESMÉ *comes in. She stops in the doorway, looking serious. They all turn to her.*

ESMÉ: It's all up this time.

MME D.: What's all up? Don't frighten me, Esmé, my dear.

ESMÉ (*weighing her words*): Madame's leaving him.

MME D. (*with a shriek*): Esmé, it can't be true!

ESMÉ: True as I'm standing here!

M. DELACHAUME *comes in, triumphant with his tray, through the service door.*

DELACHAUME: Camomile tea, with tray-cloth!

ESMÉ: Madame won't want it now. She's getting up. She says it's stupid wasting her life away like this, to no purpose . . . Well, it's no more than he deserves.

MME D.: Esmé, you surely can't think such a thing!

ESMÉ: Oh yes, I can. I'm a woman, and I can see myself in her position. Besides, we need a bit of peace and quiet in this house, all of us.

MME D.: Esmé, my dear Esmé . . . you can't do this to us! Try to stop her!

ESMÉ: I kept advising madame, as long as I could, to be patient. Now, it's more than my job's worth . . . I have to agree with her now . . .

MME D.: Oh! no, she can't do that! It's too silly, when all's said and done. I may be Georges's mother, but I am Christine's friend. I'll go and speak to her.

ESMÉ (*shouts to her*): She's locked herself in her room! She won't answer you!

MME D. (*disappearing*): We'll soon see! The poor child's always adored me.

ESMÉ (*to the others*): As long as she adored the master perhaps . . . but not now! Don't fool yourselves. If it's all over with the master, there's no hope left for the family. What do you expect? It's all very well, you keep on and on loving someone, but if that person doesn't love you in return, you know, sooner or later. . . .

DELACHAUME (*furious, strikes the table with his fist*): But by God! why the devil doesn't he love her?

MME D. (*enters, annoyed*): She won't see me, she's locked her door.

ESMÉ: What did I tell you? As I was saying, it's all up now. What's said cannot be unsaid. If the master doesn't come home tonight, madame's going away in the morning and everybody will have to clear out.

MME D.: What, in one day?

ESMÉ: Madame said that when she wasn't here, nobody else was to remain in the house.

DELACHAUME: Good Lord, that's impossible! Why, even servants get a week's notice!

ESMÉ: But you're not a servant, are you, sir? Servants are workers . . . It's not the same thing. . . .

DELACHAUME (*stiffens, quite beside himself, his monocle brought into action*): This is too much . . . Who exactly do you think you're dealing with? Let me tell you we are people of standing, only I see we made the mistake of allowing you too much familiarity; we'll see to it in future that you're kept in your place. Now, get out, girl, get out at once!

ESMÉ: 'Standing', did you say? Hm! You make me laugh . . . You're just a bunch of phoneys!

DELACHAUME (*seating himself tranquilly*): I don't know what she means. I never did understand slang.

MME D.: Esmé! Esmé! You must be patient and excuse Monsieur Edgar. You know how eccentric he is, he's an artist, you see. I am quite sure, Esmé, quite sure he didn't mean to offend you . . . Anyway, he'll be telling you so himself in a moment. Esmé, listen to me . . . what if we were to promise you something for using your influence?

ESMÉ (*before going out*): Nothing doing. Sorry, I think you are all out of luck from now on. In any case what you could manage to scrape up between you . . . (*She goes out.*)

MME D.: This time we're finished! Destitute! My courage will never hold out. I am too old to . . . er . . . I mean, I'm too young, I'm too young to resign myself to it.

JACQUES (*from his corner*): Ah! Poor Georges – who can't bear wearing the same tie more than three times. Too fastidious! He likes ringing the changes! Now he'll have to keep putting the same ones on till they look like bits of string!

BARBARA: I know it's only a detail, Jacques, but it means you'll have to start buying ties yourself!

JACQUES: I don't care a damn! I'd be glad never to wear a tie again and have holes in the seat of my pants, for the pleasure of seeing him on his beam ends! It'll be torture for him! Those hand-made brogues that cost a fortune every pair – he's seen the last of them! . . . He'll have to get what he can in the sales! And the striped trousers and black double-breasted jackets? And taxis? Not on your life! Into the crowds and stink of the underground with Georgie now! And a boss round his neck again all the time. Poor fellah! He'll just croak!

BARBARA (*wild*): You too, if that's any comfort.

JACQUES: Me too, yes, but he'll go first. Friend Georges has got me quite used to having a boss these last two years. He's made me earn my thirty thousand francs, I can tell you! . . . Mind you, I don't complain. I'd have done the same myself. When you provide somebody with a living, whether it's a servant or secretary, you've got to see he pays you back in kind . . . But now he'll have to pay in kind, Georges! And will he squeal! I remember how he squealed in the army when the N.C.O.s were swearing at him all the time. 'Hey, you there, Delachaume! Call that polishing your boots? Four days C.B.! What's that? Right – make it eight days!' Hm! he's going to find himself polishing boots morning after morning, days without end, stuck into the polish up to his elbows!

BARBARA: Shut up, Jacques! Don't be so crude!

JACQUES: You don't know what it's like to grow up with somebody who's handsomer than you are, who was always brighter at school and then gets rich into the bargain! That's what's so attractive about revolutions, I always think – even if you don't care a damn about the principles, it must be wonderful watching people who've always been carefree and confident suddenly plunged into horror and misery, and all croaking their last! And Georges'll croak, all right, he's such a sensitive chap . . . he'll just give up the ghost; I know him.

DELACHAUME (*prostrate*): If only we knew where he was! We could at least warn him that tonight is his last chance! Absolutely the last!

JACQUES (*finishing softly – in a hoarse voice*): Maybe we'll all croak, but Georgie'll be the first to go.

BARBARA (*suddenly bursts out*): I can't bear this! I followed him the other day! He's rented a house, thirty-two rue Victor Hugo, at Senlis. I suppose that's where he must be!

JACQUES (*leaps up*): Hell! why didn't you say so before, damn your eyes? I've got the car outside. Quick, all of you! We'll get him!

He drags the MOTHER *by the hand, and pushes the* FATHER *out.* BARBARA *goes out last, quickly.*

Curtain

SCENE 2

Same set as Act One. In the centre a young lady in white, ISABELLE, *surrounded by the* ACTORS, BUTLER *and* PROPRIETRESS, *sunk in their chairs.*

ISABELLE: Are you quite sure he didn't even know you an hour ago?

DELMONTE: Are we sure! Why, we arrived on the seven-ten and came straight here. We'd never set eyes on him before.

ISABELLE: And he's really rented this house for a month?

PROPRIETRESS: I don't normally let by the month, of course, but he seemed such a nice young man, the sort you'd trust without question – you know.

ISABELLE: Yes, you would, wouldn't you? (*She sighs a little and turns to the* BUTLER.) And you were going to play the old faithful servant?

BUTLER: Yes, miss.

ISABELLE (*looks at him and says pleasantly*): Isn't that dreadful?

BUTLER: Oh! I was in a very wealthy household for seventeen years, miss. Only now I work for Dufort's – I simply came in answer to a telephone call. We were asked for a number two type menu for four people.

ISABELLE: Four people? Why four? There would have been five, with Jacques.

BUTLER: Now you've broken the crust, you may as well taste the fruit, miss. The fifth person wasn't going to have anything to eat, miss.

MME DE M. (*clucking*): That was the friend!

DELMONTE: The best friend in the world! Ha! Ha!

ISABELLE: Jacques?

DELMONTE: That's right! Jacques! The wonderful Jacques!

ISABELLE: Jacques wasn't having anything to eat? Why not?

DELMONTE: For a very good reason. . . .

MME DE M. (*with a guffaw*): He hasn't got the stomach for it! He doesn't exist.

ISABELLE: Jacques doesn't exist?

DELMONTE: No more than we do! (*Hopefully.*) But we can eat, at least – can't we, Emilienne?

MME DE M.: Any time it's convenient.

ISABELLE: No, that's not true! Jacques does exist, I'm sure of it. We've talked about him every day for the last two months!

DELMONTE: Pure imagination, all of it!

ISABELLE: But I've seen his photograph!

DELMONTE: A fake! Nothing would surprise me, where that spry young man's concerned.

ISABELLE (*softly*): There's nothing left at all, then, if even Jacques is a lie? . . .

MME DE M.: How do we know he's ever going to come back? He said he was going to make a telephone call! It may have been a trick to leave us and get away.

DELMONTE (*with a guffaw*): Oh! This is absolutely priceless! (*He stops, then repeats thoughtfully.*) Priceless . . . (*Suddenly, gets angry.*) Yes, that reminds me – if he doesn't come back, who's going to pay us?

MME DE M. (*stops laughing, too*): I had a sort of feeling there was something fishy about the whole business.

DELMONTE: Just a minute, just a minute! I'm a Union man; I'll soon have them on to him. He won't get away with a trick like that, with me.

MME DE M.: What are you going to do, then, Mr Know-All? You don't even know his address.

DELMONTE: Guillotard knows it.

MME DE M.: That's what you think! He told me all he had was *this* address.

PROPRIETRESS (*anxiously*): They can't impound *my* furniture and hold *me* responsible can they?

DELMONTE: I have no idea, madame. I know nothing about it! You should take advice on these matters when you let to strangers!

PROPRIETRESS: How was I to know? He seemed to me a young man of good education, very good family and so on.

DELMONTE (*jeering*): Good family, ha! ha! Let me laugh at that one. That's us! We're his family! . . . Ha! You've got a funny eye for families, I must say!

MME DE M.: Oh dear, oh dear, there's one born every minute!

DELMONTE: He's a very slippery customer, this fellow. Ha! Very good family! . . . It hits you in the eye, really. As for you, young lady, I'm ready to believe you've been taken in, so were we – but if you were my daughter, I'd see you found something out about young men before you had much to do with them.

ISABELLE: You have no right to speak like that! How much were you supposed to get if this dinner had taken place as planned this evening?

MME DE M. (*hastily*): Three thousand francs, that's the rate for outside Paris.

DELMONTE (*quite as eagerly*): Plus travelling expenses, of course. Travelling is never included in the fee. That's another eight-fifty each.

ISABELLE: Here you are – ten thousand francs.

DELMONTE: It's a bit thick, don't you think, you being drawn into a pantomime like this and then having to pay the actors into the bargain? All right, it's your business. I'll give you the change. (*He feels in his pockets.*) Er . . . Have you got any change, darling?

MME DE M.: Er . . . I don't know, how much do you want?

ISABELLE: Please, don't bother . . . It's a small bonus for playing your part so well.

DELMONTE *looks sour and pockets the money stiffly.*

Do you usually play in straight plays or musicals?

DELMONTE: I play everything, classical and modern plays, tragedies and comedies.

ISABELLE: And you never get them muddled, mix them up at all?

DELMONTE: Never used to in the old days! Comedy was comedy and tragedy was tragedy! But with the plays we get served up nowadays, of course . . .

ISABELLE: Tell me – when you've been cast to play a good and noble father, do you usually welcome the heroine in the way you welcomed me?

DELMONTE: Oh! now that's going a bit too far! You're not going to complain at my telling you the truth, I hope? You were being hoaxed, my dear girl, diddled, swindled, spoofed!

ISABELLE: Perhaps I was, but you were being paid to swindle me, and after all it's your profession . . .

DELMONTE: Wait a minute! Let's have no aspersions on the stage, please . . . Don't you understand. I stepped out of character simply because I felt some villainy was afoot? Do you think I'm the sort to turn accomplice to a briber and corrupter? Or a petty thief who may only have been after your handbag?

ISABELLE: If that's what he wants, poor boy, there's very little left for him now. (*To* BUTLER.) What do I owe you?

BUTLER (*taking out his bill and handing it to her*): Fifteen thousand, eight hundred. Hm! (*Has second thoughts and takes back his bill.*) Er . . . that is to say, just one moment, miss . . . (*Takes a pencil from his pocket, sucks it and leans over the table.*)

MME DE M.: You know, really, as woman to woman, I think he's treated you shamefully.

DELMONTE: Shamefully! Young scamp! If I'd got him here I'd pull his ears straight out of his head.

ISABELLE (*gently*): Poor Georges! He'd thought up such a wonderful story! And when he comes back he'll find his worthy parents in a state of revolt and the old and faithful servant busy cooking the accounts. . . .

BUTLER (*straightens up*): What's that? Pardon me . . . But I . . . was . . . er . . . I was checking the figures.

ISABELLE (*smiling*): Well, how much does it come to, now you've checked the figures?

BUTLER (*coughs to give himself confidence*): Hmm . . . eighteen thousand one hundred and sixty . . . I'd forgotten travelling expenses . . . eighteen thousand one hundred and sixty . . . Twice eight are. . . .

ISABELLE (*smiling*): All right. Hurry up and take your money, then you can all three go. You've nothing to keep you here, now.

DELMONTE: Right! (*Strikes an attitude and quotes theatrically.*) 'Farewell! Farewell! God knows when we shall meet again – or who has justice on his side!'

ISABELLE: I'm sure it must be you . . . but please hurry. When Georges returns I don't think he'll be in the mood to congratulate you.

DELMONTE: That's true. (*To the* PROPRIETRESS.) What time's the next train to Paris, Lady Macbeth?

PROPRIETRESS: Hm! . . . (*Coldly.*) At this time of night I'm afraid there *are* no more trains. But if you care to come to the kitchen, we will look at the time-table.

They go out. The BUTLER *follows them.* ISABELLE *walks dreamily up and down. She wanders regretfully round the room.*

ISABELLE: All the grandmothers are part of the trick! The old servant, the house, even the furniture . . . None of it is real . . . What a pity. . . .

JACQUES *comes in upstage, warily, like someone entering a room unannounced in a strange house. Reaching the middle of the stage, he notices* ISABELLE *and stops.*

JACQUES: Excuse me, but all the doors were open and anyone can walk in – it's like a shop. I would like to speak to M. Georges Delachaume.

ISABELLE (*looks at him for a moment, then suddenly cries out*): Hello, Jacques.

JACQUES (*stops in his tracks*): Good God! Who told you my name?

ISABELLE: I guessed it.

JACQUES (*not in the least upset*): Oh! Clairvoyante? Where's your crystal?

ISABELLE: Wait a minute . . . Are you an actor? You can speak quite freely, I know all about it.

JACQUES (*this time he is rather amazed. After a moment of painful reflection he asks*): Excuse me, but this house is number thirty-two isn't it?

ISABELLE: Yes.

JACQUES: Rue Victor Hugo?

ISABELLE: Yes. yes.

JACQUES (*beginning an explanation*): You see, I'm a friend of M. Georges Delachaume. . . .

ISABELLE: Yes . . . His childhood friend, in fact. Your name

is Jacques Lemoine. You are twenty-six. You've come here
this evening to have dinner with me.

JACQUES: Oh! No! that last bit was wrong! I've just had a
meal, thank you. But it doesn't matter, don't let that put you
off. Even the best clairvoyantes make a mistake now and then.
Do go on. This is most interesting.

ISABELLE (*looking at him all the time*): Stand up straight, first.

JACQUES: What?

ISABELLE: Look me in the eyes.

JACQUES: Well . . . ?

ISABELLE (*gravely*): You're standing straight, aren't you?

JACQUES: Yes . . . why?

ISABELLE: How is it you're not taller than that?

JACQUES (*a bit put out by this conversation*): I can't really say. I'm
doing as well as I can. . . .

ISABELLE: Georges told me you were as tall as he is.

JACQUES: Has Georges been talking about me?

ISABELLE: Of course he has. Georges hardly ever talks of
anything else. Does that surprise you?

JACQUES: A little, yes. Er . . . Do you think I could hear
what my friend Georges has been saying about me?

ISABELLE (*smiling*): A lot of awful things, of course!

JACQUES: Oh! Of course! But . . . er . . . anything else?

ISABELLE (*looks at him in silence*): No . . . I'm sure you're not
an actor; you would have been straightening your tie, then,
just to try to look natural.

At these words JACQUES *does so, in spite of himself.*

BUTLER (*behind* JACQUES): Excuse me, miss, but would it be
possible, do you think, now, for me to announce dinner?
It is after ten o'clock. It would fall in with the wishes of those
other persons . . . (*Look of mistrust towards* JACQUES.) . . .
you know of. The persons . . . (*Another look at* JACQUES.)
that, er . . . you know of, miss, are as a matter of fact
obliged to spend the night in the kitchen. There is no train
for Paris until tomorrow morning.

ISABELLE: How late do Dufort's guarantee to serve their meals?

BUTLER: Midnight, miss.

ISABELLE: Well, we'll wait until midnight.

BUTLER (*gesture*): As you please, miss. However, there is no refrigerator in the kitchen, so I must warn you now, miss, that I can't be held responsible till midnight for the taste of the fish sauce. (*Goes out.*)

JACQUES: What was all that about?

ISABELLE: Strangely enough I was counting on you to explain.

JACQUES: On me! Tell me, where are we exactly?

ISABELLE: In a furnished house rented by Georges, so that he could have me to dinner this evening.

JACQUES: A four-storeyed house! At Senlis, too, of all places!

ISABELLE: You see, he meant it to be the house where he was born.

JACQUES: Where he was born? I like that! And that undertaker's assistant who just went out?

ISABELLE: That's a butler from Dufort's. He was to play the old family servant.

JACQUES: Well! Well! Well!

ISABELLE: In the kitchen there are two actors, hired. They were to be his mother and father.

JACQUES: Marvellous! And you? What was your part in all this? By the way, who are you?

ISABELLE: I'm one of his girl friends.

JACQUES: Oh! Yes! Georges has never been short of them. A girl friend from where?

ISABELLE: Nowhere in particular. That may distinguish me from the others, I hope. I met him in the Louvre, by the Egyptian mummies.

JACQUES: Mummies! Ho! Wonderful! That's the company he keeps nowadays, is it? He would find something different! He drops us all in the cart so that he can go gallivanting around museums! Well, well, well!

Pause.

ISABELLE: I wonder why he didn't want us two to meet.

JACQUES: I wonder, too. (*Pause.*) Do you know what time he's coming back?

ISABELLE: He'd left when I arrived; there was no message.

JACQUES: Charming evening! (*Sits down.*)

ISABELLE (*looks at him*): It's funny, you know. He swears that he tells you everything that happens to him, and yet he's never spoken to you about me?

JACQUES: He must have forgotten.

ISABELLE: You *are* his friend, though, aren't you?

JACQUES: His lifelong friend, don't doubt that for a moment. His only real, intimate friend. As close as could be . . . we are what you might call Siamese friends.

Pause.

ISABELLE: Is it true that you saved his life once, when he fell out of a boat into the sea?

JACQUES: No, I'm afraid not . . . I can't swim.

ISABELLE (*after a moment's silence*): Oh! . . . And the girl you were both in love with when you were eighteen, the girl you sacrified to him?

JACQUES: Me, sacrifice a girl? I don't remember that.

ISABELLE: Oh! I must find something that's true! Didn't you sell all your furniture one day just so that Georges could buy a new shirt, and some decent clothes? Didn't you?

JACQUES (*guffaws*): Did he say I sold my furniture? No? My God, that fellow's imagination! It's like the Arabian Nights when he can get a woman to listen to him. Sold my furniture! That's the latest! (*He stands up nastily.*) I'll give him sacrifice and devotion! He invents a devoted friend, to dazzle the ladies, then has the cheek to call him by my name! Well! I'll tell you what we really are, your fancy Georges and I . . .

ISABELLE: No, no, don't tell me anything! I don't want to hear!

JACQUES: Don't you really? Ah! but that'd be much too easy!

ISABELLE: *He* must tell me, then, not you!

JACQUES: Oh! No! I will. He told you *I* loved *him* and *he* loved *me* like a brother? Well, the truth is, Georges hates me, and *I* hate *Georges* . . . like poison. We're lifelong friends, that's true enough, and our nurses walked us out together. But hatred came to us with the age of discretion, and since then, believe me, we've made up for lost time.

ISABELLE: Well, what are you doing here, this evening? Why are you always with him, day after day?

JACQUES: I cling to him, little lady, as the shell clings to the rocks, and for the only reason that makes people really inseparable: self-interest . . . he keeps me.

ISABELLE: But why does *he* want you near him.

JACQUES: He needs me every day, so that he can humiliate me, so that he can send me on errands for him. Or rather, I should say, he needs my wife.

ISABELLE: Your wife?

JACQUES (*bows graciously*): Just as I have the honour to inform you, with shame on my brow! He needs my wife! You don't seem to understand me properly. Yet I'm speaking as clearly as I can. Need I be more explicit, my choice of words more picturesque?

ISABELLE: Be quiet! You're disgusting.

JACQUES: That's my speciality – I always disgust people! Someone else told me that only a moment ago. Whereas everything about Monsieur Georges has style, and style is so important, isn't it? No hint of anything common about him. Take these actors he's hired to play his mother and father – the noble parents, ha! – and this venerable old house. I'll bet he just loves it all. And the friend too – me – done with a flourish in the grand manner – nothing by halves, no – all Monsieur Georges's dreams are on a grand scale. But they are *dreams*. This is a dream. If he really had a friend like that, a man of flesh and blood, he'd have to pay heavily in solid cash for his noble, unselfish devotion.

BUTLER (*enters, distracted*): Miss . . . Miss . . . some more persons. I don't know what to do. I'm swamped!

M. and MME DELACHAUME *appear, followed by* BARBARA.

DELACHAUME: Well, Jacques, in God's name . . .?

MME D.: We were getting worried; it's nearly eleven o'clock.

JACQUES: Ah! You've come just at the right time! The atmosphere is most propitious! The very moment for a dramatic entrance! Right in the purple passage! Come on! Gather round! Do you know what this young lady has just told me – this charming girl waiting here for Gentleman Georges with tears in her eyes and hand on her heart? Georges loves me, and I love him!

DELACHAUME (*understanding nothing*): My God! What a welcome! Tell me, who is the young lady?

JACQUES: Ah! . . . She's Maria Marten in person, the mystery girl from a woman's weekly! The pale and delicate heroine, trembling and afraid, who is dragged by Gentleman Georges through dark and terrible adventures.

DELACHAUME (*decides to take no notice of* JACQUES'S *talk*): Where are we anyway?

JACQUES: In the Chinaman's house! The villain's! The doors all open of their own accord, the lotus plants are telephones, and the telephones are lotuses . . . Look at these tapestries, these green plants and bowls, these family portraits. They're all *fishy*! Very, very fishy! Careful, Edgar, careful! Look beneath your feet, that little fault in the carpet there! That's the trap door! That's their entrance! That's the way they'll come in!

DELACHAUME (*leaping away to another spot*): Who, *who*, in God's name? I don't understand a word you're saying. *Who* will come in?

JACQUES: *They* will! The others! The Chinaman's friends!

At this moment the ACTORS *appear at the back, attracted by the noise.* JACQUES *stamps with joy.*

Look! what did I say? Here they are!

The ACTORS *are bewildered and disappear.* JACQUES *gets up on a chair.*

My Lords, Ladies and Gentlemen! This house is a complete

fake! It's stuffed with Mummies and Daddies! Lift up that arm-chair. You're sure to find a Grannie underneath, and (*With a wave of his arm.*) there's a best friend in every drawer... All of it invented piece by piece to dazzle an innocent girl! Ah, no, I shall die of it, I shall burst before the night's out! (*He falls into his chair. You can't tell whether he's laughing or crying. He shouts to* BARBARA.) Did you hear that? It beats anything! Gentleman Georges invented a family. But that's nothing unusual, people do it every day. *He* had to go one better than that! *He* told her that I loved him and that he loved me! Do you hear? Don't you want to laugh? He loves me, he said. Don't you want to crack your sides?

BARBARA (*gently, looking at* ISABELLE *all the time*): Shut up, Jacques.

JACQUES: What did you say?

BARBARA: I'm just telling you it's time you shut up.

JACQUES: Shut up? Don't you see that now things have gone as far as this, we can't shut up any longer? Mme Delachaume come on, speak out! Now's the time, if ever! Put your hand on your heart, strike an attitude and quick about it! . . . Edgar, come on, make your moustache tremble, be noble and dignified as never before – this is the moment! Tell her you must have your son immediately to take back home, that the family's whole future is at stake. Come on, what are you waiting for? This is your big scene!

MME D. (*very much 'the mother' when she begins*): My dear . . . I realize, of course, that all this must be very distressing for you, as it is for us, but I am speaking to you now as a mother . . . You appear to be a respectable young girl . . . you'll understand me, I'm sure. My son has been telling you a pack of lies. You must send him back to us.

DELACHAUME (*thinking this is all true*): The boy is on the verge of breaking up his home, young lady!

MME D.: You hold our happiness – the happiness of all of us here – in your hands! Let me explain . . .

ISABELLE (*stiffens*): No.

MME D.: What do you mean? No?

ISABELLE: I don't want any explanation.

DELACHAUME: Well, if that isn't ridiculous in the extreme!

ISABELLE: I'll stop my ears up, I won't listen! I'll wait for Georges in the next street if need be, but I will not listen to your explanations!

MME D.: You're being childish. You've got to hear the whole story sooner or later.

ISABELLE: From Georges, but not from you.

DELACHAUME: Nothing will stop me telling you, young woman, that Georges is ruining his life, because of you!

BARBARA (*suddenly comes forward*): Oh, you're revolting! It's more than I can stand! You make me sick, all of you!

JACQUES: What's that? Have some tact, for God's sake! Tact, Barbara, please!

BARBARA: You're nauseating, all three of you, with your terror of losing him! You know you'll soon get your hold on him again, and take him back – very soon – isn't that enough for you? Answer me – isn't that enough?

JACQUES: My God! That wins the gold medal! Barbara defending Georges's love-affair with the beautiful stranger! Didn't I tell you it was pure novelette?

BARBARA: Why say anything at all to her? Why must you do any more breaking up and destroying? The poor girl's seen us now, all of us, and the hypocrisy in our faces? Aren't you satisfied?

MME D.: Barbara!

DELACHAUME (*not sure of what he has heard*): What did she say?

MME D.: Barbara, my dear! You can't know what you're saying! Your jealousy's got the better of you!

BARBARA: I just want him left alone for a bit! I want him left alone, happy for once!

MME D.: But you're mad, my dear – you mean, *without us*?

BARBARA (*quietly*): Yes, without us.

MME D. (*bursts out*): And that's what you call being in love with Georges!

Silence for a moment.

ISABELLE (*has been looking at* BARBARA *for a time; softly*):
But . . . who are you?

JACQUES (*bows and clowns*): My wife! I don't know what I can
have been thinking of when she came in. Do forgive me.
Allow me to introduce Mme Jeannette Lemoine, known as
Barbara, because she thinks it's posher. Say how-d'ye-do to
the lady, now, Barbie. Pay your respects!

ISABELLE: Your wife? . . . But. . . .

JACQUES: Oh! Yes! There's a big 'but'! When you scratch a
bit below the surface, life is full of 'buts'! Let me give you a
tip, my dear. Never scratch – it's dangerous. Never, never
scratch! Appearances are quite sufficient; they make a whole
world in themselves!

GEORGES *appears at the back.* JACQUES *sees him and shouts
without the slightest confusion.*

Isn't that right, old chap?

ISABELLE (*runs to* GEORGES): Georges!

MME D. (*almost at the same moment*): Georges, my boy! We've
been looking everywhere for you.

DELACHAUME: You've got to be back before midnight! Do
you hear? Absolutely got to!

GEORGES (*gesture*): Don't shout, Father. I've just come away
from there. It's all settled. (*To* ISABELLE.) I see you've
introduced yourselves.

ISABELLE: Yes, Georges.

GEORGES: This is Jacques, the famous Jacques. There is
Jacques's wife. I'd never even mentioned her to you; it was
very careless of me . . . My real father, my real mother.
Where have the others gone?

ISABELLE: They're just outside. There are no more trains, so
they can't leave until tomorrow morning.

GEORGES: Isn't that grand? Well, have you made your choice?
Which parents would you like to pass the evening with? The
false ones were quite nice, if only they'd known their parts.
But the real ones aren't too bad, either . . . you'll see. . . .

ISABELLE: Georges, why did you lie to me?

GEORGES: Haven't they told you I'm a married man?

ISABELLE: No, Georges.

GEORGES: Astonishing!

DELACHAUME: I hope that shows you that your parents have all the delicacy you seem to lack yourself, my boy. We've not said a thing.

GEORGES (*gently*): I am married, Isabelle.

ISABELLE (*tonelessly*): Are you, Georges?

GEORGES (*continuing*): I've been married four years, to a woman I don't love. A very rich woman. (*He smiles feebly. Still looking at* ISABELLE *he orders his father.*) You explain, Father. You're so good at explaining.

DELACHAUME (*not sure whether he's being laughed at or praised*): I'm good at explaining? . . . Well . . . er . . . of course. I'm proud of your marriage. Who wouldn't be? Have you ever heard of Desmond's Steel Girders, young lady?

ISABELLE (*stammers, still looking at* GEORGES): I . . . I . . . I couldn't say.

GEORGES (*quietly*): That's what I married – a Desmond Steel Girder. . . .

DELACHAUME: The biggest firm of steel girders in Europe!

ISABELLE: Is that all, Georges?

GEORGES: No. Isabelle. We're all living on my marriage. Jacques and Barbara included. The reason they've followed me out here is that my wife has threatened to throw us all out on the street if I don't get home before midnight tonight.

MME D.: Don't listen to him; he doesn't know what he's saying.

GEORGES (*continuing*): There's much worse to come. (*Laughs.*) With us, you know, there's always worse to come—

ISABELLE (*stops him with a gesture*): No, I don't want to hear even from you.

GEORGES (*looks at her, his smile gets harder; he laughs again; afte a moment his tone changes*): Afraid? I've never known you afraid before?

ISABELLE: I've never heard you laugh like that before. It's a nasty laugh. You're hurt. (*He is silent.*) Georges, have you the courage to stay alone with me just for five minutes?

GEORGES: I've courage enough for anything tonight.

MME D. (*comes forward*): Georges, dear, I know this is a very difficult situation for you, very painful, in fact; but it's nearly eleven o'clock. Paris is twenty-five miles away and we might be held up on the road.

ISABELLE: Just five minutes, Georges. I think you owe me that.

GEORGES (*to the others*): Leave us alone, please.

They hesitate and mutter to one another.

There's no need for any anxiety; in five minutes we'll all go back home together. Nothing can stop us doing that, now.

The DELACHAUMES *and* JACQUES *look at one another and make towards the door.*

DELACHAUME: All right. We'll trust you once again, for the last time. Do you hear? The last time! See you in five minutes, my boy.

GEORGES: In five minutes, Father.

They have all gone out – JACQUES *cynically closing the door.* GEORGES *comes down in silence to* ISABELLE.

What a let-down isn't it? A young man of such good family, with so many qualities? Too many qualities really, Isabelle. I wonder that didn't put you on your guard.

ISABELLE: Georges, why did you lie to me?

GEORGES: It should be as clear as daylight. I meet a girl in the Louvre; for two months I go with her every day and see the sights of Paris. It's one long idyll. You actually made me go round visiting old Paris . . . and drinking tea . . . I hate tea, always did. Well, one day I'd had too much of your tea and your pink-and-gold tea-rooms. I was fed up with snatching kisses in a taxi and holding hands over a doughnut. But what could I do? What proposition could I possibly make to a serious little girl from the Pyrenees, lost in the capital of France, supposed to be studying literature? Show her the curiosities of Parisian life? No. Make love in a shady hotel? What could I offer you? They've told you, I'm a married man; there was nothing on earth I could decently offer. So, as I'm a pretty low species of human really, I invented this nice young man, with a wonderful home, and an old and faithful servant, respectable parents – and I decided to seduce you, that's all.

ISABELLE (*gently*): Did you really think I'd believe anything as silly as that?

GEORGES (*lowers his head*): No, Isabelle, but . . . you can't blame me for trying.

ISABELLE: Georges, why did you lie to me?

GEORGES: Mm? . . . (*Looks at her in silence, then, in a different tone altogether.*) Well, the first day I lied for the sad and sordid reason I've just given you. I liked you, you were a young girl. I wasn't going to tell you who I was point-blank, and spoil it all.

ISABELLE: And the days that followed?

GEORGES: Afterwards I began lying so that it shouldn't look as though I'd lied too much on the first day. Then the nice young man you seemed to like so much would be real, to some extent.

ISABELLE: But why all this play-acting and fuss tonight, since I was going home tomorrow, anyway.

GEORGES (*smiling*): Ah! Tonight is altogether different . . . It's the little slip that catches out the murderer and gets him hanged. He's got cast-iron alibis, he removes all traces of himself with every possible care, but he gives a kiddie a fifty franc piece as he leaves the house, or he picks a flower from the dead man's garden to wear in his buttonhole . . . (*He lowers his head like a boy caught red-handed in mischief.*) Tonight's little manoeuvre was pure selfishness, just for my own pleasure, Isabelle.

ISABELLE: What pleasure?

GEORGES: Oh, very simple, just passing a real family evening at home with you – and my people.

ISABELLE (*half-surprised, half-amused*): Do you think it's as enjoyable as all that, a simple family evening?

GEORGES: I wouldn't know.

ISABELLE: You wouldn't know?

GEORGES (*gently*): I try to imagine it sometimes.

He is huddled into a corner of the sofa, hands in the pockets of his
raincoat, collar turned up, eyes closed. ISABELLE *watches him for a*
moment, quite disarmed, then goes on questioning him.

ISABELLE: You weren't brought up at home, then? . . .

GEORGES: Oh, yes . . .

ISABELLE: Didn't your parents get on very well together?

GEORGES: Not very well, no . . . Mother was always out
taking tea with her friends . . . she had so many friends! We
were always waiting dinner for her . . . When it got late
I'd fall asleep at table and the maid used to hold me and give
me my dinner. She was generally wild at having to feed me.
Father was wild about it, too. So he'd go upstairs and lock
himself in his room with his tin soldiers.

ISABELLE: *His* tin soldiers?

GEORGES: Yes. At my home it was Father who always played
soldiers. Oh! It was a funny house, I can tell you . . . Your
mother and father were serious-minded people, I suppose?

ISABELLE: Yes, Georges.

GEORGES: And they all had their meals at the same time?

ISABELLE: Of course.

GEORGES (*not ironically*): That must have been marvellous. (*He*
looks at ISABELLE *a moment, and smiles.*) Actually, people have
only to look at you to see that you were brought up in a house
that was bright and warm in the evenings, and where the
meals were calm and there was no quarrelling . . . My
lovely, radiant Isabelle . . . what a lot of happy grandmothers you must have way back behind you, there, in one
long line, holding on to each other's skirts – protecting you.
(*Pause. He smiles gently and adds.*) It may sound funny, but I
think I was a little bit in love with those grandmothers of
yours, as well.

ISABELLE (*softly, after a moment*): In spite of all those other lies,
then, Georges, it was true that you were in love with me?

GEORGES: Yes, Isabelle, *that* was true.

ISABELLE: Then I'm happy, and I don't care about the rest.

GEORGES: You're right. Let's be happy. (*He ponders a moment.*) We always ask too much of life, you know. We begin by wanting a whole lifetime of happiness, then we learn that to have a few stolen years even is wonderful luck . . . Later we reconcile ourselves to reality and could be satisfied with a single evening . . . Then suddenly we've only five minutes left, and we discover that even that is a boundless oasis in the desert . . . five minutes' happiness! (*He looks around them at the lounge, dark and yet friendly.*) It's nice in my old home, isn't it? Mother and Father have folded their newspapers at last and gone up to their rooms: and good old Jacques understood in the end, went off and left us alone . . . It's snug here. We've no need to hold hands, like beginners, to make sure the other one's still there in the darkness and silence. We're certain of one another being there. A peaceful end to a happy day . . . What shall we do tomorrow, darling?

ISABELLE: Lots of things, Georges.

GEORGES: Let's make it something silly. One of those unbelievable things that innocent lovers still do, the sort who don't know where to go in Paris . . . Visit the Invalides or the Eiffel Tower, or go boating in the Bois de Boulogne.

ISABELLE (*smiling*): We've been an ardent boating couple, haven't we, Georges?

GEORGES (*smiling, too*): Very ardent – but it was all according to plan. (*He raises his finger and sententiously plays the clown.*) All engaged couples should take a course in boating on the lake in the Bois de Boulogne. They should learn in good time how to steer the ship of married life! You know, I'm going to be a drivelling old bore after we've been married about twenty years. Will you hate me?

ISABELLE: No.

GEORGES: No . . . I can see you. You'll be very sweet, very elegant and very charming. The faithful old companion. The woman who never even thought of dyeing her hair, and ignored every one of her wrinkles. Do you agree to keep all your wrinkles and let your hair grow white, for love of me, Isabelle?

ISABELLE: Of course, Georges.

GEORGES (*sighs, relieved*): Ah! good. I felt I couldn't have lived through my five minutes' happiness without that guarantee. I would almost certainly have wasted them in making a scene . . . Maybe I'd better make a scene, anyway, on purpose, so that these five minutes really seem like a lifetime of happiness. What do you think?

ISABELLE (*smiling*): I think the wish is quite enough, darling.

GEORGES (*stops, looks at her*): Darling? What courage! You've never called me that before, Isabelle. . . .

ISABELLE (*bends her head, smiling*): I never dared to before. But we've been living together four whole minutes, already, so I . . . er . . .

GEORGES: Four minutes gone! Doesn't time fly! I was wondering where this confidence, this comfort, this feeling of peace had crept in! Of course, we've reached the stage of calm and tender affection – our golden wedding already. . . . We've been very happy together, Isabelle. And, although we haven't said it very often, I think we've loved one another quite a lot.

ISABELLE (*asks in a slightly trembling voice*): Why are you putting it in the past tense?

GEORGES (*draws back and smiles a trifle sadly*): Because our long married life is drawing to a close, Isabelle.

ISABELLE: Georges, darling – please don't pretend any more! I'm frightened now, Georges.

JACQUES (*appears in the doorway and comes in*): Excuse me, won't you? I must look like the jailer in a melodrama. The five minutes are up, Georges; your mother and father are out in the car already.

Enter BARBARA *also, slowly.*

ISABELLE: Georges, please!

She throws herself, distracted, into his arms. He looks at her, smiles, strokes her and pats her like a frightened child.

GEORGES: Don't be frightened, Isabelle. Leave me alone with them for a moment. I'll arrange everything, I promise you.

He leads her down to the door, holding her shoulder, then brusquely comes back to BARBARA *as soon as* ISABELLE *has disappeared.*

Stay behind after we've left, will you? Tell her I lied to her again because I was afraid of seeing her hurt. Tell her I don't love her and have never loved her, that she'd better go back home and forget all about this wretched little interlude as soon as she can.

JACQUES (*who has come up to him, slaps him and grips him on the shoulder*): Aren't you the lucky one not to be sentimental. Lucky fellow!

GEORGES (*goes pale and says quietly*): You're hurting me, Jacques, take your hand off my shoulder, damn you!

BARBARA (*moves towards him*): What's the matter? You've gone quite pale!

GEORGES: It's my shoulder. Unbutton the coat, will you, please?

BARBARA *rushes to do so, opens his raincoat and jacket, cries out.*

BARBARA: Georges, you're covered with blood!

GEORGES (*tonelessly, eyes closed*): Don't touch it. My shirt's stuck to me. Just unbutton the coat.

BARBARA: It's a bullet wound, Georges!

GEORGES: It's not serious. It was Christine. You know her little pearl-handled revolver? Well, this time she used it. We had a terrible scene. I tried to take it off her and in the struggle, she fell back against the marble fireplace. Everybody in the house started to shout; I rushed back here. I may have killed her.

JACQUES (*bounds up*): My God! We must go back at once! Can you walk?

GEORGES: I think I need a stiff drink.

JACQUES: A drink? Where the devil do you think I can find a drink in this place?

GEORGES: Call the butler.

    JACQUES *rings. In a moment the* BUTLER *appears.*

BUTLER: Did you ring, sir?

JACQUES: Have you got anything really strong to drink here? Perhaps a liqueur?

BUTLER (*with a smile*): Oh, sir! What a question! (*Recites – attitude.*)

  'To every meal the epicure

   Takes choicest wine and best liqueur;

     The House of Dufort, when you dine,

     Will see to all liqueurs, and wine.'

We have every possible liqueur, sir, and in particular a special old Calvados we highly recommend.

GEORGES: No, I'd like some rum.

BUTLER (*caught*): Ah! Of course, just the thing we haven't got! Nobody ever drinks it nowadays. Oh! just a moment – we have a thing called Rum Fantasy in the kitchen, which I was going to use for lighting the omelette, had everything passed off in the normal way. But I'd never recommend it, sir, for ordinary consumption.

GEORGES (*stands up*): We'll go down. Bring your bottle of Rum Fantasy out to the car, will you?

BUTLER: How many glasses, sir? One, two, three?

They go out without answering him.

(*Alone now, stunned.*) Rum Fantasy! . . . and probably drunk out of the bottle! (*He shudders with disgust and goes out, arms raised to heaven.*) What an evening! What an evening!

Curtain

Act Three

The same set. BARBARA *and* ISABELLE *are standing motionless in front of the dining-room door, which is wide open. They appear to be waiting for something. The* PROPRIETRESS *appears, holding a bowl and some dressing.*

PROPRIETRESS (*as she goes out*): We'll soon be finished. The doctor says it's just a superficial wound.

BARBARA: Do you think it's very painful?

ISABELLE: Not very, I shouldn't think.

BARBARA: I wouldn't like it to hurt him *very much*. He's been awfully spoilt. (*A pause. She looks at* ISABELLE. *Then she asks her suddenly.*) You *are* in love with him, aren't you?

ISABELLE: Why do you ask?

BARBARA: You seem so calm. He's in love with you, you know. He was lying to me just now. He's always been looking for someone like you . . . for you.

ISABELLE *shrugs her shoulders.*

ISABELLE: What do you know about it?

BARBARA (*gently, with a sad smile*): I know him very well.

ISABELLE (*pause*): You were his mistress, weren't you?

BARBARA: I wouldn't ask any more questions, if I were you. You know he loves you – so does it matter now what he used to be to any of us?

ISABELLE: You're quite right, it's of no importance to me.

BARBARA: He was everything you don't like . . . Everything that he'll never be again if only he goes away with you tomorrow and leaves all of us behind.

ISABELLE: So you're not quite sure whether he'll go with me or not?

BARBARA: Not yet, no. There's still a faint chance for me. It's a mean little chance, I'm afraid, very mean, and I don't intend to tell you what it is.

ISABELLE: Do you think you can frighten me with your mean little chance?

BARBARA: Oh! I haven't the slightest desire to . . .

ISABELLE: You're going to try and keep him for yourself. I know that! Seize on him as soon as you can . . . that's what you're waiting for. . . .

BARBARA: No . . . I shan't try.

ISABELLE: It would surprise me if you let him go, just like that!

BARBARA: The others will probably try, but I shan't. I've nothing more I want to say to him.

ISABELLE: I suppose you get a kick out of behaving as if you're making me a present of him?

BARBARA: Oh, no. I'm not the 'saintly' type. Besides, I couldn't give you my Georges, the one I know; you would never want him.

ISABELLE: You think not?

BARBARA: I'm sure of it. He's not at all a nice young man, my Georges. He's everything you must hate. He's sad, he's never sure of anything. He's unfair. He's cruel.

ISABELLE: You're lying.

BARBARA: Yes. *He* lies, too. *He's* a liar. He makes appointments and never turns up. He never keeps his promises. He's petty and mean and complains and quarrels all the time. He's a strange man, my Georges . . .

ISABELLE: What good can it do you to run him down like this?

BARBARA (*smiles*): That's not running him down . . . That's the way I loved him.

Silence. They look at one another.

ISABELLE (*suddenly*): You must hate me. Don't you?

BARBARA: No . . . It's funny. I hated you with all my heart at first, when he was always searching for you and hadn't found you . . . But I must have used up all my hate; now that he's found you, for good, I realize that I don't hate you any more.

ISABELLE: I hate *you*.

The DOCTOR *enters.*

BARBARA (*goes to him*): Have you finished, Doctor?

DOCTOR: Yes, madame. It's only a scratch, really. See that he rests and is quiet, so that his temperature doesn't go up. That's all. (*He bows – then to them both.*) Would you be good enough to show me the way out?

They hesitate, then ISABELLE *suddenly decides.*

ISABELLE: I'll show you, Doctor.

She goes out with him. Enter GEORGES. *He and* BARBARA *look at one another. He walks past her, then suddenly asks anxiously.*

GEORGES: Where is she?

BARBARA (*smiles a little*): She's still here . . . She'll be back in a moment. Lie down, Georges. The doctor said you must rest.

GEORGES (*goes to sofa*): What a stupid thing to happen. If only I'd fainted a bit later, in the car, you wouldn't have brought me back *here*.

BARBARA: Are you feeling better? The doctor didn't hurt you very much?

GEORGES: No. Where has she gone?

BARBARA: To show the doctor out . . . (*Pause. She suddenly asks:*) What are you going to do, Georges?

GEORGES: I don't know. (*He adds softly.*) It isn't up to me to decide what I'm going to do. (*Pause. He asks.*) How long is it since Jacques left?

BARBARA: Nearly an hour.

GEORGES: He should have phoned by now.

BARBARA: But there's no phone here. I had to ring through before to the house next door. Jacques probably hasn't thought of doing that.

She looks at him in silence.
Suddenly her thoughts bring tears to her eyes. GEORGES *sees her, she turns her head away, so does he. He stretches out on the sofa.*

GEORGES: I wish you wouldn't cry, Barbara.
BARBARA: I'm not crying.
GEORGES: Oh, don't pretend . . . What were you thinking about?
BARBARA (*not daring to look at him*): Just the way you and I used to play robbers, when we first went out together. Do you remember? We said we were being followed. We were on the run. We kept jumping in and out of taxis, and before we ever went into a café . . . took the most elaborate precautions. Now, I suppose, you play robbers with someone else . . .

GEORGES *doesn't reply. She hangs her head and goes on gently, ashamed.*

I hope for your sake you won't have to go to prison, Georges. And I'm being very fair when I say that. I can't help thinking that if you did go to prison, I'd be the one waiting at the gates when you came out. (*She raises her head and asks.*) You're disgusted with me, I expect.

GEORGES *doesn't answer this. Another pause.*

You don't even want to answer me?

ISABELLE *comes in; she goes to the sofa where* GEORGES *is stretched out, his eyes closed. She leans down to him.*

ISABELLE (*to* BARBARA): He's dropped off to sleep . . . exhausted . . . the loss of blood, I suppose.
BARBARA (*with a little, mysterious smile*): No, I don't think so. He always goes to sleep when he's unhappy.
ISABELLE: Why?
BARBARA: To stop being unhappy. It's a little trick he has.
ISABELLE: A trick?

BARBARA: Yes. He has several little tricks like that. Hasn't he ever begun drinking madly, with you, at about four o'clock in the afternoon?

ISABELLE: No, never.

BARBARA: Hasn't he ever laughed too loudly all of a sudden for no reason? Started to roar out his barrackroom songs enough to split your ear-drums? When he has to be gay, whatever the cost, much too gay?

ISABELLE: No.

BARBARA: You see, we're not talking about the same man at all.

JACQUES *appears in the doorway. He comes in quickly.* BARBARA *rushes to him.*

Well, what's the news?

JACQUES: Where is he?

BARBARA: There, asleep.

JACQUES (*turns round and sees* GEORGES): Well, now, isn't that wonderful! We rush around the streets in the dead of night worried out of our wits, we sweat ourselves dizzy with plans for escape, alibis and what have you, and meantime Monsieur Georges feels a bit tired, so he drops off to sleep.

BARBARA: Oh, come on, tell us what's happened.

JACQUES (*not paying any attention to her*): Do you know, I wish *he* was asking me that, pleading with me . . . I'd take my time and play the breathless messenger in a tragedy, who runs on and dithers. You know . . . 'It's awful! . . . Dreadful! . . . I can't bring myself to say it! . . . Awful! . . .'

BARBARA (*shakes him*): Tell us, for goodness' sake!

JACQUES (*changes his tone and sits down farther away*): Well – can you credit it? It was the merest bump! Only left a baby bruise! And the little wifie more in love than ever! Now, poor soul, she thinks that he must absolutely adore her to go so far as to risk a criminal offence! Dear Edgar suggested that one to her . . . I must say the old boy doesn't lack imagination.

BARBARA: Where are those two?

JACQUES: I left them sitting on the end of Christine's bed, engaged – rather prematurely, I think – in killing the fatted calf.

ISABELLE: Rather prematurely, as you say. Georges has decided to go with me to the Pyrenees.

JACQUES: You're taking him away?

ISABELLE: Yes.

JACQUES: What for? To start bee-keeping?

ISABELLE: No, to start being my lover . . . and my husband as soon as the divorce is settled.

JACQUES: What a delicate little bloom he is! The gentleman feels in need of a rest-cure in the country; so with a graceful shrug he drops us and takes the next train out of town . . . (*He turns to* BARBARA. *Clowning.*) Can we put forward any objection, do you think, to the gentleman going away for a rest-cure, my dear?

BARBARA (*half jokingly, half dreamily*): I don't think so.

JACQUES: What, then, remains for us to do, my dear?

BARBARA: Go away.

JACQUES: With dignity?

BARBARA: With dignity.

JACQUES: A gallant French exit – a smile, a hand on your heart, a foot at your behind . . . (*He has taken* BARBARA'S *arm and with one foot in front takes out his handkerchief.*) Handkerchief held high for the last farewell. 'Good-bye! and pray be happy, for you have deserved to be! You will never hear of us again.'

He stops short. Comes back to ISABELLE.

No, for God's sake! Did you really think it would be as easy as that? Just scoot off to bliss with your gay Lothario by the first convenient train? Ha! I must laugh . . . Ha! ha! ha! ha! Do you hear me? I'm laughing. And I'm making myself comfortable!

ISABELLE: What are you doing?

JACQUES (*sitting down ostentatiously*): Waiting for him. Listen. Take my advice. I quite like you. Do you know what I'd do if I were in your place? Skedaddle! Before he wakes up!

ISABELLE (*coldly*): Really? Why?

JACQUES: He's in love with you, of course, we know that. It's all hot, and sparkling, all bubble and squeak for joy at the moment . . . But he's not totally mad. Georges always come back in the end, when he has to. Up till now he's always come back after adventures like this. And there's no earthly reason why he shouldn't come back this time.

ISABELLE: I think this time you'll add to your experience. Georges won't come back.

JACQUES: If you were a sensible girl, you'd believe me. I know him. He's done this trick at least a dozen times before.

ISABELLE: Be quiet, I won't listen to you.

JACQUES: You're making a mistake. I'm trying to save you making an ass of yourself, my dear. This sleeping beauty here is a wolf in sheep's clothing, a Casanova. I imagine yours is one of those straightforward lives, everything simple and clear . . . Go to the station alone, tomorrow . . . Jump in the train and go back to your bees, your big dogs and your virtuous grannies down on the farm. (*He implores her, still clowning.*) For the sake of your virtuous grannies, sweet lady!

ISABELLE (*walks away with a shrug*): You're just being a bore.

JACQUES (*following her*): I'm boring myself, too. I'm wearing myself out taking all this trouble with you . . . but only because I feel it is my duty. In your eyes, I'm a despicable sort of cad, I know. But doesn't that mean anything to you, that a cad like me with God knows what presentiment of evil – goes to such lengths trying to warn you?

ISABELLE: No. It doesn't mean a thing.

JACQUES: You're a hard woman. If I were in your place I'd find it overwhelming. Honestly, do you believe he loves you enough to cast his old wolf-skin, chuck it out of the window and turn overnight into an absolute lamb?

ISABELLE: Yes, I do believe it, with all my heart. I believe I can teach him real happiness.

JACQUES: As if happiness were a thing anyone can learn. . . . You'll need an inhuman amount of talent. Still, how touching it all is! Don't you think so? (*To* BARBARA.) Aren't you moved? I am, really I am.

ISABELLE: Be quiet. You're only saying this because you hate him.

JACQUES (*suddenly tired of it all, too*): No, I'm not even sure I hate him any longer. I've said it too often without doing anything about it. It's just so much hot air. A few moments ago, when I started talking, I knew I wouldn't convince you. I knew he'd go away with you, but I kept on so that he'd wake up and throw me out. You see . . . once I start talking and get really wound up, there's always got to be somebody to stop me by force, and throw me out! And mind you, they're doing me a favour. Otherwise I go on and on, and wade in deeper and deeper, till I wear myself out and feel as bad as my victims about it all.

BARBARA (*after a pause, goes to him*): Come on. It's not worth the trouble waiting till he wakes up.

JACQUES: Think not? (*He gets up, very businesslike.*) In that case, I will be brief. The end of this month is going to be extremely difficult for us. Do you think you could lend me fifty thousand francs.

ISABELLE: You must think I'm rich, too . . . I haven't got any money, you know.

JACQUES (*modestly*): Five thousand?

ISABELLE (*nearly laughing*): Five thousand, perhaps. I've got just about that much in my handbag.

She takes it from her bag. BARBARA *snatches it.*

BARBARA: Jacques!

JACQUES: What the hell's up with you? Are you mad?

BARBARA (*putting the money back in the bag*): Not in the least.

JACQUES: Oh! what a delightful gesture, my dear! . . . It'll make a wonderful story. I shall tell everyone, depend upon it, especially the waiters in the cheap restaurants we shall be reduced to from next week onwards. I can see them being so impressed they'll shower us with steak and chips . . . But you've made your gesture now – so keep out of this will you?! (*He pushes her aside.*) Do forgive her, it was just a thoughtless impulse.

BARBARA: No, Jacques.

JACQUES: She was only helping us through a difficult patch. . . .

BARBARA: Well, I don't want her help.

JACQUES (*sits down, completely discouraged*): If we all played at being noble, we'd never get anywhere at all. There must be some noble people in the world, of course, but not too many, don't overcrowd 'em.

BARBARA (*suddenly after a pause*): You're quite right, Jacques, I'm a fool. If we all play at being noble, we'll never get anywhere. Georges especially – he'll never get anywhere at all. I'll take that money. It will make it easier for him that way.

JACQUES: Hurrah! Let's leave it at that! (*He sees* GEORGES *move.*) Careful, he's waking. (*He hides the notes quickly.* GEORGES *sits up, looks at them.*)

GEORGES: Where are Mother and Father?

JACQUES: With Christine. And she's as fit as a fiddle. It was only a bump, old chap; you can start all over again tomorrow.

GEORGES (*with a deep sigh – you feel he is suddenly filled with a hard kind of joy*): I don't ever want to go back there again. I don't want anything I've got there. Tomorrow I'm going to put on a different suit, and tie and shoes and shirt, get on the train, and go right away from here.

JACQUES: We know.

GEORGES (*savagely*): Why did you come back, then?

JACQUES: To wish you God-speed, dear boy. Whether we adore each other or not is beside the point. We've still got to come to some arrangement.

GEORGES (*shrugs*): You can tell Mother and Father that I shall be back in Paris soon to settle the details of the divorce. Tell

them I'm going to find a job and start work, then I shall help
them as much as I can.

Short pause.

Perhaps Father had better look round for something to do.

JACQUES: He'll look round all right, never you fear. He's been
looking round for the last thirty years.

GEORGES: I'll give them all I have left. They'll go to a hotel
at first, I expect. Mother will want to put up in a palace of
course, as usual, so as not to sink too low in her friends'
esteem. And Father will gaily agree, thinking the price they
quote for the room is by the week, not by the day, and that
drinks, coffee, cigars and everything else is included.

JACQUES: The old boy is two or three wars behind us.

GEORGES: Try to make them see that they're old now and
should be sensible; they must manage to live for at least a
few months on what I send . . . (*He turns to* ISABELLE *with
a smile.*) You'll forgive all these details, I know?

ISABELLE: You should forgive me, for staying and listening.
I'd better leave you for a bit, Georges.

GEORGES (*goes with her to the door*): Thanks, Isabelle. We shan't
be long.

She goes out. Silence. They look at one another, embarrassed.

So there we are.

JACQUES (*echoes him*): There we are, as you say.

GEORGES: What are you two going to do?

JACQUES: In the words of the old artist Edgar himself – we
shall 'take steps', old chap.

GEORGES: Will Barbara have to go back to work?

BARBARA: None of your business.

GEORGES: I'll go into what money there still is and see that
you have something.

JACQUES: Thanks. Actually, it's embarrassing having to tell
you this at a time when we're all so upset, but I was going
to mention it to you tonight at dinner . . . I've had the
tailor's bill . . . You know, for the . . . er . . .

GEORGES: Right, I'll send you that.

JACQUES (*softly*): Fifteen thousand francs.

GEORGES: But you told me it was going to be thirty thousand?

JACQUES (*hangs his head*): Yes, but it's fifteen thousand.

GEORGES (*smiles*): Good God! Jacques! Don't tell me you're turning honest, too!

JACQUES: Everybody's honest in one way or another. The trouble is, there's only one official way.

Pause. They are uncomfortable.

So there we are.

GEORGES: As you say, there we are.

JACQUES (*suddenly, in the silence*): There's one thing I'd like to know. Why did you tell her I saved your life once in a boat, a long time ago?

GEORGES: Have you forgotten one day when we were in Brittany – there was a strong current and I thought I'd never get back in my depth. You were green with fright but you managed to get the canoe out to me for all that.

Pause.

We were only twelve then.

JACQUES: How time flies . . .

Another silence. JACQUES *suddenly asks in a different tone.*

Look here, it's all finished now, so we're not going to quarrel over a detail. If I'm in the way for your good-byes to Barbara, I can disappear. . . .

BARBARA (*throws herself into his arms with a cry*): No, don't leave us. (*She turns to* GEORGES *as she still clings to* JACQUES.) She'll be getting anxious, Georges; I'm sure you ought to call her back.

GEORGES (*turns to her*): Yes. But I wanted to say good-bye to you, Barbara.

BARBARA: You said it, five minutes ago.

GEORGES: But we can't just part like that.

BARBARA: Yes, we can. I tell you we can! (*She almost shouts.*) Why pretend we've anything in common any more? What have our troubles to do with you? You can't bear the sight of us now! I've known that longer than you've known it yourself. Well, hurry up and throw us out. This hurts.

GEORGES (*gently*): It hurts me, too.

BARBARA (*gently, too, after a moment*): I hope it does, Georges.

GEORGES: It does. But all the same I must say good-bye properly. I'm leaving you Barbara – for ever.

BARBARA (*with a gulp*): For ever. Yes.

GEORGES: When a man gives a woman up the usual thing is to promise to be friends, to soften the parting. I'm not promising you my friendship. (*Lower voice. It is difficult for him to say and he says it even with a touch of tenderness.*) I can only promise you my feeling of shame . . . my hatred of what we were to one another, Barbara.

BARBARA: Your 'hatred', yes.

GEORGES: The whole bunch of us around Christine led disgraceful lives; but we two were the worst. The others were only thinking of money, but we two – in the midst of the petty wrangling and all the dirty little bargains that went on – you and I went through the motions of love.

BARBARA (*more quietly still, if possible*): The motions, yes.

GEORGES (*suddenly*): Forgive me, Barbara.

BARBARA (*looks up, slight pause*): What for?

GEORGES (*dully*): For the foul life I made you lead.

BARBARA (*suddenly shaken by a shudder of tenderness, smiles*): No, Georges – I can only *thank* you for that foul life, as you call it . . . (*A terrible silence, then suddenly she cries out as she rushes to the door.*) I'll fetch her back to you!

GEORGES (*runs after her, catches her*): Barbara!

BARBARA (*turns on him*): What is it? What more do you want me to say – that that sordid life was simple for me, as simple as this girl's happiness is to her, just because I was in love with you? Do you think that will make it any easier afterwards? (*She gets away from him, runs to the door. He lets her go. She calls.*) Isabelle!

GEORGES *does not move.* BARBARA *re-enters with* ISABELLE.

We're just leaving. We're in absolute agreement, my husband and I, on everything. Thank you for the money!

GEORGES (*leaps at this*): What money?

JACQUES (*tries to interpose*): Nothing! Nothing at all! A joke! Just a joke! A mistake.

BARBARA (*to* GEORGES *face to face*): It's something to make up for what we're losing from Christine. You don't think we'd just leave you without getting any money, do you? Really! What do you take us for?

GEORGES: I forbid you to take anything from her! I'll send you everything I've got.

JACQUES (*shrugs*): That's a good one – you've got nothing now!

BARBARA *bursts into false laughter, which suddenly stops. She then asks feverishly as though something were on her mind and she were in a violent hurry.*

BARBARA: Well, Jacques?

JACQUES: Yes, dear?

BARBARA: Why can't we go? What the devil are we waiting for?

JACQUES: True enough. Grace, my dear, style before all things . . . (*He bows like a cavalier.*) Young lady . . .

Just at this moment the ACTORS *open the door and push in their heads; with them is the* BUTLER. JACQUES *sees them.*

Come in! Come in! Don't think twice about it! Walk right in! Don't be afraid; you're at home here, remember!

They all look bewildered.

Come in, come in. This is the home of happiness and dignity, and of every pleasure in the calendar that has a proper licence from the authorities. . . .

As they come in, to BARBARA, *whose arm he takes.*

Look at that, isn't it lovely? There you have the family with
a capital F, the pure Family with nothing to be ashamed of!
Doesn't it just belch fine sentiments – or, at any rate, it
pretends pretty well. And that's the main thing for a family,
after all.

DELMONTE: What do you want with us, sir? Really, I don't
know what's taken hold of you! This is farcical!

JACQUES (*without a smile*): No, not farcical, sir – tragical. You're
an actor, I take it, sir?

DELMONTE: I am.

JACQUES: Well, you've just come in time to give us some
advice. Our scene has just come to an end, you see: now how
do you think we should make our exit?

DELMONTE: Well, hm, an exit isn't as easy as all that, you
know. Not a simple thing at all, an exit. It depends on the
situation, the character, and so on. What sort of parts have
you been playing?

JACQUES: The villains.

DELMONTE: Ah! ah! There are some lovely exits you can use
for villains . . . Albert Lambert used to go out draping
himself in his cape. . . .

JACQUES (*withdraws a step or two, taking* BARBARA'S *hand*): I'm
only wearing a jacket, it's not quite ample enough. (*Silly
waving with his jacket.*)

DELMONTE: Poor old Sylvain – he's dead – in *Arnolph*, used
to exit running, without a glance at anyone else on the stage.

JACQUES (*still withdrawing*): That won't do! We want a view
of every single face until the very last second!

MME DE M.: Sarah Bernhardt never went out at all. She just
stayed on the stage for the final curtain and the applause!

JACQUES (*still withdrawing*): There'll be no applause for us.
Besides, we've just *got* to have an exit.

DELMONTE: Well . . . er . . . Mounet was wonderful. When
he wanted a good exit he used to march to the footlights
first. . . .

JACQUES (*who has now reached the door at the back*): Too dangerous! Well, don't bother thinking up any more. We've covered

the four yards to the door. Those last four yards before disappearing, that sometimes take years to cover . . . Well . . . Nobody moved? We're going! Nobody spoke? One . . . two . . .

BARBARA (*gently, her eyes on* GEORGES): Nobody. . . .

JACQUES: Well, then! Hey presto!

They disappear as though through a trap.

DELMONTE: Dreadful! Impossible! No actor would ever make an exit like that!

ISABELLE (*happily*): They've gone, Georges.

GEORGES: Yes, Isabelle.

ISABELLE: You're free to live now.

GEORGES: Yes, Isabelle. I'm free to live now.

A noise, heavy, dull from outside. He shudders.

What's that?

ISABELLE: Nothing. The car door slamming to.

They listen motionless for a moment.

There . . . The engine's cold. It won't start . . . Ah! Now it's started . . . It's moving away . . . It's at the end of the street already. It's passed the light from the last lamp post . . . It's gone into the night, now . . . It doesn't exist any longer.

GEORGES (*looks at her, murmurs with a frightened smile*): You are terrifying, Isabelle.

ISABELLE: I am happy, Georges. There's always something terrifying about happiness.

BUTLER (*comes forward*): Excuse me, sir, but would it be possible, do you think, now, for me to announce dinner?

ISABELLE: Yes, at once.

BUTLER: At last! (*He makes the announcement as though nothing had happened.*) Dinner is served.

MME DE M. (DELMONTE *has given her his arm*): Ah! Come, children! It's five minutes to midnight . . . I think this is going to be a very strange sort of meal.

BUTLER: You are mistaken, madame, definitely mistaken! (*He recites.*)
   'A miracle, just one more
    From the firm of Jean Dufort!
       Time and distance trouble not!
       Nothing warmed up, all quite cold!'
   Oh! I'm sorry! I meant to say 'hot', of course.
DELMONTE (*giving him a friendly tap on the shoulder before passing through to the dining-room with* MME DE MONTRACHET *on his arm*): Don't worry your head about that, old chap, please! No fuss! It's only a little family dinner after all.

The ACTORS *giggle to each other as they go.* GEORGES *and* ISABELLE *follow them into the dining-room. The* BUTLER *goes out last, and closes the door.*

Curtain